MORAL UNIVERSALISM AND PLURALISM

NOMOS

XLIX

NOMOS

Harvard University Press
I   *Authority* 1958, reissued in 1982 by Greenwood Press

The Liberal Arts Press
II   *Community* 1959
III   *Responsibility* 1960

Atherton Press
IV   *Liberty* 1962
V   *The Public Interest* 1962
VI   *Justice* 1963, reissued in 1974
VII   *Rational Decision* 1964
VIII   *Revolution* 1966
IX   *Equality* 1967
X   *Representation* 1968
XI   *Voluntary Associations* 1969
XII   *Political and Legal Obligation* 1970
XIII   *Privacy* 1971

Aldine-Atherton Press
XIV   *Coercion* 1972

Lieber-Atherton Press
XV   *The Limits of Law* 1974
XVI   *Participation in Politics* 1975

New York University Press
XVII   *Human Nature in Politics* 1977
XVIII   *Due Process* 1977
XIX   *Anarchism* 1978
XX   *Constitutionalism* 1979
XXI   *Compromise in Ethics, Law, and Politics* 1979
XXII   *Property* 1980
XXIII   *Human Rights* 1981
XXIV   *Ethics, Economics, and the Law* 1982
XXVI   *Marxism* 1983
XXVII   *Criminal Justice* 1985

NOMOS XLIX

Yearbook of the American Society for Political and Legal Philosophy

MORAL UNIVERSALISM AND PLURALISM

Edited by

Henry S. Richardson
and
Melissa S. Williams

NEW YORK UNIVERSITY PRESS • *New York and London*

NEW YORK UNIVERSITY PRESS
New York and London
www.nyupress.org

"Contingency in Obligation" reprinted by permission of the publisher from *Moral Literacy*, by Barbara Herman, pp. 300–332, Cambridge, Mass.: Harvard University Press, Copyright © 2007 by the President and Fellows of Harvard College.

Library of Congress Cataloging-in-Publication Data
Moral universalism and pluralism /
edited by Henry S. Richardson and Melissa S. Williams.
      p. cm. — (Nomos ; xlix)
"Yearbook of the American Society for Political and Legal Philosophy."
Includes bibliographical references and index.
ISBN-13: 978–0–8147–9448–7 (cl : alk. paper)
ISBN-10: 0–8147–9448–3 (cl : alk. paper)
1. International law—Moral and ethical aspects. 2. International law—
Political aspects. 3. International law—Philosophy. 4. Universalism.
5. Pluralism. I. Richardson, Henry S. II. Williams, Melissa S., 1960–
KZ1256.M67   2008
341.01—dc22   2008018239

New York University Press books are printed on acid-free paper, and their binding materials are chosen for strength and durability. We strive to use environmentally responsible suppliers and materials to the greatest extent possible in publishing our books..

Manufactured in the United States of America

10 9 8 7 6 5 4 3 2 1

CONTENTS

PREFACE

Like every volume of NOMOS, this one—the forty-ninth in the series—emerged from an annual meeting of the American Society for Political and Legal Philosophy (ASPLP). The meetings of the ASPLP cycle among the three principal professional meetings for the academic disciplines that form the core for the NOMOS volumes: Philosophy, Law, and Political Science. In this case, our conference was held at the American Philosophical Association's Eastern Division Meetings in Boston, December 29-30, 2004. Its topic, "Moral Universalism and Pluralism," was selected by the voting membership of the ASPLP.

Barbara Herman, Benedict Kingsbury, and William Galston presented the three principal papers at the conference, with commentaries by Seyla Benhabib, Kenneth Baynes, Frank Michelman, Gopal Sreenivasan, Daniel Weinstock, and Robin West. Their contributions made for an extraordinarily rich and lively intellectual exchange, which has been deepened in this volume. At the conference, F. M. Kamm raised such thought-provoking questions that we asked her to develop them into a commentary on Barbara Herman's piece. Thankfully she did, and Barbara Herman has responded, with delightful consequences for the volume as a whole. William Scheuerman also generously accepted our invitation to submit a piece for the volume, which has added substantially to its discussion of moral universalism and pluralism in the context of international law.

The editorial staff at New York University Press—Ilene Kalish, Gabrielle Begue, and Despina Papazoglou Gimbel—have been wholly supportive of our enterprise and have earned our gratitude for the Press's ongoing commitment to the series.

Genevieve Fuji Johnson has contributed substantially to this volume in her capacity as Managing Editor: first, by managing the organization of the original conference and, subsequently, by offering substantive feedback on the volume, maintaining communications with the contributors, and overseeing the volume's final production for publication. She has done all this while also juggling the duties as a new Assistant Professor of Political Science at Simon Fraser University. I am profoundly grateful to her for all she has given to this as to other shared projects; but the series and the Society are also very much in her debt.

Erica Frederiksen took some time away from the completion of her doctoral dissertation in the Department of Political Science at the University of Toronto to assist with the final production of the volume. We also wish to thank Tobold Rollo for his work in preparing the index.

The ASPLP's Secretary-Treasurer, Jacob T. Levy, keeps the operation running. He's performed a tremendous service in augmenting the Society's traditions through enhancements to its website, management of its finances, efforts to broaden its membership, and intellectually engaged participation in its conferences. We are very, very fortunate to have him in this role.

Finally, and most important, I wish to express my humble but heartfelt gratitude to my co-editor, Henry Richardson. He carried much more of the editorial burden than was his due, and he did it with grace, incisive intellectual judgment, and efficiency. Though the production of this volume has called on the patience of our authors and publisher, the delays must be charged to my account, not to Henry's. I am particularly grateful to him for writing such a fine introduction. It has been a privilege to work with him.

MELISSA S. WILLIAMS
Toronto, August 2007

CONTRIBUTORS

KENNETH BAYNES
Philosophy and Political Science, Syracuse University

WILLIAM A. GALSTON
Senior Fellow, The Brookings Institution

BARBARA HERMAN
Philosophy and Law, University of California, Los Angeles

F. M. KAMM
Kennedy School of Government and Philosophy, Harvard University

BENEDICT KINGSBURY
Law, New York University

FRANK I. MICHELMAN
Law, Harvard University

HENRY S. RICHARDSON
Philosophy, Georgetown University

WILLIAM E. SCHEUERMAN
Political Science and West European Studies, Indiana University

GOPAL SREENIVASAN
Philosophy, University of Toronto

DANIEL WEINSTOCK
Philosophie, Université de Montréal

ROBIN WEST
Law, Georgetown University

MELISSA S. WILLIAMS
Political Science and Centre for Ethics, University of Toronto

INTRODUCTION

HENRY S. RICHARDSON

Taking first the simple idea of plurality, before coming to the pluralisms that emphasize or celebrate it, I note that moral universalism is hardly opposed to plurality; indeed, moral universalism is pointless without a plurality over which to range—a plurality of diverse persons, nations, jurisdictions, or localities over which morality has, or purports to have, universal authority. Far from denying the existence of such pluralities, moral universalism presupposes it. Such mere literal pluralities are not what are at issue in the essays here, of course, but rather the forms of diversity that inevitably and invariably come with human plurality. While moral universalism presupposes a plurality of persons and circumstances over which to range—else it has little point—it is also challenged by the diversity among persons' views and practices, institutions and cultures, governments and jurisdictions that arise from that plurality. The challenges that these pluralities pose to moral universalism are both normative and practical: they demand that we ask both which forms of pluralism a universalist morality *should* accommodate and which ones it *can*. And the latter, broadly practical question has conceptual and political aspects: which forms of pluralism are conceptually compatible with moral universalism, and which ones can be accommodated in a politically stable way, without capitulating to sheer political force? As this volume's essays here demonstrate in a wide variety of ways, these normative, conceptual, and political questions deeply intertwine.

1

MORAL UNIVERSALISM

The severity and the form of the challenges posed to moral universalism by human plurality depend on the nature of universality claimed. As the outset of Barbara Herman's essay in this volume reminds us, moral universality sometimes comes in a merely formal version, amounting simply to an affirmation of the centrality of rules or principles to morality. Such a formal universality is compatible with the rules being highly context sensitive and specific; it excludes only references to particulars in the strict sense: persons and places as referred to by proper names, times referred to by indexicals such as "now" or "next week." In being compatible with almost any content, a commitment to this kind of formal neutrality has seemed to many, going back to Hegel's critique of Kant's ethics, to be empty. It is today opposed, not by political philosophers or legal theorists worried about the diversity of religious and other doctrines within modern societies, but by moral philosophers who reject it on largely metaphysical or epistemological grounds.[1] These particularists hold that the basis of moral reasons, say, is not in any universal principles, but rather in the particulars of each case. For these particularists, the ultimate ground for helping Mrs. Smith who has fallen and is lying helpless in the roadway is not that one has a general duty to help people in need when one can do so without gravely endangering oneself, but, say, the fact that Mrs. Smith is now lying helplessly and vulnerably in the roadway. Interesting as the debate between particularists and their opponents now is,[2] for present purposes, we may set it aside. At least for the sake of argument, all of the contributors here accept moral universalism in the sense in which it stands opposed to moral particularism. Each accepts that there are objective moral principles that are formally universal. The question that each raises is rather whether there is also an importantly universal content to morality. As Herman puts it, the question is whether there is "universality in the content of obligation as well" (p. 17, this volume).

To get universality into the content of obligation, or of morality more generally, one must specify the domain across which it is purportedly to range. On this dimension, the essays in this volume have a distinctive focus. Most commonly in moral theory, the question is whether moral principles hold universally across all persons. While this layer of concern presumably does always lie in the background of any discussion of moral universalism in politics, it is not here in the forefront. The challenges here addressed do not stem directly from the diversity of individuals' views, characteristics, or commitments—the sort of challenge that has absorbed much recent attention from liberal theorists of toleration and their critics,[3] a challenge posed to liberal justification by what Rawls calls "the fact of pluralism."[4] If people's moral, religious, and evaluative beliefs and commitments did not differ in the ways that comprise the fact of pluralism, then perhaps the issues treated in this volume would not arise; nonetheless, this kind of pluralism is not directly under discussion here. Rather, the potentially problematic pluralities considered here are all plural claims to authority of one kind or another: the normatively tinged claims of multiple nations, legal systems, or religious and other associations to some form of deference and allegiance, at least on the part of their citizens or adherents. The issue here being one of accommodating pluralism to the objective, universal core of morality, a thoroughgoing moral relativism is not on the table. Our contributors generally assume that there are some objective moral truths and set themselves the task not of defending this objectivity against a relativist's challenge, but of asking how best to assimilate political, legal, and religious and otherwise associational pluralism within an objectively universal morality. In the broadest terms, then, the question addressed here is whether deference or allegiance to plural authorities of any of these kinds can be reconciled with, or accommodated to, the invariant, objective core content of a substantively universal morality.

On a purer form of universalism than is represented here, the pattern of any possible reconciliation would be simple to derive. Any such deference or allegiance to plural purported authorities would be licit if endorsed by the universal principles of morality and illicit otherwise. Consider a simplified Kantian picture: the universal content of morality—as Herman also reminds us— would be "pure" or a priori, and hence invariant across possible worlds and across types of rational being. While the principles of universal morality might imply that, in certain circumstances, this or that government, legal system, or religious association ought to be deferred to, the moral principle that generates this result must be formulatable without reference to any such contingent social structure. Although Kant allowed that an understanding of anthropology and a schema of practical judgment might help us bring the universal principles of morality to bear on our contingent circumstances, still, these principles remain, at their core, invariant across nations, legal systems, and constellations of religious and other social associations.

On this simplified Kantian picture, there is clearly no such thing as moral authority. There is only reason, identically present in each person, and needing to be freed from its "self-imposed tutelage," its deference to authorities.[5] It is perhaps an indication of the influence of Hegel's critique of Kant's ethics that so many of the contributors to this volume both accept the possibility of morally significant authorities of one kind or another and see these residing in various aspects of the social forms within which we live. Or perhaps it is just that we have lost confidence in this simplified version of the Kantian solution and, having also denied the authority of pure reason, are not sure how, if at all, to locate morally significant authorities.

By "morally significant authorities," I do not mean "moral authorities." Possibly no one in this discussion believes that there is anyone or any social body with the authority to issue a binding *moral* judgment, that there is anyone who can authoritatively tell it like it is, morally speaking. The authorities here in question are not interpreted by this volume's discussants as claiming moral authority as such. Instead, they are taken to claim political, legal, religious, or associational authority. The question is whether any of these ways in which authority is socially exercised has interesting implications for the content of morality. For the implications to be interesting, they presumably must not be deducible from some invariant and universal moral principle plus the facts. For instance, from the moral principle that one ought to obey the commands of one's legitimate sovereign plus the fact that one's legitimate sovereign has commanded one to pay a poll tax, one may deduce the conclusion that one ought to pay a poll tax. In such a pattern of derivation, the sovereign's command is indeed authoritative, and does indeed have implications for what ought, morally, to be done; but this implication is not interesting, for here the sovereign's command is like any other factual condition that activates a moral principle. That being so, there is no reason to think of the sovereign's command as shaping or modifying the content of morality, which remains invariantly universal: the variable element is simply one part of the circumstantial facts to which morality must be applied.

As a model for what a more interesting form of morally significant authority might be like, consistent with the acceptance, for the sake of argument, that there are universal principles of morality, we might look to Aquinas's idea of a "determination (*determinatio*) of certain generalities" of natural law.[6] In addressing how it is that the universal content of natural law bears on the civil laws of the world's many nations, Aquinas crucially distinguished two ways in which this can occur. One is via the sort of deductive route I have alluded to both in characterizing the claims of a simplified Kantianism and, just now, in explaining why some ways that social authorities might end up having moral significance would be uninteresting. The second, however, is the determinative route. Sometimes, as Aquinas pictures things, the civil authorities in a given state are called on creatively to interpret a precept of the natural law by making it more specific.[7] Even in the absence of a meta-principle declaring that such interpretations or determinations of the content of principles by legitimate civil authorities are to be taken as binding, they can—perhaps in some of the ways innovatively explored by contributors to this volume—come to have morally binding force in their localities. Although Aquinas's suggestion, here, is hardly radical—and, indeed, some of our contributors go farther in carving out room for moral creativity—it does illustrate how a social body that purports to issue authoritative guidance may in fact end up exercising morally relevant authority that is actually interesting, in that it contributes normative content not deducible from the invariantly universal core of morality.

Whether or not there exists any valid or legitimate form of morally significant authority, the pronouncements of popes, rabbis, and imams, the rulings of courts of law, and the statutes and edicts of national governments will inescapably shape what Herman here calls the "lived morality" of the world's myriad localities. These interventions, each *claiming* a kind of authority, will shape the "basic practical skills," the tacit perception of available options, and the "background conditions for everyday life" that people internalize in becoming moral agents (Herman, pp. 23–24, this volume). Although we moderns are nervous about the very idea of moral authority, that does not mean that we can escape these many ways in which authorities of other kinds influence how morality is locally lived. The question pursued in this volume, in these terms, is whether such morally significant authority is ever valid or legitimate and, if so, under what conditions. Can universal morality *cope* with such pluralities of claims to other kinds of authority, and how, if at all, do the authoritative pronouncements of such diverse and plural authorities contribute to the content of moral requirements?

POLITICS AND PLURALISMS

The *political* issues raised by our contributors, as they grapple with this question about accommodating pluralisms of various kinds, fall into two broad categories. There are questions about whether political realism may successfully be resisted while carrying out such a reconciliation, and questions about how to recast liberalism if plural authorities are to be recognized. The authors of our three core chapters, Bernard Kingsbury, Barbara Herman, and William Galston, variously set these modes of engagement with politics. Kingsbury and Herman each seek to make room for pluralism of authority while resisting political realism. Galston, in his recasting of the ideal of liberal toleration, insists on the plurality of moral authorities.

Recurring to the understanding of invariantly universal morality that comes with the simplified Kantian picture described above, we can see why committed moralists as well as hard-bitten observers of politics might converge in thinking that when political currents generate variations that apparently depart from the core content of universal morality, these developments should be frankly viewed as the triumph of political power, political will, or political necessity over universal morality. Our contributors focus on two domains in which this tension between morality and political power are likely to be present: in international law, in which nations confront one another in ways that can seem only superficially moralized, and in moments of political revolution and upheaval, in which cataclysmic political change threatens long-accepted modes of lived morality and new "modes and orders"—the realist would say—are imposed.[8] Realist accounts of international law and domestic political struggle are both familiar and seemingly easy to grasp.[9] Those who react against such political realism simply by insisting on the demands of universal morality tend to seem hopelessly utopian. Here, Kingsbury and Herman avoid that trap, each setting out to walk moral universalism across the knife-edge of according moral significance to those plural authorities whose de facto influence the realists stress while nonetheless resisting realism.

For Benedict Kingsbury, this effort is the crux of his answer to the question of how international law ought to be conceived. Although this is a question about law, it maps readily onto the issues about morality that are the common concern of the essays in this volume. In international law, the theoretical debate has long raged between cosmopolitan and realist poles. For the cosmopolitan about international law, international law's core grounds and content, or both, are to be drawn from universal morality. Only such a basis in universal morality, it is argued, can distinguish international law from the brute use of force. For the realist about international law, by contrast, there is nothing more fundamental than the power relations among plural nation-states and, now, various other kinds of international actors, such as the multi-national corporation. Kingsbury holds that it is a mistake either to attempt to deduce the central norms of international law from universal morality or to reduce international law to being a modus vivendi among nation-states. The third possibility is to look to the idea of law for norms that have significance beyond being the residue of compromise. He finds such norms in international law's complex commitment to publicness: to laws being an expression of a public and speaking in its name (pp. 174, 176, 181 this volume). In international law, this commitment is complex because multiple publics—not all of them national—are in play. Innovative and intersecting international law-generating bodies, such as the European Union and the World Trade Organization, also help generate, in effect, new publics to which this new law ought to answer. That public law ought to express the will of a public and to speak in its name is both a normative commitment specific to this type of law, as Kingsbury emphasizes, and one that plausibly has moral significance. Hence, on this kind of middle position, while the content of international law could not be read off of, or deduced from, the principles of universal morality, still those principles can be seen as constraining the legitimate processes whereby international legal authority is exercised.

Whereas the plurality that international law addresses is above all that of nation-states and other "jurisgenerative" bodies, and hence is arrayable, to a first approximation, on a world map, the plurality with which Barbara Herman deals in the first instance is one locality's plurality of forms of lived morality as they change over time. Herman notes that while lived morality needs to be stable over time in order to become properly internalized, thus equipping individuals with adequate moral skills and moral perception, lived morality is also locally lived, in forms of life that are subject to change. Sometimes, indeed, change is urgently called for. Herman does not address a Callicles or a Machiavelli who might purport to reduce all of morality to a hardheadedly realist basis, but she does focus on a type of case in which realism rears its head again, even once universal morality is granted general sway, namely in moments of political crisis in which years of systematic injustice have come to a head. At those moments, it might be thought, one should listen to the realist's appeal to "political necessity," even if the aim is to rebuild the framework of a just society on the ruined foundations of the old, unjust one. To test this question, Herman takes the case of post-apartheid South Africa, where such an attitude was certainly to have been expected. She argues, however, that there not only was available a pathway of renewal within universal morality, but that, with the institution of the Truth and Reconciliation Commission (TRC), it was actually taken. As she describes it, this path involved a "moral improvisation" that shifted the permissible routes of redress for the many decades of violence and injustice suffered by the victims of apartheid. Nelson Mandela's supererogatory forswearing of revenge set an example, making possible a course in which the rights of redress of the many victims were neutralized.

Although the target of Herman's analysis is a change in morality over time, consistently with a framework of universal morality, it is clear that, so long as the South African case is not unique, different local improvisations of this kind will result in a plurality of divergent lived moralities. Another country that, like South Africa, had long perpetrated systematic injustice against an oppressed group, but that lacked a leader like Nelson Mandela, might not be able to improvise its way into a moral neutralization of rights of redress. What Herman is describing, then, is not just how the content of morality can evolve, consistently with a universal core, but also how, again consistently with a universal core and without any relativism, morality can come to have different content in different places. In these many places, lived morality claims a kind of authority over how life is to be lived. Herman sketches how to reconcile these claims of the moral practices of our many human localities with the universal morality underlying each of them.

While not denying the existence of this kind of local variation, William Galston reminds us that our localities each tend to be normatively complex. A political theorist such as Galston might find the idea of "lived morality" too much of an abstraction, insofar as it characterizes morality without reference to any of the preachers, politicians, pundits, or philosophers who claim the authority to articulate for us how we ought to live. A central tenet of the liberal pluralism Galston defends here is that, so long as individuals' free alignment with any of these purported authorities is protected by robust rights of exit, political society ought to cede to its non-political competitors considerable sway in determining how their adherents' lives are to be led. Galston's approach is "empirical" at least in the sense that it starts from a close examination of how life is actually lived in modern societies. One observes, in effect, that the lived morality that people in most places internalize allows for a kind of render-unto-Caesar, render-unto-God compartmentalization that allows for multiple types of authority. Galston defends this multiplicity or pluralism of authorities as appropriate, both by undercutting arguments for "civic totalism"—the view that all authority ultimately rests with the state—and by suggesting that this kind of plural authority appropriately reflects the plurality of distinct, ultimate values that Isaiah Berlin so eruditely extolled. Galston recognizes and indeed affirms, however, that his liberal defense of allowing sway to multiple authorities does rest on a "minimal universalism" of moral commitment—one that elevates certain ultimate values over others and helps explain why this kind of liberal pluralism is appropriate for all liberal societies.

What kind of authority is Galston discussing? It is not political authority as such: that is what Galston seeks to limit to make way for

other authorities. Obviously it is not clerical or any other kind of associational authority. Political institutions, religious bodies, and other associations each share in the kind of authority that Galston has
in view. It seems to be authority, or purported authority, over how
we ought to live. This is, then, a kind of moral authority or purported moral authority. Compatibly with a modernist's view that none
of these institutions or associations can speak authoritatively—that
is, infallibly or "unsecondguessably"—about the content of morality, one may recognize that each, in varying ways, claims authority—
that is, obedience or allegiance—in articulating principles, ideals,
and models of how one ought to live. Accordingly, while Galston's
concern is principally with politics—specifically, with reining in the
tendency to civic totalism—in the background of his view is a quite
general understanding of moral authority, namely that it does not
rest entirely in any person, faculty, or body, but is irretrievably and
appropriately dispersed across a plurality of those.

DETAILS OF ACCOMMODATION

Frank Michelman's contribution to the present volume accepts
Herman's contention that the South African TRC involved some
kind of moral improvisation but differs with her about how to ana-
lyze it in detail. The issues of relative detail that he raises have general importance for our understanding of how moral universalism
might accommodate itself to plural authorities.

How much room there is for such accommodation crucially
depends on whether the scope available for plural authorities
to shape lived morality is limited to what counts as a determination or specification of universal principles. Universal principles
may need determination because they are vague, because they
are highly abstract, or because they explicitly require that people
or societies adopt one sufficient means from a disjunctive list of
alternatives. As Herman mentions, T. M. Scanlon "argues that
where there is a region of activity that requires moral regulation,
and there is more than one legitimate principle that can do the
job, the fact that one of these principles is generally, even if not
universally, accepted in a community can be sufficient for it to obligate all" (p. 40, this volume).[10] Call this "Scanlon's community-
acceptance principle." Herman argues that this principle is too

conservative to cover the case of the TRC, however, because it involved a rejection or suppression of broadly accepted norms of redress in favor of a new approach. But what exactly did that rejection or suppression involve?

Michelman argues that the crucial moral change in the South African case was a shift, not in the moral rights of the victims of apartheid, as Herman suggests, but rather in the moral duties of the South African legislators who instituted the TRC. Michelman grants that the creation of the TRC made redress through the courts effectively unavailable to the victims. But did that shift their moral rights? He doubts this, for by removing an effective legal pathway for pursuing such a moral right of redress, the creation of the TRC made it practically unnecessary to modify these persons' moral rights and odd to say that they had an obligation not to pursue them (p. 55, this volume). Conversely, as F. M. Kamm here reminds us—in addition to raising myriad important questions about the content of Herman's moral analysis—the mere practical unavailability of a means of pursuing or defending a moral right does not mean that the moral right does not exist (p. 66, this volume). Michelman argues that, instead of a shift in the victims' rights, what occurred in the creation of the TRC was a shift in which moves were morally permissible for South Africa's legislators. He suggests that at an initial phase, shutting off the victims' legal right of redress would have given the victims a valid moral complaint against the legislators, while at a later phase, "procedural-moral" reasons may have entered via the democratic process to have shifted things so that such a moral complaint would no longer be valid (p. 56, this volume). To consolidate this shift, he suggests—transposing Herman's language into the key of deliberative democracy—that the democratic process must have come to favor one of two "competing casuistries": the one favoring the TRC rather than the one favoring a more vengeful policy.

Michelman's recasting of Herman's example forces us to reconsider what it means for local divergences in lived morality to be compatible with the invariant, core content of universal morality. Different specifications or determinations of that core content will all be compatible with it; but it may seem that a moral change that has the effect of canceling the victims' rights of redress cannot be a change simply from one determination of that core content to another. Either these rights were not truly grounded in universal morality in the first place, one might think, or else their cancellation is a violation of universal morality. Yet even if Scanlon's community-acceptance principle cannot explain the moral change that interests Herman, it illustrates how it might have been the case that universal morality derivatively required local rights of redress before the TRC, compatibly with a moral change arising that sidelined them. Further, as Kamm's essay suggests, meta-principles more abstract than Scanlon's might explain how contingent shifts in the means available for effectively realizing morally necessary regulation can entail shifts in what is morally required or permissible. More specifically, Kamm argues that the case of the TRC as set out by Herman exemplifies a common meta-principle for transforming supererogatory acts into obligatory ones, namely, reducing the costs or sacrifices imposed by the act. As the rich exchange between Kamm and Herman brings out, the creation of a new moral obligation on a societal scale cannot hinge on balancing civic goods against individual rights. At most, a spirit of civic benevolence combined with the creative moral example of one or more heroic individuals can leverage individuals' capacities to imagine their rights differently, and so to accept a different content of obligation.

Excesses of Accommodation?

As we have seen, each of the three core chapters argues that, in some important way, moral universalism can be accommodated to an important type of pluralism, while Michelman further probes how changes in what morality requires—and hence possible local divergences in moral requirement—might come about. While the remaining contributors raise specific themes and issues of their own, almost all of them, in one way or another, argue that the three core authors have been too accommodating of pluralism. In various ways, the remaining authors argue, variously, that moral universalism is robust enough not to need to accommodate pluralism, that pluralism's claim to be accommodated is weak, and that the costs of accommodating it are too high.

What makes moral universalism robust against any need to accommodate pluralism might lie in the subtlety of its structure or in the power of its demands. F. M. Kamm, who, as I have noted, emphasizes that there seem to be universal meta-principles governing the introduction and withdrawal of norms of lived morality, highlighted its potential conceptual subtlety. If so, she points out, universal morality may be more able to remain invariant in the face of variable contingent circumstances than at first appears. Put in slightly more political terms, her claim is that universal morality can remain a stable, conservative influence without hamstringing our ability to respond flexibly to changing circumstances. William Scheuerman, in his illuminating response to Kingsbury's essay on international law, argues, in that domain, for the strength of universal morality's demands. His argument is in the conditional. He maintains that Kingsbury's attempt to steer a middle path between universalist cosmopolitanism and a realist capitulation to plural powers places him unstably on a knife-edge: if universal principles are robust enough to generate a requirement that international law be public in Kingsbury's two senses, then they will also be robust enough to require more by way of international democracy and international distributive justice than Kingsbury admits.

Another basis for resisting the universalist's accommodation of pluralism is to question why it is called for in the first place. This is the principal mode of Daniel Weinstock's chapter, which analyzes the normative assumptions of liberal pluralisms such as Galston's. Weinstock distinguishes what he calls "autonomy liberalism," which holds that all should have the opportunity to live autonomously, from "toleration liberalism," which argues for an unrestricted range of choice of modes of life. Galston's liberalism, he suggests, is of the former kind. As Weinstock interprets it, it rests normatively on its commitment to Berlinean value pluralism: while being willing to elevate the value of autonomy, it denies that there is any general way of reducing the plurality of ultimate values to a single basis for choice. Weinstock points out, first, that value pluralism of this kind is a definite normative commitment, at odds with relativism on the one hand and value monism on the other. As such, a commitment to value pluralism is not compatible with neutrality about fundamental moral matters. While autonomy liberalism may not aim to be neutral in this way, it does tend to look to value pluralism to support the importance of ceding normative authority to the many religious and civic associations to which people in a liberal society become attached. Weinstock's principal aim is to undercut this purported argument from value pluralism to liberal pluralism. He argues that there is no necessary conceptual connection between the existence of plural ultimate values and the existence of plural social institutions having normative authority.

The final sort of response to universalist accommodation of plural authorities represented here is the claim that, even if there is some call for some such accommodation to be made, the moral costs of such accommodation are too high. In her powerfully argued response to Galston, Robin West urges that his liberal pluralism would give too much sway to the kinds of religious and familial authorities that long have oppressed and inflicted violence against women and vulnerable minorities. As she sees it, to accept the moral significance of these forces that claim authority within lived morality is to take a step backward to the kind of quietist liberalism that for centuries condoned such practices as "chastisement" (wife beating). On her reading of the history of U.S. liberalism, it was precisely deference to such plural authorities, and not a commitment to individual rights, that led to liberals shutting a blind eye to this kind of horror.

According to West's critique of Galston, too hasty an embrace of moral pluralism can generate a failure adequately to protect vulnerable groups' interest in equality and freedom. In a comparable fashion, Gopal Sreenivasan and Kenneth Baynes warn that Kingsbury's pluralistic understanding of inter-public law gives inadequate weight to democracy, and therefore also to the principles of legitimacy that democracy supports. Kingsbury does not claim that his conception of public international law is democracy promoting, but he suggests that it is at least neutral with respect to democratic values. Sreenivasan demurs, arguing that international law on either Kingsbury's model or the *jus inter gentes* model can function as a serious threat to democracy by constraining democratic publics' capacity to legislate on behalf of their understandings of the common interests of citizens. On Sreenivasan's reading, Kingsbury's principle of publicness could counteract this threat to democracy only if it were interpreted robustly as protecting the permanent and fundamental common interests of all affected—but to strengthen the principle in this way would shift it significantly in the direction of moral universalism.

Is a pragmatic pluralism grounded in a normative principle of publicness or is publicity a sustainable middle ground between cosmopolitan universalism and realpolitik? Like Scheuerman and Sreenivasan, Kenneth Baynes argues that as soon as we identify rule-of-law principles, including the principle of publicness, as normative criteria of law's legitimacy, we are set on a path toward moral universalism. The patterns of international law-formation that Kingsbury thematizes constitute a partial and incomplete "thickening" of rule-of-law principles in international society, representing a growing norm of mutual accountability between international actors and an increasing interpenetration of legal orders. Citing Habermas's arguments for the internal connection between the rule of law and democracy, Baynes believes that these dynamics both encourage and demand "the development of democratic institutions at the global level" (p. 229, this volume). Kingsbury's emphasis on the local and partial character of international "publics" is motivated, Baynes suggests, by a pragmatic concern to speak to what is possible in human affairs, to temper our normative aspirations with a sober assessment of empirical realities of power inequalities and deep moral disagreement.

In this respect, the debate between Baynes and Kingsbury, like the debates between Herman and Kamm, or Galston and Weinstock, return us to old questions in moral and political philosophy concerning the tension between what is practically realizable and what we imagine humans at their best to be capable of, between political necessity and the demands of morality, between the real and the ideal. Our authors agree, however, that the phenomena of moral pluralism cannot simply be explained away as expressions of human imperfection, as if they were flawed instantiations of universal moral principles. The fact of pluralism is not evidence for the impossibility of universalism. The practical realization of universal moral principles will not look the same in every time and place, and yet the claims of universal morality—equality, justice, the rule of law, perhaps toleration and democracy—do provide meaningful critical standards against which to measure actually existing practices. It seems inescapable that our guiding question in this introduction—whether a plurality of morally significant authorities can and should be accommodated by universal morality—must be answered in the affirmative, though that does not settle the question of which authorities have a valid claim to recognition. Although this is a genuinely common issue across the contributions to this volume, it is of course possible that differences among the types of plurality that concern our different authors—plural international legal actors, plural moral localities, and plural voices within a given community that claim moral authority—will mean that different answers to these abstract questions will be appropriate for international law, for the comparative moral analysis of different times and places, and for domestic politics. Even if the answers thus vary, however, it is clear from the interlocking discussions here that the issues that arise about accommodating universal morality to plural authorities in these different domains all illuminate one another.

NOTES

1. See, for example, Jonathan Dancy, *Ethics Without Principles* (New York: Oxford University Press, 2006).

2. For interesting recent developments, see, for example, Mark Lance and Margaret Olivia Little, "Defeasibility and the Normative Grasp of Context," *Erkenntnis* 61 (2004): 435-455; and Pekka Väyrynen, "Moral Generalism: Enjoy in Moderation," *Ethics* 116 (2006): 707-741.

3. See, for example, *NOMOS XLVII: Toleration and Its Limits*, eds. Melissa S. Williams and Jeremy Waldron (New York: NYU Press, 2008).

4. John Rawls, *Political Liberalism*, rev. ed. (New York: Columbia University Press, 1996), 36f.

5. Immanuel Kant, "An Answer to the Question, 'What Is Enlightenment?,'" in *Kant: Political Writings*, ed. H. S. Reiss (Cambridge: Cambridge University Press, 1970), 54-60.

6. Thomas Aquinas, *Summa Theologiae*, I-IIae, Q. 95, a. 2.

7. For an updating of this idea of specifying norms, see Henry S. Richardson, "Specifying Norms as a Way to Resolve Concrete Ethical Problems," *Philosophy and Public Affairs* 19 (1990): 279-310.

8. The phrase is Machiavelli's, as highlighted by Harvey C. Mansfield in *Machiavelli's New Modes and Orders: A Study of the Discourses on Livy*, new ed. (Chicago: University of Chicago Press, 2001).

9. Political realism becomes more difficult to grasp insofar as it claims to be prescriptive.

10. Herman cites T. M. Scanlon, *What We Owe to Each Other* (Cambridge, MA: Harvard University Press, 1998), 339ff.

1

CONTINGENCY IN OBLIGATION

BARBARA HERMAN

This paper begins with an exploration of a set of tensions that arise between some ambitions of moral theory and the role of morality in the regulation and construction of ordinary life. It ends with a conjecture about moral justification in a moment of radical social and constitutional transition, and a challenge to the view that when such moments are politically necessary they may be normatively discontinuous with morality. The route from beginning to end is by way of an account of various kinds of contingent obligations. The idea is that in coming to terms with contingency in obligation within morality we acquire resources to extend the reach of moral justification across the putative gap between morality and political necessity.

An important strand of modern moral theory aspires to capture the connected standards of universality of rule or principle and the unconditional nature of obligation. This can come to be regarded as the source of an ideal of sorts: that there be universality in the content of obligation as well.[1] Our moral lives, by contrast, are run through with obligations that are contingent, in form as well as content, specific to here and now. We are answerable to moral demands that arise from evolving institutions as well from the vagaries of human life. One response from the side of theory might find our moral lives to that degree imperfect. I doubt that could be right. A different response would take the measure of the contingency as a challenge to the ambitions of moral theory.[2] Once

we appreciate the many different ways in which obligations are
contingent, where things genuinely could have been otherwise, it
might be wondered how we could support the claim of objectivity
thought necessary for the unconditionality of obligation. In some
cases the answer is easy, but not in all. My plan is to approach the
topic of contingency in obligation in the spirit of this challenge,
examining contested claims from the bottom up. I regard the ways
we engage with morality in both ordinary and unusual circumstances as providing data, and adopt the working hypothesis that
some of the difficulties we encounter may have their source in the
ambitions of moral theory, or in the way we interpret them, rather
than in the facts of moral life. Reversing the angle of inquiry can
often reveal occluded aspects of things; in this case, one hoped-for
effect of the shift is some increased insight into the conditions that
can give rise to moral obligations.

Some of the questions I will consider may appear more empirical than philosophical. This oddity of method is appropriate to the
subject: ethics is a boundary discipline, beholden both to its internal standards (of correctness in judgment and action) as well as
to the conditions of the practical world it orders. This can leave
it open, in particular cases, to contest which sort of question we
ought to be asking.

Consider, in this light, an initial piece of data and the consequences that flow from it for moral theory. Knowing in advance
where our obligations lie, what claims of duty we may encounter,
is not just practically useful for planning, but essential—arguably
necessary—for living a coherent life.[3] If compelling moral demands, personal or impersonal, may be lying in wait for us around
any corner, we would have to set ourselves to anticipate and manage them; and if we cannot know in advance what they are, it is
reasonable to think even the best of us would be rendered less
able to invest ourselves, our energy, and attention in the projects
and relationships that make life worthwhile. A great deal of practical uncertainty of any sort tends to be bad for us; moral uncertainty is especially problematic because moral demands, when they
do show up, can override other concerns. This fact, on its own,
pushes moral life to be conservative, resistant to change. And because most of us live locally, embedded in complex social and institutional networks, the conservative content of morality that we

encounter will also often be local: promises are to be made *this* way, help to be offered like *that*.

These features of moral life—that it resists change and has a local face—have other sources as well. Morality is important in and to our lives: it is to be maintained against strong passions, and it can require the sacrifice of valued interests. Such importance would be belied if morality were inconstant or readily changed.[4] And since it is part of morality's work to mold and direct institutions and relationships, it must appear in a form that fits with what they are locally like, else it would not be able to provide the constancy of direction that is among the conditions of flourishing for both institutions and individuals.

But the story of what we want from morality—the kind of thing we want it to be—contains elements that suggest the constancy or stability of morality and its local face may not be in total harmony. We might want the stability of morality to arise not from its pragmatic encounter with local mores or our psychological needs, but to reflect the fact that it tracks or expresses some objective truth about the way things ought to be. The local aspect of lived morality suggests, if not full-blown relativism, something other than the universality of moral principle that is often regarded as the telltale of objectivity.

There is also the matter of moral correction and moral change (they are not the same). One might think that the more local the shape of our moral understanding, the more likely it is to be wrong, in large ways and small. This would create problems at different levels. There is the potential challenge the occurrence of local error sets for moral stability (assuming errors discovered are things to be corrected). But also, the very unavoidability of local error might make one think that the project of looking at "lived morality" cannot belong to philosophical inquiry. At best, perhaps, it belongs to its less-formal department of engineering or office of pragmatics—applied ethics in a literal sense. But is this right? Inquiry directed at determining correct moral principles and standards is certainly sharply different from a project of understanding the conditions needed for agents in actual social settings to absorb morality and negotiate moral requirements. But why think it follows that the latter kind of inquiry is normatively, and so philosophically, limited?

Suppose that the Doctrine of the Double Effect is a true principle of permissibility (harms that arise as unintended but fore-
seen effects of overall beneficial action count less than they would
if intended). The lesson of double effect would be lost in a moral
space that was dependent on strict performance standards (imagine a society in which traditional forms of action play a central
and extensive role in social life). Where trust depends on external
signs, claiming that one's intention was not directly engaged with
a harm caused may not be a credible way to mark a moral difference.[5] But even if this were a social or psychological fact, it would
not challenge the correctness of the doctrine's standard. What is
left to ask is whether it is necessarily a good thing to have (or bad
to lack) the doctrine playing a significant role in moral practice.
How could that be a philosophical question? One might equally
ask: How could it be anything else? It is certainly not an empirical or sociological question ("a good thing" in what sense?). It is
a question about the contingency of moral content and its significance for claims of obligation. I don't see how we can understand
what morality is about without answering it.

If one of the projects of morality is to make the world different, more habitable, more ordered, shaped by our understanding
of what is right and good, then the situated agent, living in some
specific social space, has to be in the forefront of philosophical reflection. Against an assumed background of objective moral principle, we will ask agent-centered epistemological questions: How
should we decide what to do, how to be, given where we now find
ourselves? There is precedent for asking the question this way in
Kant: morality as a philosophical subject must have its pure or rational part, where we investigate the nature of its authority and
the objective principles that lie at its foundation, *and* it must have
an empirical part, where we come to grasp what we are to be like
and what we are to do—here and now, and toward the future.[6] But
then we do need to make philosophical (as well as practical) space
for thinking about moral correction and change, and so find a way
to manage the contingency in obligation that results.

As we shall see, not all contingency in obligation raises problems. Sometimes the contingency is in secondary principles or
meta-rules of response to moral failure, but there is unconditional
obligation at the ground level for agents acting. Less easy to accom-

modate would be ground-level obligations that impose significant burdens but that arise in ways that cannot be anticipated: where the kind of thing we may be required to do is not in or implied by our lexicon of duties.[7]

I think there are difficult obligations of this kind, and that they come about chiefly in conditions where creative solutions to moral difficulties are needed or attempted, often in the space between individual morality and politics. At the limit, there are occasions where the morally innovative or improvisatory acts of some can obligate all. Such a class of obligations would raise questions at many levels: about the closure of moral theory, about the stability conditions for coherent moral action and character, about the conditions of legitimacy for the creation of new obligations, and about their justification.

In what follows, I start out by describing some of the relevant data about our moral lives and circumstances that include the easier to tolerate aspects of contingency in obligation. After canvassing a range of harder cases and the resources morality requires to manage them, I take up the more radical idea of allowing for moral improvisation in moral theory and deliberative reflection. This will in turn provide a framework for examining the very different kind of contingency where political necessity can seem to override or supplant the authority of moral justification. I approach this topic by way of a real case: the obligations that arose with the creation of the South African Truth and Reconciliation Commission. Although the context is political—the establishment of a new constitutional community in post-apartheid South Africa—and with the creation of the Commission came abrogations of fundamental rights and the imposition of new obligations, I aim to show that justifying what was done by appeal to "political necessity" is not necessary, and that using resources drawn from other forms of contingent obligations, the contested actions can be located within the extended scope of morality, and that the new obligations, though radically contingent, are morally justified.

I

Resistance to contingency in obligation, or to any moral novelty, runs deep and has its source in the way morality figures in our everyday life. The normal moral agent—someone well brought up, with no errant psychological spikes or troughs—will have integrated determinate moral concerns and moral limits into the content and structure of her projects, even into the possible objects of her desires.[8] In ordinary circumstances, she will move seamlessly in the space of pragmatic and moral reasons. For the most part, moral questions will not and need not arise because her actions and choices are already responsive to the moral norms that apply. Politeness, offering a helping hand, queuing, honesty, respect, and the like, are not separate from what a decent person wants to do.

Some of this just belongs to practical competence. We make judgments and valid inferences without overtly thinking about them, either because we just "see" connections, or because we have acquired some appropriate habits of response—the way an experienced driver responds to a skid, or a competent chess player engages a defense. Although we might say that someone who responds in this way does so "without thinking," we also take her reasons to be accessible, or reconstructable: we know a lot about what we are doing, and why we do this rather than that. There is nothing peculiar to morality in this, though morality may require that we be able to look at things in a finer grain, or with more focused attention, depending, for example, on the kinds of responsibility we have for things going wrong.[9] A little lack of attention to what we are doing in wandering through a market is of negligible significance, a benign absentmindedness or fugue; we can't be so easy on ourselves where what is at stake is important to what we care about, or where our attention is under moral direction.

A different source of moral seamlessness, one most intimately related to our agency, runs even more quietly in the way we approach choice and decision. There are reasons not to careen into people as one passes through a crowded lobby, and there are reasons to express gratitude for a favor done. If you ask me why I said "thanks," or avoided collision with someone in my path, the reason I retrieve does not explain why I did "this rather than that," for there was no *that* for me in the space of possibilities. This restriction of the space of possibilities (of actions as well as objects of action) partly constitutes our moral character and is a necessary condition of virtue. Decision in such cases is not a result of choice or calculation. In accounting for this, we are drawn less to analogies with skills and more to field features of perception. From where I stand, there is no path through the space now occupied by someone else, just as there is no question about whether to express gratitude—though some, to be sure, about how best to do it. However we account for this field feature, the plain fact is that the world of the normal moral agent has a moral shape.

Though morality aims to shape the world of human action, parts of it are made to order. Whatever the account of fundamental principles, morality is responsive in certain obvious ways to the basic needs of human existence. But while it is neither arbitrary nor contingent that pain and suffering figure centrally in moral thought, how they count, and whose pain and suffering counts, may be, to some extent, an open question. I do not mean that we just decide these matters—that there are no standards here—but rather that there may be some indeterminacy, something we must fill out. Between the blue blood's hangnail and the loss of a species of toad there is a lot of space for working out costs and harms and responsibility. But even if the standard of obligation we arrive at is in some sense negotiable, because we are in better (or worse) circumstances, or understand and are able to do more, it is a standard nonetheless—not an arbitrary rule—as there is justification for the lines being drawn where they are. The fact that even core morality has to be filled out in these ways does not render it less objective, nor less fixed from the point of view of the acting agent.[10] Another locus of moral contingency has a different explanation. When land, or the means of production, are owned privately, we are in a specific space of rights and permissions that shapes much of what the world looks like to us. But while property must be stably organized in some way to establish rightful possession, there is no unique way of doing this: things could have been—and still can be—otherwise. This kind of contingency of obligation is well accommodated by a two-level theory: abstract principles reflecting fundamental needs, interests, and values, which offer direction for the construction of more determinate rules and practices. Although which rule or standard adopted is contingent, again, for the normal agent acting, the obligations and duties are set.

However, the same features that morality must have if we are to be able to live in its terms—that it can figure in the acquisition of basic practical skills, organize perception, and set the background

conditions for everyday life—are, when internalized for these purposes, sources of tension and resistance if the content of our duties
ought to change, or if we are presented with a region of moral concern with which we have little experience. Our practical skills, our
sense of salience and confident response are most at home in set
practices. Yet, somewhat paradoxically, it is just these abilities that
must be called on if we are to be appropriately responsive to new
reasons in unfamiliar circumstances: to absorb significant change
without harm we require the stability of character and moral self-
confidence that normal moral life provides. So there is something
a bit perplexing here in the terms of fit between good or normal
moral character and developing demands of obligation.

It strikes me as doubtful that there is *an* ideal type of character
fit both for negotiating normal action and conditions demanding
change. Indeed, there are as likely to be many ideal types as there
are to be any. We require certain abilities, but neither the route
to them nor the psychological configuration in which they reside
need be of one kind. One reason for this is that normal character
development is not cost free. We each come to adult agency with
a mix of tendencies: some beneficial, some inclining us to cause
harm.[11] If we are lucky in life—in choices and circumstances—our
flaws may not tarnish our record. If we are not lucky, the very tendencies that give us confidence in action may turn out to be ones
we ought not rely on.

One kind of bad luck can occur when social circumstances
evolve in morally unexpected ways. Patterns of behavior that were
normal and inoffensive may be revealed to be sites of injury; something once thought charming comes to be regarded as demeaning, even an expression of aggression or dominance. Reasonable
claims of innocence are no protection against fault.[12] When this
happens, reactions are often defensive, and sometimes hysterical;
the world can come to be an alien and hostile place, and acting
well can seem out of reach. The comfortable fit of seamless requirements and confidence is replaced by a moral demand that
we not only acknowledge uncomfortable truths, but also remake
ourselves in their light.

If a significant degree of self-knowledge and self-reform is morally required, the recognition that much of our self-knowledge
only comes through trial and error, while self-reform is, at best, an

uneven process, ought to bear on how we frame notions of responsibility, blame, and obligations of self-improvement. We do not expect people to know themselves ab initio, but we do expect them to learn from their mistakes. Likewise, though we cannot expect people to develop independently of their upbringing, we do expect them to move beyond the limitations of what they are taught. Our account of character and obligation will then have to have a view about how to make responsible moral agents—what sort of upbringing, in what conditions, produces agents who are able to generate and respond to new knowledge about themselves and their environment. The processes are interdependent: the content of known morality is reflected in our moral training; moral training includes abilities for self-shaping; these abilities make us responsible for creating and sustaining our moral character in the face of new knowledge; and so we must become trainers of ourselves. If ever there were a virtuous circle, this is one.

Of course, more than increased self-knowledge is involved. If the world in which the normal agent acts throws up new questions, unanticipated relationships, and human-made circumstances, we should expect to have obligations to initiate moral inquiries, to expand the base of relevant knowledge, to engage with and excavate morally relevant history. This too will put pressure on our moral understanding, on the type and content of the obligations we take ourselves to have, as well as what we need to be like in order to meet them.

II

Details aside, many of these points are obvious. Normal moral agents are made out of messy stuff; the contexts of action are to some degree opaque; ways in which we change the world (including ourselves) will often turn around and change morality. A natural response might be a reminder that the lived morality of actual agents is not the morality of philosophical or moral theory. And perhaps we might say this in the same spirit with which we say that our ordinary experience of and beliefs about the world is not science. But hard science is not an ideal of ordinary belief, whereas many regard the content of moral theory—at least its principles and procedures of deliberation—as something to be purposefully realized in our actions and practices. This is perhaps why some think that the facts of unavoidable failure and limits of our practical abilities and our moral knowledge, when coupled with the contingencies the world (and other people) may throw at us, point to a different kind of two-level moral theory, not now abstract principle and rules of application, but a moral analog of what, in the case of political institutions, Rawls called "nonideal theory."[13] There's a lot to be said about nonideal moral theory. I want to say only a little.

Parallel to the political case, nonideal moral theory negotiates two regions of difficulty. First, there is a moral analog of institutional noncompliance. Without assuming anything very bad about people, there is an expectable degree of moral failure: promises will be broken, lies told; anger will erupt into violence. Second, parallel to the problem of unjust institutions, there are the seriously immoral actions of some that pose practical and moral threats to others— where, for example, violence or coercion compel people into situations in which impermissible actions or ends are (rationally or morally) unavoidable. Nonideal theory will then introduce strategies for managing propensities to failure within the normal (norms of apology, blame, and repair), and principles for permissible resistance and response to wrongful actions, including, especially, resistance and response to those kinds of actions that make persons of moral integrity vulnerable to the purposes of wrongdoers.

Morality could also be nonideal in a more ordinary sense. Failures of agents might show lived morality to be in some way deficient if they arose because attempting to follow moral rules or ideals imposed large psychological and material burdens, or routinely involved one in moral conflicts, or because the circumstances or the moral rules made it too hard or too time consuming to determine what to do. Or it might be nonideal because of the uneasy fit between morality and the social institutions in which moral action takes place: for example, economic institutions that produce severe inequalities can make the unadjusted individual burdens of care too high. Considerations of this sort are sometimes brought forward to favor "common sense" and rule conceptions of morality, so that the interface between agent and principle is made simpler, or burdens are shifted from individual to group.[14]

Of course not all moral failures are at the level of individual moral action. We might have available to us a set of principles that would get us closer now to a better state, but which, over time, would do less well than some other set whose flaws have more immediate untoward effects.[15] Or we might have a region that calls for procedural regulation and no fully adequate procedure is available. We might have practices that in one case or another fail to realize their defining purpose, but overall guide well. Though a moral practice is constituted by its rules, it is justified by its purpose. Given unavoidable imperfections or shifting demands of circumstances, it is in principle open to change, adjustment or fine-tuning of the rules (different metaphors will suit different occasions). Most practices can survive such changes; they are organic in that way. But practices must also be somewhat resistant to change and challenge: if they were not, their rules would lack authority.

In the political case, nonideal theory presupposes as an ideal an objective to be achieved (for Rawls, the "well-ordered society"). In the moral case, it is hard to say whether we should be looking toward a moral order of things (a kingdom of ends) or perfect virtue, if they are different, or even if there is a sense in which the ideal in morality is something we are to promote. (I doubt that it is. If what made one think that lived morality calls for nonideal theory is that its requirements need to be adjusted to the limits of agents *as* human agents, then it really is hard to get a grip on the notion of the ideal.) We may be morally obligated to promote just institutions, so that given an appropriate conception of justice, and of the limits of social life, there is a well-formed notion of the ideal that nonideal theory is to promote. But we have no similar obligation to promote the institutions of morality (whatever that would mean).[16]

That morality must have ways of responding to the fact that ordinary agents may not always act well, or that we have practices that both require and resist adjustment, does not by itself point to an ideal condition where things would be otherwise. It seems equally sensible to think that the point of morality and such facts of human limits are in important ways co-determining. More malign failures do not in the same sense belong to morality: from its point of view, action that undermines the grip or sense of moral principle is always unexpected, even if not uncommon. That is why normal morality cannot prepare us for all the ways moral action may be subverted, or for what to do when we seem compelled to actions morality (even strategically adjusted morality) does not permit. For different reasons, but to similar effect, normal morality cannot tell us how to respond to new circumstances or unexpected revelations about familiar ones. But of course we will have to respond in each kind of case.

This leads me to think that what is at issue in many cases is less about ideal and nonideal theory than about the need for principled ways to extend morality beyond the boundaries of normal moral action. For that we will require access to deliberative resources—fundamental principles of action and volition, or conceptions of our relations to one another—that support general standards of correctness for actions and practices. We do not appeal to such principles in ordinary judgment, but they provide the terms of justification for the obligations and duties we take ourselves to have and thus make possible, if anything can, the extension of our moral understanding into unfamiliar territory.

III

In most of the regions so far canvassed, contingency in obligation is handled in one way or another by additional rules (or action-guiding principles). In some cases, the rules are socially or situationally specific determinations of higher-order principles; in others, they are reactive responses to kinds of failure that are frequent enough and/or serious enough to require set terms of response. But not all contingencies are susceptible to this sort of management. Whether because they are more extreme, and so disrupt the very idea of establishing rules (global catastrophes and the other "what ifs" of the overheated moral imagination), or because they are singular and seem to challenge our terms of justification, some moral contingencies require a different kind of resolution.

As noted earlier, among the problems one might fear contingency in obligation would introduce is instability in the content of ground-level duties and obligations. Instability is to be distinguished from mere variability of moral requirement. That can be normal, a function of changing conditions that affect action and our relationships or commitments to others. Making a promise, I cannot know with certainty what I will have to do. Being a parent, I cannot know what will be required of me as my child develops, has unexpected needs, or extends my liability. In a sense, this form of uncertainty is already contained in the obligation taken on. If I am not prepared to adjust my activities as events develop, then I have not undertaken the obligations responsibly in the first place. Typically, in incurring an obligation, we accept an authorial position: a commitment to make the narrative of self and some others come out "just so."[17]

Among the things we learn quickly is that our authorial control over the happenings in the world, even in our immediate environment, is limited. It is not just that we have limited powers; our actions are hostage to the unexpected. In the face of this, a prudent agent takes steps to minimize vulnerability: we trim our projects and ambitions; we construct a social world that helps make the effects of others' actions more predictable and our own intentions more likely to succeed. We do not obligate ourselves if there are too many intermediate steps, or our success is dependent on the unpredictable actions of others. Still, unexpected actions and events are inescapable, and if something significant hangs on it, they can alter what we may plausibly have committed ourselves to do. However, while the normal moral agent cannot be assumed to know or anticipate what is happening right now halfway around the world, or what lies she is being told by authorities, or what increases in knowledge will show to be morally salient, things will happen, things probably are happening, that will make what she should do different, and even different in kind, from what she can now expect. This introduces a different order of uncertainty and contingency in the range and content of our obligations—not something that we can, with prudent foresight, prepare for. One curious effect of absorbing this is that it makes morality—at least, moral knowledge—more like science than we typically think. The problems and questions we are taxed to answer expand. We may uncover new moral particles or systems or facts about our psychology that our "old science" cannot accommodate. We revise the way we understand the connections (causal and moral) between material conditions and obligations. And we know that the expansion of our knowledge will continue.[18]

It will follow that although lived morality (our ethical life) is by its nature parochial, as it must be in order to play its role in anchoring the conditions of everyday life, morality itself is not parochially limited. This creates an in-principle tension between the

moral facts, as it were, some of which are visible, others newly encountered or excavated, and the desired or desirable seamlessness
and stability of ordinary life. While not all tensions are signs of
something gone wrong—they are inherent in many normal processes of growth and development—the tension between the conditions of ordinary lived morality and the scope of morality tout
court is not a piece of a natural process, though it is, or is now, a
tension we cannot avoid.

We might then think of the morality we live as a working model—an expression of moral understanding at a time, articulated in
terms that cohere with the social and political institutions in which
most of our action will take place. The coherence is not primarily
about cognitive consonance. Many social institutions—law, educational, welfare agencies—are moral institutions: they exist to do
moral work, or to make moral action and relations possible.[19] Some
moral practices are elaborated in terms that make little sense apart
from local ways of life (the significance of the handshake). This
degree of embeddedness partly explains why we cannot expect
lived morality to change easily, not even in response to increased
moral awareness and discomfort. Because so much moral work is
done without much thought, or done for us, even the appearance
of something new to consider can be disorienting.

This is most easily seen at the outer limits of moral embedding,
in the norms of manners and etiquette. It can be difficult to think
of these norms as part of morality since they regulate modes of
dress, patterns of socializing and eating, historically meaningful
rituals of civility. These are not the kinds of prescriptions we think
of when we bring "morality" to mind, yet they provide the visible
form and many of the daily terms of a moral way of life. It is not
far-fetched to say that manners and etiquette articulate the out-
ward form of respect—moral business, if anything is.[20]

There are predictable costs at this end of the spectrum. The
embeddedness of etiquette in the minute details of living partly
explains why it can so easily devolve into high silliness; it goes seriously wrong when it vies for the content and not just the form of
our (usually non-intimate) relations. And since etiquette is often
also used to provide marks of class, it can seem important to reject it outright (or just ignore it); at the least we should not con-
fuse this aspect of its concern with moral ones. Still, one needs to

proceed with care in deconstructing etiquette's social pretensions: they are often ossifications of something with a point, and not as costlessly rejectable as we (or righteous adolescents) might think. The way we meet and greet one another, how we behave in groups and public meetings, what we signal with what we wear, must have conservative inertia if they are to perform their function.[21]

Although ordinary morality is essentially conservative, it does change. What drives change is no one thing, and some of the sources of moral change can be both elusive and morally complex. Certainly not all moral change is for the good. And some changes only appear to make things morally different, especially when they are not well integrated into agents' moral understanding. On the negative side, we know that fear or trauma can cause persons or groups to regress. A strong shared emotion sometimes renders ordinarily decent individuals open to actions they could not straightforwardly countenance. What they then do may be hard to explain in terms of their standing intentions and goals—hard for them as well. Better explanations will appeal to psychological effects: some kind of causal mechanism that affects individuals when they are in group situations. Historical examples are all too common: mob violence, massacres, lynchings, various acts of religious and ethnic extremism, all participated in by ordinary persons. Such episodes may even attain a perverse kind of normality for some sustained time.[22] Positive change also can occur in the absence of a deliberative cause and without a sustained effect on moral life. Individuals, even whole communities, can rise to something that surpasses their own expectations of what is possible. Many of the best-known examples of extraordinary actions are taken in response to actual or threatening eruptions of violence, human and natural.[23] They too can become normal for a while, yet they rarely bring lasting change to the morally ordinary. Like their physical analog, when the rush of moral adrenalin abates, the new powers and interests are lost and devolve into tales of heroism.[24]

From the point of view of moral theory, both kinds of alteration are matters of psychology that need to be monitored and managed. Lessons may need to be learned, cautions and barriers introduced. However compelling at the time, they may not represent a route to moral change that morality itself can recommend. This can happen if the change relies on abilities and character traits that cannot survive the moment, or if the actions are not ones that could flow from or even fit with agents' understanding of their obligations.[25] This is not to say that there are no questions about obligations one might come to have when such temporary moral phenomena occur. It may seem easy to know what to do or avoid when the issue is others' evil, but it is less obvious what we are obliged to do when surrounded by members of our community caught up in a desire to do some extraordinary good. It seems unlikely that those not part of the emotional surge could be obligated to act in accordance with the new, temporary standard.[26] But I think they may not act in what were the old, ordinary ways, if this now would compromise the good attempted. Collective increases in public kindness, or a willingness to help strangers, or to rescue the persecuted, would seem to impose obligations on all in ways that even widespread acts of personal heroism do not.

The kind of change that morality can most readily welcome arises from deliberative responses to new or newly available (or newly effective) knowledge about events or changes (that may or may not themselves be the product of intention or plan). A new possibility of action is identified as a way through or around some moral difficulty which either the new conditions or the new knowledge generates. It may not matter *how* a possibility is identified; it matters a great deal that a connection be made with available resources of obligation and justification as a condition of affirming the possibility. Such interventions may then work their way into shared moral knowledge and practice. (School integration in the 1950s, partly as a response to psychologists' reports about the stigmatizing effect of racial segregation, is an example.) If, as we do with our knowledge of the physical world, we have reason to expect our moral knowledge to in this way increase and change—knowledge of what may be required of us, as well as of the possibilities and difficulties of successful action—then an openness to the ongoing intentional alteration of the landscape of obligation ought to be an integral part of the morality we live, and itself a source of distinctive obligations. This kind of openness does not ignore the concern for stability. Only some forms of stability require conservation; others involve maintaining balance, or securing a new equilibrium. The question is then not about stability per se, but about the right kind of stability.

IV

This comparison with our physical knowledge might suggest a simpler theoretical account. Wanting to sustain the objectivity of moral judgments and the stability of practices, I have emphasized the role of deliberative continuity: we deal with moral contingency and change by reknitting the moral fabric, as it were. The focus is on how things are for *agents*, whose choices and responses, guided by deliberative principles, construct a moral world. But suppose one thought that moral theory could accommodate the full range of cases because all possible obligations and duties are, in quasi-Leibnizian fashion, already contained in the concept or extension of our moral principles. It is a tempting picture, for it treats contingency as of mainly practical interest, on a par with adjusting one's financial practices to the ongoing interpretation of the tax code. On such a view, although we do not and cannot know what all our obligations and duties will be, for any set of circumstances, what duties there are is determined by the moral principles that apply. Our efforts may be partial and approximate, but the epistemic norm for moral judgment and deliberation is getting something right in the matching sense.

There are many reasons to resist this picture, but chief among them is that it leaves no place for the (anti-rigorist) idea that individuals and groups can produce moral responses to circumstances that were neither epistemically nor in any other sense "already there"—that their choices and actions can enact new norms, something created or improvised. We might want to go further and say that not only can a new obligation not be conditionally contained in prior moral principle, but it also need not be a uniquely correct response in the circumstances. So, for example, the suspicion that judgments of merit were affected by gender bias in orchestral auditions or in the refereeing of academic journal articles led some to introduce blind review (hearing but not seeing a performer; excising identifying information from a manuscript). Once introduced, I think it was clearly obligatory to adopt such measures, whether or not there might have been other means of acknowledging equity concerns (point systems, quotas).[27] Partly this was because the remedy was compelling, but also, an improvised remedy will often transform the way past norms of action are understood, potential-

ly changing the significance and/or content of known rules and
principles, so that what might have been another means no longer
seems so (e.g., once the problem is identified *by the solution* as one
of bias in judgment, not of numbers). All of this adds to the reasons for thinking the explanation of contingency is not a matter of
epistemic access. Even failed moral improvisations—ones that are
not intrinsically flawed, but which fail, for example, because of bad
timing, or lack of sufficient fit with prior values—can create new
spaces of moral possibility.

The phenomenon of improvisation, though a bit mysterious, is
not really exotic. Most of us are familiar with the moment in the
work of a group when someone recalls a past strategy or looks something up that enables the group to solve a problem. Much more unusual is the person who can, at the same kind of impasse, see a novel
way of acting that will not only solve the problem, but through her
grasp of the problem and its solution, transform a group's conception of its powers and even of its charge (even more rarely, this may
happen collectively). Most forms of moral problem-solving are well
understood in the first way: involving factual discovery and reliance
on precedent, they pose no strain on any reasonable conception of
how morality works. But not all are like this.

I think that morality, and so moral theory, must allow for improvisation, both in its sense of system (that it is open to change not
only *at* the bottom, but *from* the bottom), and in the way it acknowledges (and educates) the abilities of agents to effect moral change.
In this respect, morality is unlike other practices with which it is often, at least formally, compared. It is not like games, which typically involve fixed systems of rules; and it is not like the law, which can
change, but only through the activities of designated authorities
(judges, legislatures, etc.). No one has authority to change moral
norms. Changes that morality can countenance come by way of
the responses of individuals and groups that mark out a direction
of action that is held open to challenge on grounds of correctness
of fit (fit both with the problem to be solved and also with the
rest of morality) and of the legitimacy of costs imposed. It may be
that a novel response, once understood, will fit easily with familiar
moral principles. But it may also happen that in appreciating the
force of an improvisation, one is moved to rethink or reinterpret
familiar principles and values. Sound methods of moral justifica-

tion need not regard the prevailing understandings as fixed. A culture's reflective engagement with these challenges is one way an appropriate demand for stability can be met.

V

To demonstrate the fruitfulness of this approach, I want to turn to a more extreme kind of case, where contingent phenomena seem to require not just a revision of moral understanding but the partial abandonment of moral strictures. Explanations of a normative divide between morality and politics are often made in these terms: political necessities can give us reasons to do things that morality cannot countenance.[28] In times of war or civil upheaval, rights may not be upheld, commitments kept, or justice done. The rationale is the overarching need for peace and security, or social order, or a change in regime. Because the goal is of such weight in terms of human goods (or evils avoided), it supports a permissive stance towards means. When the crisis is over, this rupture between politics and morality is repaired.

It would be more than odd to regard this realpolitik as good in itself. It arises, when and if it does, because of the limits of morality, whose rules prohibit the actions deemed politically necessary. While I won't argue against the possibility of such necessities, I do want to suggest that with a more capacious understanding of morality's resources, and in particular the possibility of moral improvisation, the "necessity defense" might be less frequently needed. And that would be good in itself.

To explore this possibility, I want to examine the issues as they arose in the debate over the establishment of the South African Truth and Reconciliation Commission (TRC)[29]—a set of temporary, extra-judicial commissions through which victims of apartheid's violence could formally register crimes committed against them, perpetrators could seek amnesty, and some amount of reparations would be provided to victims. The legacy of grievous injustices of apartheid presented a range of obstacles to the possibility of shared moral life that ordinary morality and existing institutions lacked resources to overcome. The TRC was designed to bridge that gap. It is an especially apt case for my purposes, since those who created the TRC explicitly intended by so doing to obligate

others—specifically, to forgo redress for claims they had against
perpetrators of immoral, criminal acts, and to accept the regimen
of the TRC in its stead. Given the circumstances in which the obligations were to be introduced, the question of their legitimacy
arose naturally, and political necessity was one immediate answer,
though not one the principles endorsed.

The TRC has been viewed variously as a baldly political compromise introduced to avert a civil war, or as a situation-specific transition stage in the institution of constitutional democratic rule, or
as a local modification of the post-Nuremberg structures used to
provide an accounting of state crimes. I think the record shows
that it was no *bald* compromise; it is hard to imagine a more articulate or morally anguished public debate, regardless of the existence of some backroom deals. I also think its creation was a piece
of a strategy for constituting civil society, but it was not for that an
act of political necessity, nor something to be subsumed under the
rubrics of irregular or reparative justice (though the procedures
were irregular and reparative). The costs imposed were morally
significant, and it would be best to offer a moral justification, if
there is one. The question is: Of what kind? I will argue that the
TRC can be understood as a moment of moral improvisation, and
as such prompts an account of the moral costs and benefits that
reframes the issues involved. Pragmatic considerations can figure
in its justification, but not so as to make the brunt of the argument
instrumental—doing what had to be done for some pressing end.

There is always some danger in trying to do philosophical work
with an historically specific event. However, the wariness that is in
order when one is adducing as argument a flow of interconnecting
events and actions is to a considerable extent addressed in this case
by the great care of the participants took to publicly acknowledge
and justify the moral complexity of their decisions. And there is a
related advantage. Distinctions that might seem artificial in a philosopher's example here lie on or close to the surface of the historical record. It is an unusual moment in which thoughtful efforts
were made to use available morality to introduce moral change.[30]
So if there is a risk, I think it is one worth taking.

To make the case for the TRC as an example of successful moral
improvisation, I need to show three things: that the creation of
the TRC is not to be regarded in purely political terms; that its

origin was in an improvisation that created obligations not latent in the moral world (in ideal or nonideal terms); and that nonetheless these obligations could be justified in the moral terms of the world they changed. The contingency of the obligations was at both ends: the source is in no rule or principle, and the outcome is a set of obligations whose justification, though moral, is tied to time and place.

In the moral story of the TRC, the moral improvisation comes in two steps. First, there was an act of individual creativity. It is credibly claimed that Nelson Mandela's stunning refusal to seek retribution for the grievous wrongs he suffered did much to create the moral possibility of social order and democracy in post-apartheid South Africa.[31] What he did, and was seen to have done, is to offer himself as a model of moral self-transformation. In refusing both the natural desire for revenge and any formal claim for just retribution, he created a possibility of self-movement from the status of victim of unjust violence to the status of citizen of a state (one not yet fully existing) committed to an ethic of forward-looking civic benevolence. But Mandela's act was not of a kind that many others could repeat. It required unusual moral heroism, and its success depended on Mandela's special public position. What Mandela and others saw, however, was that *given* his example, an institution might be constructed, the TRC, that would make generally available a less heroic avenue to the same transformation of moral status, from victim to citizen. (And this would be so even if it was also true that some of the actual argument for and the resulting form of the TRC was a product of naked political bargaining.[32])

The second step introduced the obligations. In particular, with the institution of the TRC, all persons would be obligated to forgo normal routes of judicial redress for a wide class of crimes committed against them. Instead, they would have access to the TRC, either directly through public testimony and/or confrontation with the perpetrators of wrongs before the Commission, or by filing affidavits, or symbolically and indirectly (given the testimony and the affidavits) through the creation of a new history whose framing theme turned what had been merely private stories into a public moral narrative. For those friendly to the work of the TRC, it is this symbolic and indirect moral possibility, with its wide inclusiveness, that provided the key element in its justification.[33] (Accounts of the TRC that emphasize forgiveness thus mistake its grand ambition.)

Critics of the TRC argued that the obligation to forgo judicial redress was not a necessary condition of an important moral possibility, but, very much to the contrary, an additional injustice, one that undermined the legitimacy of the claimed obligation, and so also, of the TRC (perhaps the TRC could obligate, but it could not obligate the relinquishing of *these* rights). If neither the act of creating the TRC nor the TRC itself could impose this obligation, and the imposition of the obligation was not a morally necessary action (no one argued that it was), the contested obligation was at best genuinely contingent, and, absent further justification, vulnerable to the criticism.[34]

In fact, with the TRC came an array of new obligations. Victims (their families and allies) were obliged to forgo not only revenge but also retributive justice, accept not only the possibility of amnesty but also a future in which they would share a normal social world with the unpunished guilty. Perpetrators were obliged to accept the amnesty process as a condition of their peaceful inclusion in the social order, a process that carried risks: of the roughly 9,000 who applied for amnesty only a few hundred met its conditions—that the deed for which amnesty was requested had been politically motivated and that a full public account of it be given. Archbishop Tutu expressed the odd gravity of the first condition this way: "You are able to tell the amnesty committee that you are proud of what you did, albeit that it constitutes an offense under law."[35] It did not matter what the actual intention of the torturer was, or his personal moral guilt. What did matter was the conceptualization and subsequent repudiation of the political motive and its legitimizing source. For those who did not receive amnesty—because it was not granted or because they would not apply for it—there was risk of civil suit and criminal prosecution. Last, there was something like a general obligation to participate in the construction of a moral history: to resolve conflicting memory and private story into an emerging public narrative that would provide a shared truth, if in parts a permanently contested truth, on which a morally sound politics could be built.

Even though the occasion for these obligations was a radical political transition, and the obligations were given specific content by a quasi-parliamentary process, I do not think their nature or their justification is best dealt with in political terms. If we take political obligations to be those whose main line of justification derives from political institutions, the justification of (basic) political institutions and the obligations incurred in establishing them is not political, but moral. Since from the point of view of justification the TRC is not a political institution, but part of the formation conditions of political institutions, its justification depends on the legitimacy of the obligations it imposes, and *their* justification will depend on showing *both* that they promote some vital social good *and* that they are continuous with first-order moral standards and principles. That is why it will not help to argue that there is a standing obligation, political or moral, to bear costs in order to establish or re-establish political order, for it is precisely the justification of being obligated to bear those costs that is in question.

The question of justification is most acute with the obligation to forgo retributive justice, since what it required innocent victims (or their families) to forgo does seem to be precisely what they had a fundamental right to in virtue of their violated innocence. Especially given the continued operation of regular courts, how could persons become obligated not only not to exercise but not to claim their legal rights? It is true that in emergencies a state may suspend some rights. But in this case, the additional fact that so many agents of the state were perpetrators of the crimes in question undermines its authority to justify the amnesty on those grounds. If the TRC was to be part of a process of legitimation and inclusion, its role would be compromised if the obligation to forgo retributive justice and accept the conditions of the amnesty could not be justified in a way that answered the moral complaint. The problem is particularly difficult because of features shared with more radically contingent obligations: the obligation was unforeseen and unforeseeable; it was not chosen or voluntarily adopted by all affected; and it was not the unique solution to a state of moral conflict.

Let us focus first on non-uniqueness. We have already seen one kind of non-uniqueness with two-level theory, where obligation follows from institutions that give form to a higher-level principle that could have been expressed differently. But the TRC was not such an expression; it introduced an obligation that altered the moral terrain, imposing significant burdens, and it was just one of a number of possible obligations that could do the moral work. Why couldn't victims rightly object if they were to be so obligated, at considerable cost, when some other obligation was available, morally equivalent, and would impose lesser burdens on them? In a different but related context of non-uniqueness, T. M. Scanlon offers a decision principle that is suggestive.[36] He argues that where there is a region of activity that requires moral regulation, and there is more than one legitimate principle that can do the job, the fact that one of these principles is generally, even if not universally, accepted in a community can be sufficient for it to obligate all. Those who are inconvenienced by the accepted principle, or just prefer another, have no legitimate grounds to object to it, no reason based in its non-uniqueness to resist it.[37]

If there were a way to extrapolate to the TRC, we could then say that both principles—the principle of retributive justice and the principle of amnesty (requiring that retribution be forgone)—might be morally supported, and yet only one, though either one, could obligate. However, the conditions of Scanlon's principle are not satisfied by the TRC, since it is the option of retributive justice that is already in place. On its own, Scanlon's principle is conservative.

The attraction of thinking about the TRC using some analog of Scanlon's non-uniqueness principle is that we would not have to judge the decision for amnesty as legitimate only if so deciding tracked a balance (in which some fundamental claims are outweighed). Nor would we need to describe the contested principles as representing an underlying conflict of duties (in this case, one looking backward, one forward). That is, if there really were different routes or principles that were morally legitimate, each supported by equally sound moral considerations, then in choosing the amnesty condition, the value of punishing gross violators of human rights would not need to be judged less weighty than the forward-looking goals of reconciliation and the constitution (or reconstitution) of civil society. It is doubtful this would assuage feelings of outrage at losing the opportunity of "seeing justice done," but it would address the sense of moral offense that individual entitlements are being swept off the stage for the collective good.[38]

Now to do its work, Scanlon's principle, or any analog of it, has to appeal to something to give reason to elect one of the competing principles. First-order reasons are exhausted in support of the principles. The reasons to favor one principle over the other are, in a broad sense, pragmatic. But pragmatic considerations cannot trump or outweigh either principle, so there is a puzzle about how they enter at this stage.[39]

Moreover, not just any pragmatic consideration would do, as if there were a wide-open consequentialism at the level of principles. That the adoption of one of two morally legitimate principles concerning punishment, or privacy, would have a positive effect on GNP seems irrelevant to the decision between them, though the same effect would not be irrelevant with respect to a pair of principles about fair taxation.

Overall, what we need is a way to fully acknowledge all the moral considerations that are reflected in the competing principles, without weighing and balancing—an analog of Scanlon's principle would do that—*and* find criteria of relevance for the introduction of pragmatic considerations. We do not want to say that individuals who would make a claim for retributive justice—claims that could be honored—not only are blocked from pursuing their claims, but are also obligated to accept principles requiring them to forgo their claim, on grounds that just appeal to numbers, or even general welfare. Fundamental moral claims should not be discounted in that way.[40]

To figure out how to proceed, I want to turn away from the TRC for a bit, and look at another area where weighing and balancing has been a problem which has a kind of solution we can draw on. The cases of interest are ones where rationality seems to require that agents violate one moral prohibition so that there will be fewer violations of the same or some other prohibition (lying to prevent lies, or lying to protect a life, or to prevent a murder). There is either weighing kinds of wrongs done, or numbers of wrongs done, in a way that seems paradoxical. One appealing way to avoid the idea of minimizing bad doings by doing something bad is to rethink the nature of the harm to be averted. If the wrong-making feature is of a kind that sums, then weighing and balancing is hard to resist—e.g., when the wrongness of lying is its effect on trust, or damage to the institution of truth-telling; or the wrongness of killing is the loss of a life or to security. A different kind of account will claim that the reason lying is wrong, when it is, is because of the relation between liar and victim, or because of the principle about

treating others on which the liar acts. Inappropriate relations and
attitudes are not kinds of wrong that sum. If A lies to B and C to D,
even if effects and reasons are the same, there is no state of affairs
that is twice as bad as A lying to B; there are simply two lies—two
persons relating to others in ways they ought not. And if the lies
don't sum, it is not clear how preventing more of them could be,
in a simple summing way, better. Of course, if there is sufficient
reason to prevent each, and one can, one ought to prevent both.
But whatever obligation I might have to prevent lies from occurring would not derive from the primary obligation that I have not
to stand in lying relations to others.[41]

Still, don't lies sum simply as the items they are? This one and
then that one are two lies. They may well sum if we are doing the
demographics of lying, but that by itself is not a summing over value
that introduces a requirement of rationality. If I am obligated not to
lie—not to stand in a lying relation to another—then if a lie is ever
justified to prevent other lying, it is not by way of a balance sheet.
One can argue in similar fashion about harms: causing harms and
preventing harms by harming are, morally speaking, sufficiently different kinds of action that they cannot speak directly to a balance of
reasons. That is, we have reasons not to harm, and *different* reasons
to prevent harmings from occurring. How the different reasons involved interact will be a delicate casuistical question.[42] Of course casuistry of this sort is a familiar feature in moral thinking about harms—
how a harm is caused, with what intention, or to what end, affects the
moral valence of an action. Situations involving large numbers can
present a distinct set of reasons: great losses are not simply sums of
small ones; nor are our relations to them the same. And so on.

The general idea in moving away from weighing and balancing
in this way is to preserve the integrity of reasons on all sides. The
competing reasons are now of different kinds, with different justificatory reach; each gets its own hearing, on its own terms. It is a
revisionary casuistry that can recognize the force of a value claim
against the contrary pressure of numbers.

In the case of the TRC, we accepted from the outset that both
alternatives capture a valid ordering of reasons. A decision between contending principles cannot be made by a further casuistry of reasons if all the reasons that bear are already included in
the arguments for them. It was at this point that we looked at the

idea of a decision procedure—an analog of Scanlon's principle—that could introduce pragmatic considerations in a way that avoids grounds for complaint. Of course a decision procedure is no better than the argument it represents. If it were to offer a principle that in these circumstances bypasses the minority claim without supplying sufficient independent reason why doing so is justified, then we would not have advanced beyond the unacceptable pragmatics of majority preference.

Here is where our excursion into revisionary casuistry bears fruit. The key move was to rethink the terms of argument that lead to weighing and balancing. In the case of the TRC, I believe, we have mistaken the significance of the majority in the argument for a principle of choice. We are unable to get past moral complaints against the amnesty principle so long as we see the choice for the TRC as a matter of majority preference or will—an inappropriate pragmatics. How else might we regard it? First, the object of choice is not merely an independently valid principle of obligation, but also one whose supporting reasons offer a vision of a future accepted by those who will, by means of the principle, act for that future together. In such a case, one might almost argue, *can* implies *ought.* And second, in contrast to the other cases we have looked at, the agents here saw themselves faced with a novel situation, where, as I would put it, there was need for improvisation.[43] Now any valid moral improvisation will be constrained by, among other things, shared moral history: those who are to act on its principle have to be in a position to experience it (hear it) as obligatory. That is why the mix of political, religious, and traditional experiences and values brought to the decision between principles does not make the decision other than moral, and certainly not impure. These beliefs properly inform the decision, for they partly constitute the abilities agents have for action and sacrifice, and so inform their vision of what is possible. This is one of the ways Mandela's exemplary action clearly made a moral difference. By drawing on shared values and experiences, his singular action revealed a creative potential in the abilities and values people already had. Absent Mandela's example, the institution of the TRC might not have been able to generate a legitimate collective obligation.

Does this mean that it was not right to say, as we did initially, that the circumstances prior to the creation of the TRC supported more than one legitimate principle? The argument as it now stands is that more than one principle could have been justified—that is, is supported by sound casuistry—but only one principle was practically viable, or a real possibility. Even if the counterfactual were true (had the other principle been chosen, it would have served as well), real possibility is determined from the point of view of those making the decision, and not all possible futures can be imagined, or imagined well enough. The actual conditions of moral life are thus part of the argument determining moral possibility—in this case, they provide a criterion of pragmatic relevance.

However, if this shows a different way to support the decision for the TRC, we still need to account for the status of the moral interests represented by the option forgone. In some resolutions of moral conflict, a correct judgment about what to do does not remove the competing source of obligation—there are remainders, and if we can act in light of them, we should.[44] In the case of the TRC, however, any reassertion or continuation of the forgone retributive claims would seem to be excluded by the amnesty provision itself. And yet key elements that supported those claims remain. Vicious illegal acts will not be punished; guilty persons will circulate with impunity among not just the innocent but their victims. True, that just is the effect of an amnesty. But in these circumstances, it seems hard to resist the argument that because of the abiding moral cost in forgoing retribution for those who supported the path not taken, the amnesty violates *some* ongoing moral claim. At the time, some who were concerned about this issue argued that the conditions of the amnesty—that perpetrators come forward and publicly admit to wrongdoing in the pursuit of political ends—were weakly retributive insofar as they created vulnerability to shame and public censure.

I doubt that the forms of public censure available could have been an adequate response to the retributive claims. Moreover, it is not clear that this role was consistent with the reparative ambitions of the TRC. But neither of these points addresses the real issue. If any part of the retributive claim is met, or acknowledged, then the decision to forgo retribution is not effective. So, either there is an abiding retributive claim, which undermines the legitimacy of the amnesty decision, or the amnesty decision somehow cancels the retributive claim.[45] That is, the claim cannot be acted

on—conceptually cannot (nothing would count as satisfying it)—
or the reasons that had supported it no longer do.

To this point, I have treated the retributive claim as self-evident.
In the last stage of the argument, it will be helpful to think a bit
about the values that support it, and to introduce a revisionary casuistry here as well. We say that a victim of a crime has a claim in
justice to seek the punishment of the guilty perpetrator. Take this
to be a legal fact. Behind the legal fact is a more complex story.
Consider one familiar version of it.[46] In broad strokes, there are,
on the one hand, social needs: for deterrence of harmful acts, for
making the social fabric whole again, and for institutions that embody ideals of fairness and the rule of law. On the other hand,
there are moral concerns. Only the guilty should be punished;
some notion of proportionality in punishment. But, morally speaking, there has to be more. If we suppose that the desire for revenge
is a natural response to wrong or harm done, it is an open moral
question whether such a desire should be turned into or reflected
in a moral reason or claim.[47] Now, a legal system that makes retributive claims possible can be seen as creating a moral substitute
for, or a translation of, the desire for revenge. It both asserts a monopoly of force, blocking the natural expression of the desire, and
offers an interpretation of what it is about the desire that matters:
say, the recovery of the moral or social status of the victim. The
interpreted desire can then be captured in a judicial system that
gives a legal status to the victim, by treating her private harm as
a legitimate cause of public action, through a system of trial and
punishment for accused wrongdoers.

Suppose some such account is plausible. We could then see the
(morally) improvisatory TRC (including the decision for amnesty)
as introducing a competing method of capture for the interpreted
desire, the effect of which is to cancel the retributive claim. That is,
the decision for amnesty will give the desire for revenge no retributive expression. The truth about injury and moral harm will still be
publicly acknowledged, and the victims' status regained, but not by
way of the institutions of retributive and compensatory justice.[48]

It is a strength of this account that the considerations that favor
the decision for an institution like the TRC do not support it as a
permanent substitute for the formal systems of criminal and civil
justice. They belong to conditions of transition where a break with

the past is called for and normal institutions cannot accommodate
that role. A well-founded legal system expresses a community's
commitment to the rule of law. That is why enforcement of laws
can restore a community. But where the commitment is what is at
issue because the community needs to be constituted, and those
who were not entitled to share in that commitment need to be
enfranchised, there is moral room and reason for extraordinary or
quasi-judicial action. For the TRC, the argument that seems most
to the point is that in the circumstances of transition from a regime that routinely violated human rights to a democratic system
of government, the restitutive moral function of retributive justice
could not be realized. There was therefore a need, for a time, for
a different way of publicly negotiating past wrongs done that managed the entry of disenfranchised victims into the class of citizens.
Given the goal of securing equal moral status, the abridging or
balancing of fundamental moral claims was not a morally possible
means to this end.[49] By contrast, the public creation of a moral history through the testimony and affidavits received and broadcast
by the TRC was an enfranchising act in that it changed the basis
on which moral status was acknowledged. Thus, given a justification for the TRC based on the absence of conditions of civility and
trust that allow ordinary systems of justice to perform their status-
securing function, its legitimacy depended on making a credible
claim to (re)instate them—though once re-instated, they are different, since situated in a different moral history.

VI

There are several things to note by way of conclusion. First, I take
the extended web of moral justification offered on behalf of the
TRC to support the claim that legitimate collective obligations can
be generated by morally improvisatory acts. In general, the resump-
tion of normal moral life will close the arc of the improvisation. The
contingent obligations it introduces are replaced, or absorbed and
no longer experienced as anything new. In either case, what now
counts as normal is no longer what it was; hopefully it is better,[50] and
stably so. Retrospective reconstruction may seem to show that the
change was latent in the community's core values. Inevitably, there
will be such connections: improvisations are constrained by their

starting points, and when they are to result in collective action, they are also constrained by the values and abilities of those who are to act. But all of this connectedness does not defeat the claim that what has been done is something moral, and something new.

Second, there is the role of what I have been calling "pragmatics" in making obligating decisions between contending principles: considerations such as stability, psychological fit, historical viability, and so also the sheer need to resolve political and social crises to create or restore moral conditions of ordinary life. I have argued that they can enter determinations of basic rights and claims, but only *after* their justification is complete, and only so long as they fit or enhance the work of first-order values. In this way pragmatics can extend, not just compete with, moral justification.

Last, we have seen how the reach of morality extends beyond the norms of ordinary moral life. Political crises can introduce unexpected normative questions, but the political context does not necessarily make the questions political—in the sense of belonging to a special sphere of argument—nor show that the resources of morality are inadequate to answer them. The discussion of the TRC shows one possible creative extension of these resources: the improvisatory intervention and the resulting reorientation of justificatory argument. It is really something we should expect. Fundamental moral values and principles have greater potential for organizing our affairs than can be realized or even appreciated at any given time. It is this potential that is tapped for new procedures of justification when contingencies might seem to outstrip moral argument.

NOTES

1. One might wonder whether there is the thought here that all good persons should act in the same way—recognizable as such to one another.

2. Or, as a challenge to conceiving of morality in these terms. One might, for example, use the Hegelian distinction between *Moralität* and *Sittlichkeit* to traverse this domain, the first marking a set of timeless obligations and rights, the other the obligations that belong to historically specific forms of life. While sensitive to many of the moral phenomena I describe, this kind of division tends to miss the contingency that occurs at all levels of obligation.

3. This piece of data shows up in different moments of philosophical discussion: in arguments about integrity and the need for space free of positive moral demands; as a background condition in accounts of flourishing; as a limit on the scope of our responsibility.

4. See, for example, H. L. A. Hart, *The Concept of Law* (Oxford: Clarendon Press, 1961), 169ff.

5. This is not all arcane. Taboos can be a moral form of strict liability (sexual activity with minors). And sometimes, where temptation to abuse is high, we may want to rescind individual authority (military interrogations offer an instructive example).

6. Immanuel Kant, *Groundwork of the Metaphysics of Morals* (Cambridge: Cambridge University Press, 1998), 4:388-389. From the side of the pure part, this is the subject matter of "*Sittenlehre*"; from the side of psychology or sociology, "practical anthropology."

7. The sense of "implied" here is deliberative: even if after the fact one might show something to follow as a consequence, if the reasoning was not available—not just difficult, but practically beyond reckoning—then the consequence is not deliberatively implied by what we know.

8. I use "normal moral agent" as a term of art. She is the subject addressed by the non-heroic elements of a moral theory, or, what amounts to the same thing, the object of good parenting. The elements of character of a normal moral agent will not be the same across times and places, but the feature of fit is constant: hers is the character that is at home in her social world. In some severe circumstances, there may be no place for a "normal" agent; in others, what is normal will hardly be moral. Although morality ideally provides guidance in all circumstances, it would produce an order—a moral order—in which most of us can most of the time be at home.

9. There may also be differences in the extent to which we can recover our reasons in the moment, a matter of deliberative agility, even creativity, at the limit.

10. Some might dispute this, pointing to elements of morality—respect for persons, for example—that are immutable. But what respect for persons amounts to is not always the same; what is immutable is that respect play a central role in justifications of the ways we may treat each other.

11. We have regions of high sensitivity and of likely negligence; we tend to replicate past injuries. So we may harm without intention to cause harm; yet when we do, we should not say it is accidental.

12. We may then have good reason to respond differently to first offenses than to repeated ones, especially when repetition occurs in the face of what has become obvious.

13. For useful discussion on this topic, see Christine M. Korsgaard, "The Right to Lie: Kant on Dealing with Evil," *Philosophy and Public Affairs* 15

(1986): 325-429, Liam B. Murphy, *Moral Demands in Nonideal Theory* (New York: Oxford University Press, 2000), Seana Shiffrin, "Paternalism, Unconscionability Doctrine, and Accommodation," *Philosophy and Public Affairs* 29, no. 3 (2000): 205-250, and Tamar Schapiro, "Compliance, Complicity, and the Nature of Nonideal Conditions," *The Journal of Philosophy* 100, no. 7 (2003): 329-355.

14. E.g., obligations of individual beneficence replaced by private charities and social welfare institutions.

15. Issues of this sort have recently been raised concerning the rationales for preventive war and the need to curtail civil rights in order to fight terrorism.

16. Even if there are better norms of friendship than those we have, our obligation is to be (or to help others be) better friends. The idea of an institution of friendship is no more than a façon de parler.

17. We might use this metaphor as yet another way of marking the difference between negative and positive duties: negative duties tell us that the narrative may not unfold this way (by this means), or over there; positive duties set us on a path: to get Jamie into college, Joey out of harm's way, the package into Mary's hands.

18. One might think that the very idea of morality changing is suspect, or worse, an opening to some kind of relativism about moral claims and judgments. But even if we thought that fundamental moral principles were fixed—a priori or eternal—the conditions of their application are not, and that creates quite enough space for there to be pressure for change on the lived morality of individuals (this is easy to see for the principle of utility; I think it no less true for the morality of the categorical imperative).

19. Some of this is familiar: we cannot make promises or exchange goods without the institutions of promising and property. Some is less so: we may have obligations (e.g., of beneficence) that we cannot fulfill without moral risk or fault unless there is institutional mediation (see Jonathan Garthoff, "The Embodiment of Morality" (PhD diss., UCLA, 2004)). Of course, there is a danger on the other side as well: reliance on public devices of caring may make persons less morally sensitive, and less able to act well when they must act on their own.

20. For a useful discussion, see Sarah Buss, "On Appearing Respectful: The Moral Significance of Manners," *Ethics* 109 (1999): 795-826.

21. A function that includes in an essential way the possibility of its iconoclastic subversion.

22. One would like to think that when the frenzy is over and normal life resumes that there is shame. This does not always seem to be the case. There is ample evidence of pride (souvenirs kept in plain sight, stories told to children, a willingness to re-enact, if asked), and remorse, if it occurs,

may take generations, or the externally imposed intervention of courts and tribunals.

23. Sometimes it is ordinary life that is temporarily transformed. The French village of Le Chambon during World War II is a famous example, where, under the leadership of local minister André Trocmé and his wife, Magda Trocmé, ordinary citizens risked their lives to protect Jews fleeing from the Nazis. The story is vividly told by philosopher Philip Hallie in his *Lest Innocent Blood be Shed: The Story of the Le Chambon and How Goodness Happened There* (New York: Harper and Row, 1979).

24. Interviews sometimes suggest after-the-fact puzzlement and even surprise at the extent of their extraordinary actions. In other cases, a possibility for human interaction is glimpsed and then mourned, and once again, inspiring stories are told. It would be interesting to know under what conditions change of this sort can enter ordinary morality through acts of retrospective integration.

25. The comparison with supererogatory action is instructive. Supererogatory actions go beyond duty, but they do not surpass an agent's moral understanding and remain connected to the content of obligation. Though they too may call on abilities and will that an agent cannot normally access.

26. Though they might become so obligated if it becomes permanent.

27. This is why it will not do to say that all the moral business lies in a standing obligation to do what one (permissibly) can to remedy injustice. That misses the obligating nature of what is actually done.

28. Some might argue that what I call political necessity is really a species of moral justification, at the limit, where morality condones or even directs the violation of its central standards. It's a view that doesn't so much beg as give up on the moral question. A different way of ducking the problem is to claim that political justification is of its own kind, so that given its distinctive subject, one should not expect congruence with morality. Though we should not expect states to operate on the principles that govern personal relations, that is a reason to extend our understanding of morality, not to leave it behind.

29. The TRC was created by an act of Parliament in 1995 (fulfilling the directive of the postamble of the 1993 Interim Constitution to establish some mechanism and criteria for granting amnesty for conduct "associated with political objectives and committed in the course of conflicts of the past"). The first hearings were in 1996. The work of the Commission officially ended in April 1998 (though the amnesty phase went on until July 2001); its *Final Report* was issued in November 1998. The moral question begins with the postamble.

30. I don't claim that the debates got all or even most things right, nor that it was the moral force of the deliberative conclusion that carried the

day. But the public discussions leading up to the TRC were remarkably clear about what was at stake, morally, if less clear about how or whether they resolved the moral problems introduced by their decisions. One of the purposes of this discussion is to suggest that the moral resources they had available to them were in fact adequate to the task.

31. The nature of the circumstances in which a charismatic individual can be morally effective is a question for social science. How the change affected can be legitimate and correct is the business of moral theory.

32. Chiefly, balancing the moral and personal costs of amnesty with the needs for public order, given that any viable future state would not only contain perpetrators and victims, but would have to rely on the good will of both, especially if, as was reasonably believed, police and military would not tolerate purging malfeasors.

33. Analogous claims are made about the need for international war crimes trials. The claim is not (or not just) that ordinary criminal trials might not be successful, or would be too dangerous. That risk could be seen as part of what makes the use of the criminal justice system necessary—a way of bringing horrific acts within the orbit of ordinary justice. The justification for these abnormal judicial activities is more commonly that some moral possibility needs to be opened (or closed) that exceeds the orbit of ordinary justice, some difference negotiated between criminal liability and accountability per se. It is exactly the nature and extent of this sort of justification that is in question in the case of the TRC.

34. The issue of authority to introduce the change is unusual in this case, since the TRC was established through public and open discussion. And if that was done well, there may be no authority question that is not tied to the question of moral legitimacy (i.e., some things may not be changed or foregone, no matter what the process).

35. As quoted in Charles Villa-Vicencio, "The Road to Reconciliation," *Sojourner's Magazine* May-June (1997), http://www.sojo.net/index. cfm?action=magazine.article&issue=soj9705&article=970522.

36. T. M. Scanlon, *What We Owe to Each Other* (Cambridge, MA: Harvard University Press, 1998), 339f.

37. Uniqueness *is* necessary for the meta-principle legitimating the authority of lower-order principles.

38. This was vivid in the complaints of Steve Biko's family. See, for example, the discussion in Antjie Krog, *The Country of My Skull* (New York: Three Rivers Press, 1998), 47.

39. Moral arithmetic isn't straightforward: one can't argue that since the principles are equal, pragmatics just adds a little weight-of-reasons to one side. The objections to deciding against a basic moral claim by appeal to numbers or welfare or pragmatics would just re-enter.

40. Scanlon's own use of his principle is left unclear: it might be that the pragmatic concerns are the values of stability or continuity, or merely the preference or comfort of the majority.

41. Interestingly, with this shift in perspective, it may cease to be clear what kind of obligation we have to prevent lies. It is not obvious that it is in itself a good thing to prevent a lie by altering the circumstances that would prompt it. Knowing that I tend to lie about my score in some game, you do not risk doing something wrong in asking me how I did. There would be something odd about the direction of concern. (Of course if my lie would injure someone else, there might be a moral reason not to ask.) While we are not to be indifferent to the moral content or effects of each other's actions, we do not have surrogate responsibility for their choices.

42. If we may not kill to prevent more killing, the reasons to prevent killing are not outweighed by the reasons not to kill, as if the value of life were numerically overmatched by the value of virtue.

43. Even if an existing institution had been embraced, it would have been for new reasons, and so represent a decision for a different principle.

44. Suppose we can act to save either A or B, both drowning; we cannot save both. We decide to save A and allow B's fate to unfold as it will. If B drowns, there is no moral remainder. We did what we could. But if B miraculously hangs on, we have further obligations toward him. We cannot now let B drown, even though our earlier decision to let B drown was without fault. The obligation continues past the decision point of action. However, the continuing presence of the obligation need not warrant action of the same kind: there may be new considerations that bear, including the effects of the first action. If B hangs on, but A needs to get emergency care to survive, the earlier choice to save A seems to encumber decision, even when B's need to be saved reasserts itself. So the fact that the obligation continues does not return us to the original choice situation.

45. This is not a general claim about remainders and residues. It is a special feature of this case that if the retributive claim survives, the principle that blocks retribution fails.

46. To make a point, I borrow liberally from chapter 5 of J. S. Mill's *Utilitarianism*.

47. I say "turned into" rather than "acknowledged as" to reflect the idea that desires alone do not support reasons or claims.

48. This sort of argument led some who supported the amnesty from criminal liability to want there to be room for civil suits seeking damages. The third arm of the TRC, the Committee on Reparation and Rehabilitation, was partly designed to capture that aim.

49. Thus rather than setting a limit *for* morality, it is a task *of* morality to set the terms in which such a goal can be an obligating target of our individual or collective action.

50. Better from its own as well as from the prior point of view.

2

MORAL IMPROVISATION, MORAL CHANGE, AND POLITICAL INSTITUTIONS

COMMENT ON BARBARA HERMAN

FRANK I. MICHELMAN

On grounds that look strong to me, Professor Herman argues that morality and moral theory must allow for contingency and change in moral norms.[1] And, yet, as Herman observes, "No one has authority to change moral norms."[2] It follows that change in this field must occur—and Herman maintains that it does occur, tendering cases in point[3]—through processes that do not rely on anything like the kind of arbitrary normative creativity (within certain bounds, let us say) that populations in legally ordered countries cede to public official bodies clothed with powers of legislation. In this respect, "morality is unlike . . . law."[4]

Moral change and creativity rather must and do arise from non-institutionalized, socially embedded, reason-descrying processes of "improvisation,"[5] a mode of normative alteration that is *not* available to law, which "can change . . . only through the activities of designated authorities" such as legislatures and judges.[6] And conversely, to repeat, official enactment by constituted bodies is *not* a mode of normative creativity available to morality: whereas legislatures and common law judiciaries have authority to change legal norms, no one has the authority to change moral norms. Hence whatever it was that imposed a certain set of previously non-existent moral obligations on victims of apartheid-era criminality in South Africa, it cannot have been any official body's "act of creating the TRC."[7]

I do not here take issue with any of these claims.[8] Rather, my aim in this brief comment is to establish certain limits on their meaning, or refinements thereof, by examining closely how they apply to the South African case that Herman analyzes.

I want to start with a question about the alteration in moral norms that by Herman's account—persuasive to me—has been improvised into existence in harness with the legal establishment of the TRC and its amnesty provisions. Herman speaks of this alteration in terms of moral obligation. What has come newly into existence, she says, are "obligations" of victims "to forgo normal routes of judicial redress" for apartheid-era crimes, obligations "not to exercise [or] to claim their legal rights."[9] I have trouble seeing this. Through acts of official bodies that undoubtedly had authority to determine law in South Africa, the laws of that country incontestably had been altered by the end of 1995 (or of 1996 at the latest), in such a way that the choice to go to court no longer was open to the victims.[10] To speak of a moral obligation on their part to refrain from doing what it was no longer open to them to do seems odd. Nor would it be consistent with the rest of Herman's argument to think that the new moral obligation that interests her is an obligation on the victims' part to forgive.[11] So in what does the new moral obligation consist?

It seems to me that the term "new moral obligation" has to be stretched a little to fit the victims' situation. If we think of obligations—and normally we do—as constraints on choices among courses of action that agents otherwise have open to them, we'll be unable in this case to name anything that the victims are supposed recently to have come under obligation to do or not do (as distinguished from something that they have been stripped of the ability to do). There literally is *nothing* they can do now to resist the redress-stripping action that the South African legislative polity has taken, absent a legislative reversal. Barging into the courthouse, forcing judges at gunpoint (or persuading them by argument, the force of the better reason) to issue orders granting redress against perpetrators, cannot work; the so-called orders would be legal nullities unless and until the legislative authorities reversed their decision for amnesty. Well, then, how about a new moral obligation on the victims' part not to agitate politically for a legislative reversal of the amnesty law? I do not read Herman to claim or argue that any such obligation has come into existence.

I suggest, therefore, that what has been improvised in this case is not moral obligation but rather the moral probity of a certain sort of legal change, to wit, a change that strips the victims of the access they previously would have had to judicial redress. Looking at matters from the standpoint of a victim, what has happened is that whereas formerly I would have had a valid moral complaint against a law closing the courts against my claim for redress, today I no longer have such a complaint. One might try to cast this in terms of moral obligation, by saying that the victims newly have come under obligation to bear no moral grudges against this law of amnesty, but why bother?

I don't think it detracts at all from what Herman wants to say about the openness of morality to improvisation, and the advantages to theory of recognizing that openness, if we forgo obligation talk in this case and rather say that there occurred in South Africa a telling change in moral states of affairs (MSA). In MSA-1, enactment of a law stripping the victims of access to judicial redress gives rise to a valid moral complaint on the part of the victims; in MSA-2, it does not. The transition from MSA-1 to MSA-2 is, I take it, the occurrence that Herman wants to show—does show— contains an indispensable element of moral improvisation.

Let us now ask: Is that transition conceivable in the absence of an official act of legislation, wiping out access to judicial redress for apartheid-era crimes? It seems it had better be, if we want to uphold both the claim that the transition incorporates and instances on moral improvisation and the claim (differentiating morality from law) that no one has authority to change moral norms. Official legislative action is ipso facto action that someone has authority to take. If the moral transition depends on such action, then either someone has authority to change morality or the transition is not a case of moral improvisation. Or so it may seem; there will be more to say about this later.

No problem, you say. The transition from MSA-1 to MSA-2 quite clearly can occur—indeed, it must occur—without benefit of legislative action. MSA-2 is the moral state of affairs in which the legislative action we have in mind, closing the courthouse doors to certain actions for redress, gives rise to no moral complaint from the victims. It is, in other words, the state of affairs in which the South African legislative polity has a moral permission to take such action. The transition to MSA-2, you say, therefore cannot be dependent on the occurrence of the official action because the moral transition must precede, at least notionally, the legislative action for which it carries permission.

That reasoning would move too fast. It excludes the possibility that certain actions, in certain circumstances, are sufficiently world-changing to create or give rise to their own moral permissibility. Excluding such possibilities would seem to me squarely contrary to the spirit of Herman's inquiry. And indeed it is a possibility of that general kind—a legislative action giving rise to its own moral permissibility—that I now want to develop in relation to the South African case. So far as Herman's account of that case discloses, or so it seems to me, the transition in morality would not and could not have been consummated in the absence of the legislative acts establishing the TRC and the amnesty rules.

By saying so, I do not mean to deny that the lawmaking acts in this case are distinct from the moral improvisation that is also a part of the case.[12] Neither would I affirm that a moment of institutional decision is essentially involved in all possible instances of social improvisation in the genesis of moral transitions or altered moral obligations. To the contrary, Herman gives persuasive examples of improvised moral alteration unassisted by institutional acts or events.[13] My suggestion is only that a moment of institutional decision is essentially involved in a certain subset of such cases, those involving the phenomenon that Herman calls moral non-uniqueness—these being cases that pose to the community a choice that cannot be settled by the moral reasons already relied on to establish the moral acceptability of each of two or more mutually exclusive, alternative practices.[14] But neither, then—to finish up with these disclaimers—do I mean to suggest that we see here any departure from the general proposition that no one has authority to legislate moral change.

We need to pinpoint the moment of moral improvisation in Herman's account of the South African case. So far as I am able to see, it occurs with—consists in—the rise of recognition that the TRC amnesty procedure can serve as a "competing method of capture" for a certain "interpreted desire" that points at the moral end of redress.[15] The improvisation resides in the recognition that a sound moral casuistry can support displacement of judicial redress by an aptly circumscribed amnesty, *even though*—and this is important—an "equally sound" casuistry of reasons remains, at least for a time, to support the claim to redress.[16] A previously nonexistent, "competing," and "equally sound" moral casuistry in favor of amnesty having been improvised, the South Africans' choice to remap the field of legal claims, defenses, and immunities still imposes moral "costs" for which a moral justification is required.[17]

Until that justification is supplied and accepted, has any moral change yet been consummated? It does not seem so. It rather seems that moral change, post-improvisation, now hangs in the balance, pending "cancellation" of one of the competing casuistries by the other. Sound moral improvisations "create new spaces of moral possibility," but they nevertheless can "fail," for reasons, say, of "bad timing, or lack of sufficient fit with prior values."[18] In other words, moral possibility is not yet moral change; the moments of improvisation and change are not necessarily coincident. Improvisation of the moral possibility of amnesty potentiates cancellation of the moral claim to redress, it does not yet execute it. That is what a case of moral non-uniqueness is like.

I make no attempt to estimate what fraction such cases comprise the full set of cases in which moral improvisation occurs. I only observe that these, where we find them, are cases in which the contingency of cancellation still impends, post-improvisation. And cancellation, it seems, must merge in justification, or vice versa. As long as the moral costs of denying redress persist or "abide"—and they do, in the immediate aftermath of improvisation of a competing, equally sound moral casuistry—those costs will bespeak "a moral justification, if there is one."[19] By some still-pending, further modulation of, or reference to, moral sensibility or moral environment, we get beyond the (improvised) stage of recognition that each of two alternatives, amnesty equally with redress, has support from a sound moral casuistry. Herman is clear about this need to push on. It is what prompts her to take up for consideration—and eventual rejection, as inapposite to this case—of Scanlon's "conservative" proposal as an answer to the need.[20]

To recapitulate: the local history of morality that is calling for explanation revolves around—it does not consist in, but it revolves around—a fact of local legal history: displacement of a legal practice of honoring claims to judicial redress by a legal practice of amnesty. Each alternative, the one displaced and the one that displaces, can be supported by a casuistry that establishes its moral possibility. Redress is the practice that is in place when the question arises, so a conservative principle—deferring to "stability or continuity, or [perhaps] merely the preference or comfort of the majority"[21]—would militate in favor of retaining it. What else is there, then, to justify morally a social choice in favor of displacing it?

Until we have in hand a further moral explanation for a social choice in favor of amnesty over redress, we will not have explained how the transition from MSA-1 to MSA-2, the moral change (although not the moral *improvisation*) that interests Herman, can have been consummated. Where two alternative practices both can find support in equally sound moral casuistries, a moral cost—Herman tells us—is involved in the displacement of one by the other for which (further) moral justification or cancellation is required. Until that further justification or cancellation is in place, MSA-2—the moral state of affairs in which enactment of a law stripping the victims of access to judicial redress does not give rise to a valid moral complaint on the part of the victims—does not hold.

But "[a] decision between contending principles cannot be made by a further casuistry of reasons if all the reasons that bear are already included in the arguments for them."[22] So what sort of consideration possibly might answer to the need? A public decision procedure is an obvious possibility to consider.[23] Of course, it would have to be a procedure itself supported by moral reasons—a decision procedure being "no better than the argument it represents."[24] But perhaps the represented arguments can have reference to the procedure *as a procedure* and still be moral arguments—arguments independent, as Professor Herman says, of the "pragmatics of majority preference" or "will."[25] Can they indeed? If my argument to this point is correct, then those inclined (like me) to endorse Herman's nomination of the South African case as an instance of moral change brought about by moral ("legitimate") means had better hope so.[26]

What might such procedural-moral reasons be like? Might the fact that the procedure followed is the one that was duly constituted for such occasions be a moral reason? Perhaps it can be, assuming certain further conditions are satisfied, including that "the object of choice is . . . an independently valid principle of obligation,"[27] and perhaps also that the choices (both of the policy and of the procedure used to choose it) may reasonably be understood as expressions not of majority preference but rather of the predominant judgment regarding what is and is not practically possible and likely, and also morally defensible, in the circumstances.[28]

Herman is clear that there was, in South Africa, a "decision for" amnesty,[29] and this obviously was a decision made by institutionalized, formal-legal means. She is clear in affirming the legitimacy of this institutionalized choice between equally morally supportable alternatives, where "legitimacy" is a term of moral commendation.[30] It is tempting—to me, at any rate—to close the case by reading Herman to affirm that certain properties of this institutionalized decision making, perhaps including its deliberative, judgmental character, are a factor to be cited in support of the legitimacy of the choice that was made.[31]

Suppose we do so read her. Do we thus cause trouble for Herman's claim that the transition from MSA-1 to MSA-2 shows us a genuine instance of moral improvisation, as part of the genesis of theretofore non-existent moral obligations? Not that I can see. We say that certain features in certain, recent South African institutional events are indispensable from a full and complete explanation of how a certain class of recently valid moral demands could have been cancelled. We do not thereby deny that a substantivemoral defense of the cancellation—that is, of its moral possibility, to use Herman's term—*also* would be indispensable from a full and complete explanation of it. That is, the full explanation might have to include a recognition—both by South Africans and by us, their moral critics—that displacement of a legal practice of redress by a legal practice of amnesty has support from an "equally sound" casuistry of reasons that establishes its moral possibility. As I have said, it is just there, just at the stage of producing the casuistry soundly capable of establishing the moral possibility of the displacement, where we find moral improvisation at work in the case that Professor Herman has presented to us. So we would have here a true case of moral improvisation in the genesis of moral change. It would further be a case of a normative occurrence that is "not to be regarded in purely political terms"[32]—whether "political" here means institutional-processual or amoral-pragmatic. It also, though, would be a case in which institutionalized acts and events have played an indispensable part.

But where, then, would stand the proposition that no one has authority to change moral norms? Also unscathed, I think, although here a bit of shiftiness may be needed to stay out of trouble. For suppose we agree that the moral probity of the TRC amnesty depends on the moral adequacy of the procedural aspects of a historically actual, institutional choice to replace redress with amnesty (given that the moral possibility of doing so existed, by dint of improvisation). Affirmation of the procedure's moral adequacy is itself, after all, the expression of a moral judgment, made according to moral standards and norms that no one has authority to change.

NOTES

1. See Barbara Herman, "Contingency in Obligation," this volume, pp. 17–53.
2. Ibid., p. 34.
3. See ibid., pp. 22, 22–23, and 23–24.
4. Ibid., p. 34.
5. See, e.g., ibid.
6. Ibid.
7. Ibid., p. 38.
8. Might I elsewhere be inclined to take issue with any? If so (and I am not sure), it would be with the claim that law changes only through the acts of designated authorities. Since what is under discussion here is how morality changes, not law, I need not grapple with the latter question now.
9. Ibid., pp. 37–39.
10. The official process involved three steps: [1] the enactment by the old-regime Parliament of an Interim Constitution, Act 200 of 1993, containing a general directive to the Parliament being constituted by that Act to adopt a law providing for amnesty; [2] the Act of the newly constituted Parliament—Promotion of National Unity and Reconciliation Act 34 of 1995—establishing the TRC and fixing the conditions of amnesty; and

[3] the decision of the Constitutional Court in the *AZAPO* case, Azanian Peoples Organization and Others v. President of South Africa and Others 1996 (8) BCLR 1015 (Constitutional Court of South Africa), construing the Interim Constitution to authorize legally the specific action taken by Parliament, thus confirming the legal validity and effectiveness of the amnesty provisions as enacted. For discussion of the official-authority status of these bodies, see Frank I. Michelman, "Constitutional Authorship, 'Solomonic Solutions,' and the Unoriginalist Mode of Constitutional Interpretation," in *"Meaning" in Constitutional Interpretation,* eds. Graham Bradfield and Derek van der Merwe (Cape Town: Juta, 1998), 208-34, at 215-19.

11. Whether the victims became newly obligated to forbear from direct acts of "revenge" would depend on whether there had been some previous interval of time when they did not stand under such a moral obligation, a question Herman does not go into. See Herman, "Contingency in Obligation," p. 37.

12. If, as I urge, the moral transition in this case could not have been consummated without the concurrence of certain institutional acts and events—certain acts and events of lawmaking—it must follow that the character of the institutional process producing that consummation must have measured up to what is morally required of an institutional process (arguably, that it be a properly democratic or deliberative one) in order that it create morally acceptable law in the circumstances under consideration. If my general stance is right, the possibility is open that the use or exercise of the institutional process employed in this case itself gave rise to the moral acceptability of reliance on that process for the purpose for which it was used here—the process can "be justified in the moral terms of the world [it] changed." See Herman, "Contingency in Obligation," p. 37. That processual concern, however, is not the site or focus of the moral change to which my argument will be addressed. Rather, I focus, as Herman does, on the substantive transition from MSA-1 to MSA-2, assuming—until the very end—the legitimacy of the lawmaking process throughout the relevant time span.

13. See supra note 3.

14. "First-order reasons are exhausted in support of the [competing] principles." Herman, "Contingency in Obligation," p. 41; see also ibid., p. 42–43 and 47.

15. Ibid., p. 45 ("The truth about injury and moral harm will still be publicly acknowledged, and the victims' status regained, but not by way of the institutions of retributive and compensatory justice.").

16. See ibid., pp. 40, 44.

17. See ibid., pp. 36, 39. Such a view of the matter seems presupposed by Herman's commendation of Scanlon's proposal for avoiding assign-

ment of differing moral weights to the competing demands for amnesty and for redress. See ibid., pp. 41–43.

18. Ibid., p. 34.

19. Ibid., p. 36.

20. Ibid., p. 40.

21. Ibid., p. 52 n. 40.

22. Ibid., p. 42.

23. "Either there is an abiding retributive claim, which undermines the legitimacy of the amnesty decision, or the amnesty decision somehow cancels the retributive claim." Ibid., p. 44.

24. Ibid., p. 43.

25. Ibid., p. 43.

26. See, e.g., ibid., p. 31, 34, 36.

27. Ibid., p. 43.

28. Compare Herman at p. 44 and note 30: "I don't claim that the debates got all or even most things right, nor that it was the moral force of the deliberative conclusion that carried the day. But the public discussions leading up to the TRC were remarkably clear about what was at stake, morally, if less clear about how or whether they resolved the moral problems introduced by their decisions."

29. Ibid., p. 40.

30. Ibid., p. 38, 39.

31. Herman points out that even if "more than one principle could have been justified—that is, is supported by sound casuistry," it might have been the case that "only one principle" (she is thinking of amnesty) was "practically viable, or a real possibility." Granting that the opposite might also have been the case—"had the other principle been chosen, it would have served as well"—Herman adds that "real possibility is determined from the point of view of those making the decision, and not all possible futures can be imagined, or imagined well enough" (ibid., p. 44). That seems to me to invite an inference that the fact and quality of the decision making—the form and qualities of the institutional action—make up a part of a full account of the occurrence and legitimacy of moral change in this case.

32. Ibid., p. 36.

3

MORAL IMPROVISATION
AND NEW OBLIGATIONS

F. M. KAMM

After the end of a conflict between states or within a state where one side wins, how should one deal with those on the losing side accused of crimes either in the conflict or in conditions that led to conflict? In this chapter, I consider arguments of Barbara Herman's arguments in her complex, enlightening, and stimulating piece, "Contingency in Obligation," where she justifies a particular answer to this question. Her arguments concern the moral justification of the Truth and Reconciliation Commission (TRC), established in South Africa after the conflict to end apartheid. It is an example used to illustrate her views about how creative solutions to moral problems can come about and, thereby, generate new obligations.

In the first section, I will begin by considering what I take to be her view of morality and how it allows for creativity in the form of improvisation. Then, I will consider how she understands the particulars of the South African situation. In the second section, I will offer some reflections on her discussion. I shall claim that one of her arguments can be simplified and that focusing on that simplified argument lets us characterize in general terms (which Herman does not employ) one strategy that those seeking new morally acceptable solutions to problems can pursue. This strategy, however, removes much of the sting that Herman initially sees as involved in the uncertainty that we may face new obligations at any time. I shall also consider other aspects of her argument that I find more problematic, including her notion of obligation and her view on how to deal with balancing arguments.

I.

(A) Herman's View of Morality

I think that Herman believes that basic components of a universally required morality (such as respect for persons) do not amount to principles that deductively imply particular conclusions in particular circumstances (e.g., what acts or intentions are permissible or obligatory). I believe she refers to this as contingency at the high level of morality, in that there is no principle or rule from which we simply deduce conclusions. She differentiates between the universally required components of morality and what she calls "lived morality." The latter are the norms that people accept as correct at a given time and place. These may change into new norms that are also in accord with components of universal morality, as people see—but do not deduce—a new way to be true to the universal components in dealing with a new problem. The nondeductiveness and the newness of the solution amount to the creative, improvisational aspect of morality in her view.

She thinks that there is also contingency at the ground level of morality in that there may be more than one way in a given situation to be true to components of required universal morality. (This sort of contingency could also, I believe, be present in a system in which conclusions were deducible from principles, for it is possible to deduce a disjunction of equally good alternatives from a principle. So I do not think this contingency at the ground level is necessarily connected with the contingency at the high level that Herman describes.)

Her further claim, which she investigates in detail, is that even when there are several genuine moral options in how to deal with a new problem, people can come to have new obligations that "impose significant burdens" (p. 21) in virtue of the acceptance by others of one of the merely optional routes, even obligations that eliminate certain of the moral rights they previously had. She emphasizes that the fact that we might face new, unexpected obligations in life can be unsettling, as morality is valued in part because of the predict-

ability it introduces into social life. A standard way in which unexpected ground-level moral change occurs is when we discover
that conduct we have taken to be permissible or even obligatory is
wrong. (This description seems to apply to the case she describes
where people discover that behavior they had "thought charming
comes to be regarded as demeaning, even an expression of aggression or dominance" [p. 24]). Changing such bad behavior can be
very unsettling and burdensome but still necessary. However, these
are not the cases on which Herman focuses. She wants to focus on
change when there are genuine options, not change away from
doing what is shown to be morally wrong. In particular, she wants
to focus on changing from one permissible option (not a wrong,
impermissible one) to another permissible option.

(B) Herman's View of South Africa

The TRC allows amnesty for those confessing to crimes that were
politically motivated. Herman thinks the TRC is a morally justified
alternative to retributive justice (RJ). She also believes that the TRC
was not required, as RJ was also a morally permissible option. But
given the acceptance of the TRC, all citizens (even those opposed
to it) lose a moral right held under the previous "lived morality" to
seek RJ, and they acquire a new moral obligation not to pursue RJ
against politically motivated crimes that amnesty covers. (That is, if
someone requests amnesty, his victim is not at liberty to refuse to allow him to get it. Amnesty is not granted merely on condition that
one's victim is willing to go that route.)[1] Furthermore, she is most
concerned to argue that the moral right to seek RJ is not merely
overridden or outweighed owing to the necessity of pursuing some
greater good, as this would leave a residue of maltreatment of those
who would wish to exercise the right.[2] Now let us consider in greater
detail how Herman argues for her views about the TRC.

II.

(A) Available and Unavailable Options

She first reminds us of cases in which either of two options is perfectly morally acceptable, such as driving on the right or the left.

We must choose one, however, and when we do, everyone acquires a new obligation to drive on the side chosen, even if it is not chosen by everyone. However, she notes that in the driving case, the chosen option does not conflict with a status quo right, in the way that moving to the TRC conflicts with people's recognized right to seek RJ. But what if a society already had a rule requiring one to drive on the right, and then decided to change this rule? Presumably, it would not be difficult to generate a new rule in this case either. Herman's real concern should be that the right to seek RJ is not as easily changed as the right to drive on the right, in virtue of its nonarbitrary moral content.

We might ask whether there are other differences between the TRC and the driving case as well. Consider two. (1) In the case of driving, a choice must be made; we cannot have people driving in both ways at once on pain of too many accidents. Must a choice be made between amnesty and RJ? Theoretically, a society could permit those victims who are willing to allow their accused oppressors to have amnesty to do so, but also allow those victims eager to pursue RJ against their accused oppressors to do so as well. Then the society as a whole would not pursue one policy. Herman's argument, therefore, would have to make clear why only one of the two options must be chosen. For if both could be combined, the complaint of those who wish to pursue RJ would seem to be even greater if they are not permitted to do so. I do not think that Herman makes it entirely clear why the two options could not morally be combined, though, as we shall see, she presents facts that suggest why it was not a realistic possibility.[3]

(2) A second difference between the driving case and the TRC is suggested by Herman's description of Nelson Mandela's refusal to seek RJ even in the absence of confession under amnesty of his accused oppressors. She describes what he did as an act of "moral heroism" that exemplifies "civic benevolence" (p. 37). It was his act, she believes, that made it conceivable for many people to think of themselves as capable of doing something somewhat less heroic but also an instance of civic benevolence, namely giving up RJ for amnesty plus confession by accused oppressors. Herman's characterization of Mandela's act suggests that the TRC is also morally superior to RJ. By contrast, neither driving on the right nor left is morally superior.

At least two issues are raised by the (supposed) moral superiority of civic benevolence. (1) The first is that even if a course of conduct is superior, this does not imply that it is obligatory in principle. Herman agrees. However, Herman also seems to take the position that when many in a community are willing to take a nonobligatory superior course, then "can implies ought" (p. 43). This suggests that she thinks that at least for these many, the less noble course is, in fact, impermissible. (If adopting only one course [rather than a combination] is necessary, the fact that many [supposedly] find themselves with an obligation to pursue TRC, given that they are willing to do so, will also put pressure on allowing only the TRC.)

To conclude that in this way, for many, the noble cause becomes obligatory, and the less noble impermissible, would be more radical than Herman acknowledges. It is another way, less emphasized by Herman, in which her account might give rise to new contingent obligations. Namely, if one in fact feels capable of, and wants to do, a nonrequired noble act, one acquires an obligation to do it. I think this radical conclusion would not be correct. Suppose I find myself psychologically able to give up my kidney to a stranger and I even desire to do this truly noble act. I do not think it becomes impermissible for me to not do it, wrong of me not to act on my desire. For suppose that I let my desire to go back to sleep interfere with my capacity and desire to give my kidney. I do not think I thereby fail in an obligation to give my kidney. (The capacity and even desire to do a noble act does not function in the same way as the reduction in cost needed to do the noble act might function to turn the merely permissible into the obligatory, I think. We shall consider the latter option further below.)

Notice also that if a new obligation were generated in this radical way, it would not have the unsettling characteristics Herman describes as associated with unexpected changes in obligations. For the existence of the new obligation would depend on a change in one's own desires and capacities, and stem from and be consistent with them.

(2) A second issue raised by "civic benevolence" is what exactly it is, and whether it is a nobler course. Suppose that only a few people had committed politically inspired crimes and it would be possible to use RJ to punish them. It would be benevolent of black

South Africans to use TRC instead, but it is hard to believe that they would have done so. (Herman agrees that the TRC was not about the superiority of forgiveness by individuals.) Perhaps this is because "civic benevolence" is really only at stake if the *society is the real object* of people's benevolence, for example, if people institute amnesty because they do not want RJ to lead to civil war when large numbers of contested, politically inspired crimes are at issue. However, Herman also notes that the police and military would never have allowed RJ against their members. This is one reason to believe that widespread RJ was not in fact a real possibility and so civic benevolence to avoid civil war was not really needed.

In such a context, I think it is better to describe the TRC as something that could have been the creation of people who were motivated by civic benevolence, but that, in fact, the TRC need not have been the product of such motivation and, indeed, may not have been what most preferred. It is still true that its objective properties might make it the nobler course, even if this does not ensure noble motives of those who participate in it when widespread use of the other (RJ) option would be blocked by powerful forces. (One reason to worry that the TRC is not the nobler course is that it may cheapen the value of South African citizenship. This is because even if one has committed grave crimes, one need not forfeit any of the rights that other citizens have.)

(B) Justifications for Ruling Out Retributive Justice

Having further characterized the options in the South African case (though not necessarily in the way that Herman does), let us return to consider one argument Herman presents for the justifiability of the TRC even when it removes a right to RJ as an option once someone requests amnesty for a politically motivated crime. First, as noted, she thinks that Mandela's example changed the TRC from a nobler permissible option that was a theoretical possibility to a psychologically real possibility for many in the populace. Second, she also thinks the TRC was a way to change the status of blacks from "victim" to "citizen." (Of course, it was also a way of turning accused oppressors into ordinary citizens.) This is, I think, because she believes that the confessions would provide a shared moral history, presumably endorsing the black cause as the foundation of a new community of which blacks would be citizens.[4] The only drawback Herman sees with endorsing the TRC as the only system for dealing with political crimes for which amnesty is requested is that it seems to conflict with the rights of those who still want to retain RJ. The justification of the TRC will not be complete, she thinks, until this problem is dealt with. She considers some ways to deal with it.

(1) One possible answer to this problem is to argue that a greater good justifies imposing a cost (of an infringed right) on some. This is what she calls a balancing argument wherein we weigh the right against the greater good, the right loses, and some people have to bear the cost. Herman tries to avoid this balancing approach quite generally when seeking to explain either why a right does not stand in the way of a greater good (as in the TRC case) or why it does.[5] However, it seems especially important not to override rights in the South African case, where one is attempting, for the first time, to recognize the equal rights and citizenship status of black South Africans.

As an example of a case where a right does stand in the way of a greater good, Herman discusses why it is not permissible to kill someone in order to stop many other people from being killed. Her nonbalancing answer has two components. First, she says the wrong involved in killing does not sum, so more killings are not necessarily worse than fewer. I do not think this is correct. For if I had to go to one island where I could prevent ten killings or to another island where I could prevent one killing (other things equal), I should go to the first island. I think that this is because it is worse if there are more rather than fewer people killed. Furthermore, if I had a forced choice between going in one direction where I will kill ten people with my car or another direction where I will kill one other person, I think I should do the latter. The second component of her answer, to why it is not permissible to kill one person to stop other people from being killed, is that the reason why it is wrong to kill someone is different from whatever reason there is to not allow people to be killed. I think this is correct. However, I do not think that the particular reason she isolates for not killing is quite right.

She focuses on the faulty relationship killing creates between me and the person I would kill. But suppose I have set a bomb that will kill ten people unless I throw another person on it who will be blown up instead. I will be involved in ten faulty relationships if the bomb goes off, yet I should not use the one person to prevent this. I think this is not because faulty relationships do not sum. I think it is wrong to kill the one person because if it were permissible, then he would not be as highly inviolable a person as he really is. Further, this would be true of every person including those who would be saved from being killed. By contrast, if we do not prevent others from being killed and they are, in fact, violated, this does nothing to show that it is permissible for them to be killed or, in other words, that their inviolability is not great. The requirement to not kill one to save others from being killed shows, I believe, that respect for the inviolable status of persons may take precedence over what actually happens to people (i.e., that many people will be wrongly killed). This is also a nonbalancing argument.[6]

(2) Having rejected a balancing argument, Herman proposes another solution to deal with the problem of rights to RJ that might stand in the way of the TRC. She argues that when everything significant that is gotten by a victim from RJ is also gotten by him by way of TRC, there is no longer a ground for his claiming the right to RJ, and there is also no cost (that is supposedly outweighed on the balancing model) imposed on anyone who loses the right. A right to RJ may have been part of the lived moral life of the community without the TRC, but it is not a right that is a part of fundamental universal morality. This is because something else may accomplish for the victim what RJ is meant to accomplish for the victim.

Let us consider this solution in more detail. Herman suggests that RJ is meant to help a victim regain his status in the moral community and the TRC does this too. My first concern is that this is not the distinctive point of RJ. The victim may regain his status simply by everyone agreeing that he has been wronged and someone else is indeed the criminal (even without confession by the criminal). RJ may provide this, but it is not necessary for providing this. Rather, RJ is necessary in order to make the criminal pay for his crime with some nonmonetary loss and this is its distinctive point. Possibly, the victim even has a right to have the person who wronged him pay for his crime, and only RJ could satisfy this right.[7]

If the victim has such a personal right to have the criminal pay for his crime, then the TRC will not provide a victim with all he is personally entitled to have. So it is important for Herman's approach to the problem of depriving people of RJ that there is no such personal right to have the criminal pay. Suppose there is no such right. Then even if the point of RJ is to have the criminal pay (though not because the victim has a personal right that this happen), his not paying need not be a personal wrong to the victim. Hence, even if Herman's view of what RJ is about is not complete, it is possible that what the victim is entitled to get from RJ is also gotten under TRC. This can be so even if not everything that is gotten from RJ is gotten under TRC—because the criminal does not pay for his crime in a nonmonetary way—so long as, in failing to get what RJ alone can give, the victim would not be made to bear any cost that he has a right to avoid or lose anything that he has a right to have.[8]

Though Herman does not say so, her way of dealing with the problem of the supposed costs to the victim of using TRC rather than RJ seems to me to be an instance of a common strategy for turning supererogatory acts into obligations. It is also a common strategy for turning unjust impositions into permissible ones. That is, we can sometimes turn a supererogatory act (or omission such as not taking advantage of RJ) into an obligation (not to take advantage of RJ) by reducing the costs of the act. Similarly, an imposition on someone (that makes it impossible for him to seek RJ rather than merely giving him an obligation not to seek it) might be unjust if this were very costly to him. However, we can sometimes make such an imposition on someone, which makes it impossible for him to do something not be unjust by reducing the costs of the imposition. (Consider an analogy: it would be unjust of me to kill someone to save others' lives, but it might not be unjust to pinch him to do so.) Herman adopts an extremely demanding version of this strategy, in that she wishes there to be no costs to those who give up RJ. But notice that even if the person imposed on pays some cost (e.g., in being pinched), there may be no negative *moral* remainder, if it is clearly someone's duty to undergo such a cost for the sake of the end in question. Then there is also no mere overriding or balancing going on.

This strategy of creating new obligations shows us the difference between (a) having new obligations because there is now no large sacrifice associated with doing certain things that previously would have involved big sacrifices, and (b) having new obligations because big sacrifices not previously required are required. That one has many new obligations that come about in manner (a) is not a source of complaint. For example, previously we may have had no obligations to those at a great distance because the cost of helping them would have been high. But now, with rapid and cheap transport, the cost has gone down and so we may have new obligations, but not ones that are burdensome. Similarly, it is said that with great wealth comes great obligations. Suppose that prior to being wealthy one would have had an obligation to give away 1% of one's income if this would help the needy. Suppose that such a small amount of money wouldn't have helped them, and so one actually had no obligation to give it. Now one may also have an obligation to give away 1% of one's new wealth if this would help the needy. But this amount will be useful, so one comes to have new obligations. But in reality there has not been much of a change in the burden imposed on one, given one's new wealth.

That we can identify such a general strategy suggests that creativity and improvisation in generating new obligations may conform to certain patterns. It suggests that certain universals (e.g., turn a high cost into a low one to make an obligation) play a part in the transformation rules for going from one moral solution to another. It also suggests that one could discover more structure in creativity and that there may be a limited set of general moves that one could try when thinking about new solutions to problems, even though many different institutions or acts might satisfy these moves.

Notice, however, that this particular strategy for creating a new obligation is designed to make the existence of uncertainty as to what our obligations might turn out to be very nonthreatening. For the new ground-level moral regime is allowed to come into existence only if it makes us not significantly worse off (in ways that we are entitled not to be made worse off) than we were under the old regime. So it defuses some crucial concerns associated with instability that Herman emphasizes at the beginning of her chapter when she speaks of new obligations that "impose significant burdens" (p. 21). (Above we saw that this would be true for a different reason, if it were the case that new obligations arose only when they were consistent with our desires to do what is ordinarily supererogatory.) But then this means that the explanation and justification of the TRC that she gives show it not to be a case of the sort she was supposed to be discussing, namely, one where significant burdens are imposed and "difficult obligations of this kind . . . come about . . . where creative solutions to moral difficulties are . . . attempted" (p. 21).

The example and explanation that she has given of how to bring about a new contingent obligation raises the following possibility: generating in other people new unexpected obligations in selecting one of two permissible options is permissible only when it does not impose significant burdens. This is only a possibility, however, as there may be other permissible ways of bringing about new obligations, as a result of choosing one of two permissible options, despite severe dislocations they produce. For Herman says (only in passing, p. 22) that when some in a community find it possible to do heroic acts that do great good (e.g., saving victims from persecution at great risk to themselves), while others do not have to do as they do, the others may not go about their lives as they always have, if this would interfere with the heroic acts. This suggests that they might have to bear significant burdens, and not merely do things differently while not being made much worse off than they would have been, as a result of not being able to do what they have always done.

This sounds like the balancing argument that Herman rejected in arguing for the TRC. What might distinguish cases where balancing is permitted is that the burdens do not involve any denial of that to which someone has a right. After all, we do not have a right not to be made much worse off, if, for example, people refuse us access that we previously had to their property because they are now hiding victims of persecution. Hence, there may be another class of cases where significant burdens not involving transgression of a right may be imposed via a balancing argument at least when one of the permissible options chosen is morally superior to the other.

(3) We have considered the solution to the problem of eliminating RJ that Herman gives when she assumes that RJ is not only morally permissible but a real possibility, and some want it but most do not. In discussing civic benevolence, I raised the possibil-

ity that RJ was not a real possibility because powerful forces would have stood in its way. But for other reasons Herman also comes to retract her original assumption that RJ was a real possibility. Let us consider this aspect of her discussion.

First, having said that both RJ and TRC are theoretically moral possibilities, she claims (p. 44) that, in fact, only the TRC option was psychologically a real possibility for most people. (It is not clear to me why this is so, assuming that just preferring one alternative does not make another alternative psychologically unreal for one). Indeed, she thinks that they "experience it [i.e., the TRC] (hear it) as obligatory" (p. 43). One explanation for why Herman thinks that they experience it as obligatory is her view, examined above, that "can implies ought" when one finds oneself with the capacity for doing a noble deed. (I argued that this is not true.) A second alternative explanation suggested by Herman's discussion is that South Africans are obligated to do either TRC or RJ, many are psychologically unable to do RJ, and hence those many are obligated to do TRC. On the first explanation, RJ becomes, in fact, impermissible because the psychological reality of the nobler TRC gives a duty to do it. On the second explanation, the TRC is experienced as obligatory merely as a consequence of RJ having no psychological reality.

What I find especially puzzling about the second explanation is that Herman raises it before she presents her solution to the problem of eliminating RJ that I have already described in B(2), namely that everything important gotten by a victim from RJ can be gotten from the TRC. I think this is puzzling because if the community was actually incapable of pursuing RJ, and if ought implies or presupposes can, how could those who lose out on RJ complain that they failed to get something to which they had a right from the community (i.e., something that the community was obligated to give them)?[9]

Related to this puzzle is a concern about when Herman thinks people cannot do something (in a sense that relates to the claim that ought implies or presupposes can). Her account seems to heavily imply that contingency in obligation can result from theoretically permissible options not being "psychologically real" for people. (Notice that in this respect, the contingent obligation is not the one that some people have to not pursue

RJ, but the contingent obligation that the greater number supposedly have to use the TRC. This is another type of contingency in obligation that her account implies but that is not her
primary focus.)

I think this an overpsychologizing of "can't." For a psychopath
all permissible options might be psychologically unreal. Does
this mean there is nothing he is actually permitted or obligated
to do? Presumably not. Some people might be unable to conceive
of themselves as responsible voters. Does this mean they are not
permitted or obligated to vote? Presumably not. One reason those
who want RJ might have a complaint against those who want the
TRC exclusively is that the fact that RJ is psychologically unavailable to those who want TRC does not mean that they are truly
unable to support RJ in a way that would neutralize obligations
to those who have a supposed right to RJ. This is one reason that
we have to give another argument (as described in B[2]) for why
those who have to forego RJ have no complaint. When an option
is psychologically unreal for someone, this is more like his being
unwilling to do it than his being unable to do it, in the context of
the view that "ought" implies or presupposes "can."

It is still true, however, that if someone will not do one of only
two permissible options, he comes to have an obligation to do the
other one, and this obligation is contingent on his choice. But,
again, as this new contingent obligation arises from a predilection
or choice of the agent himself, such contingent obligations should
not be threatening for agents seeking to avoid dislocations associated with changes in ground level moral life. Such contingent
obligations are not instances of difficult contingent obligations for
which Herman was supposed to be arguing.

A third reason Herman comes to offer for thinking that RJ was
actually impossible goes beyond its psychological unreality for
many in the community. It implies that RJ was not even a theoretical possibility in the circumstances, though not because RJ was a
morally inadmissible option. For she says (p. 46) that a constituted
community may commit itself to pursue RJ, but the problem in
South Africa was to constitute the community (implying it was not
yet constituted). This suggests that she thinks that RJ requires a
community to pursue it, and there was no community that could
pursue RJ; even that there were no citizens who could pursue it

but only victims of a previous community.[10] (This would seem to be the real meaning of her view that victims had to be turned into citizens.) If only after one is a citizen of a community could one pursue RJ, one would need something else to make one a citizen besides RJ. Herman seems to think that one can create a community by way of the construction of a moral history for a community, from those who give testimony and confessions during amnesty proceedings. She finally suggests, therefore, that as a conceptual matter TRC is the only possible route when a community is being formed.

I do not think that this could be correct. Suppose Jewish people who had been abused citizens of Nazi Germany tried to hold trials of their persecutors in a postwar Germany in which no amnesty had been given and no confessions served as the basis for an historical narrative of the new state. I think there could already be a new state with former victims as citizens who could, as a conceptual matter, pursue RJ. They need neither the results of RJ nor the TRC in order to be full-fledged citizens. This would be so even if there was no community in the sense that those to be tried accepted the legitimacy of the new order. Why should the legitimacy of the new order depend on its acceptance (via such signs as participating in a TRC confessional proceeding) by people accused of crimes in the old order? Citizens may think it right to bring such people into the new community as full-fledged members (rather than as convicted criminals) by civic benevolence and amnesty, but not because it is literally impossible to do anything else if a new state capable of RJ is to exist.

Even if ordinary courts could not pursue RJ for practical reasons, this need not mean that RJ could not and should not be pursued. For non-state courts such as international war crimes tribunals could still be convened to pursue RJ. Indeed, Herman herself says (in note 33, pp. 51–52): "Analogous claims [to those about the TRC] are made about the need for international war crimes trials. . . . The justification for abnormal judicial activities is more commonly that some moral possibility needs to be opened (or closed) that exceeds the orbit of ordinary justice." Hence, contrary to Herman's final suggestion, RJ is not ruled out as a conceptual matter even if it must be pursued in an "abnormal judicial context" such as an international court.

Conclusion

I conclude that if it were true that victims have no fundamental right to have criminals pay for their crimes in nonmonetary ways, Herman will have provided an argument that eliminates a significant complaint of those who lose RJ. However, I think that if her argument is correct, it also shows that the TRC is not a case of the sort she had intended to investigate, namely where "significant burdens" are imposed on some in virtue of new obligations that they have because others choose one of two permissible options. This is because her argument depends on showing that the TRC, as much as RJ, gives victims all they are entitled to have. I also do not think she shows that RJ was not a possible option (either on its own or in conjunction with the TRC) because of its actual (versus theoretical) impermissibility to those who are capable of a nobler option, because of its psychological unavailability to many, or because of its conceptual impossibility in transitional contexts.

More generally, I isolated and focused on three ways in which Herman's account suggests that new, contingent obligations can arise consistent with deeper, universal elements of morality: (1) When some people want to do something, this can create new obligations in others. (This is the one to which she gives most attention.) (2) If one is capable of and wants to do something noble, this may make one obligated to do it. (I argued against this.) (3) If one of (only) two permissible options is psychologically unavailable to you, you acquire an obligation to do the other option. (I suggested problems with this claim.) I argued that none of the examples given in Herman's chapter of these ways of generating new obligations should worry people who are concerned about the dislocations and burdens of ground-level moral change. This is, in part, because certain transformation rules (e.g., unjust impositions can be made just by eliminating costs) may be part of the deeper, universal elements of morality. It is also, in part, because a desire or psychological predilection to fulfill a new obligation reduces the burden of fulfilling it.

NOTES

1. Herman does not discuss the fact that people are at least encouraged to give up another right—that against self-incrimination—with the establishment of the TRC.

2. One immediate possible objection to her claim that the citizens acquire a moral obligation not to pursue RJ (made by Frank Michelman in his comment on Herman, this volume) is that the legal possibility of pursuing RJ was eliminated once the TRC option was chosen, and it does not make sense to say that people acquire a moral obligation not to do what it is impossible for them to do anyway. I think one could respond to this objection as follows: suppose it can be shown (for one reason or another) that South Africa is morally justified in pursuing the amnesty option alone, and that one would have an obligation morally not to do what conflicts with this even if it were legally possible to do so (for example, because all legal loopholes had not been closed to RJ). Then if pursuing RJ would conflict with the amnesty, one would have a moral obligation not to pursue it, even if it were legally possible to do so. Further, on these grounds, one might justify taking the further step of making what it would be morally impermissible to do into what it is also legally impossible to do (by closing the loopholes).

3. She herself notes that South Africa did allow pursuit of civil suits as well as amnesty for politically motivated crimes.

4. One danger with the confession process, I would note, is that some of those accused might confess to what they did not do, merely to avoid the travails of a trial, and the shared moral history will then not be based on the firmest evidence.

5. However, earlier in her paper, it is not so clear that Herman would always reject such a balancing approach. She says (p. 22) that when some in a community find it possible to do heroic acts that do great good, others are not obligated to do as they do. Yet these others may not conduct their business as usual if doing so would interfere with the heroic acts; they must bear some costs as a result of not being able to go about their lives as they have always done so that a great good may be accomplished. Perhaps Herman is only opposed to imposing costs in this way when the costs stem from transgressing a right to do something and not otherwise. I shall have occasion to repeat this point in the text below (at p. 74).

6. My discussion here draws on my discussion of this topic in other places, for example, in my "Harming Some to Save Others," *Philosophical Studies* 57, no. 3 (1989): 227-260, and in my *Morality Mortality*, Vol. 2 (New York: Oxford, 1996).

7. The victim's right might be better thought of as a right to pursue punishment of the criminal or the right that society pursue this.

8. Of course, if the victim supports RJ on grounds independent of what he has a right to just because he thinks the criminal deserves to pay, he will not be satisfied by the TRC. But he has no personal right to have the community decide for retribution, as opposed to amnesty, per se, unless victims have rights to have the perpetrators of crimes against them be punished.

9. A possible answer to this is that Herman does not think that ought implies or presupposes can.

10. She says, "In the circumstances of transition . . . the restitutive moral function of retributive justice could not be realized" and that there was "absence of conditions of civility and trust that allow ordinary systems of justice to perform their status-securing function" (p. 46).

4

CONTINGENCY AT GROUND LEVEL

A REPLY

BARBARA HERMAN

Morality as the subject of philosophical study is often only indirectly related to the morality that persons live.[1] Theory to practice is pretty much a one-way street. From the side of theory, we could not say what a moral life would look like, though we could point to various norms and principles that frame or define it. A good person respects others, avoids violating their rights, is responsive to threats to their welfare, and so on. While some actions (or action kinds) are morally forbidden regardless of context, it is only within a specific social world that we can tell what respect for others looks like, or appreciate the requirements of friendship.[2] If a good person is lucky, she lives in a social world whose norms and institutions do moral work, don't threaten moral well-being, and encourage right action. But if she is not so lucky, the demands on her may not comport so easily with theory-driven expectations.

One of the aims of my essay "Contingency in Obligation" is to consider whether there might be distinctive questions for moral theory that arise from within moral practice. The point of asking the question in these terms is to suggest that morality, and so moral theory, might be incomplete: that the connection between unchanging universal values and ground-level obligations relies on facts or premises that can introduce variation in outcomes at the level of duties and obligations, permissions, and burdens.[3] After the fact, adjusted patterns of justification will make theory whole again, hopefully not in an ad hoc manner, but in ways that reveal deeper or more complex moral structures. To navigate this terrain one needs to attend carefully to the moral phenomena, and to be open to rethinking some moral features one has regarded as fixed.

One such feature that I identify is stability—that persons have a legitimate interest in the constancy of the moral elements of their world. This is not to say that there are per se moral reasons to resist change. That some group of persons might be seriously discomfited to learn that they cannot go on in their old ways does not weigh against correcting wrongdoing. But the issue is sometimes not simple: moral correction is rarely like fixing an arithmetic error on a balance sheet. Once identified as wrong, some kinds of action must simply cease being done (nonconsensual sex in whatever context, for example). But if personal and social relationships are built on norms that sanction gendered disrespect, while behaviors need to change, there are reasons to make the change in ways that are attentive to preservation and repair, and so more slowly. Here practice makes demands on theory for intermediate principles; they are contingent demands, at least in the sense that things might have been, or we might have been, otherwise.

Issues of this sort tend to arise where wrongful practices are entrenched, where moral problems have no unique solution, or where, depending on the history of conflict and the importance of a shared future, even the moral imagination of the parties, some but not all possible options are available to agents. In complex cases—what often makes the cases complex—all options involve morally significant costs. When costs get large, perhaps extending to the violation or abrogation of rights, arguments tend to engage a familiar palette of justifications—practical necessity, rights overriding rights, moral balancing—all of which suggest some resignation about morality's ability to solve its own problems. The TRC looked like an ideal case for working on these issues: the difficulties were and were recognized as being fundamental moral ones; a solution to the moral and political problem of transition was devised that was in key ways circumstance specific; the recognized challenge to the TRC was that the costs it would impose were ones, it was claimed, that victims had a right that they not bear. If the TRC was morally justified, then some rethinking of that claim would be necessary.

In her comment on "Contingency in Obligation," F. M. Kamm takes me to be arguing that the TRC, though it involved loss of rights, was an institution of civic benevolence which became obligatory when large numbers of people, disenchanted with the normal institutions of justice, felt it was the only route they could take to a viable South African state. She then offers what she believes is a better moral account of the situation that involves neither rights violations nor appeals to what people think they can do. While I think that at many junctures Kamm mistakes the nature of my argument, her own account introduces valuable elements that improve our understanding of cases like the TRC. In what follows I will try to extricate them from the elements of the criticism I find inapt. I'll begin by highlighting three of Kamm's claims.

K1. A transformation rule. Lowering burdens can transform optional good actions into obligatory ones. Before the TRC is devised, persons have a right to have their claims in justice honored: it would be supererogatory of them to forgo their claims. If the TRC provides a morally comparable resolution to victim's claims, then the burden of forgoing their criminal justice claim is lessened, and what had been supererogatory could become obligatory.

K2. A real possibility condition. The TRC is not a real case of contingent obligation if either the system of retributive justice truly was not workable or the majority simply resisted the option of retributive justice.

K3. Moral excellence cannot obligate. That some would forgo rights for the sake of building a better society does not make it morally required for others to do so.

K1 provides an important insight into the structure of moral obligations. While I don't think it always explains how the shift from options to obligations takes place, I agree with Kamm that it often does. The question is whether it makes the best case for an obligation to accept the TRC. K2 poses a challenge to the claimed role of the majority in determining what was obligatory. It depends, I think, on an overly narrow view of appeals to psychology—specif-

ically, about the way things look to agents who have to choose or
act. The good reasons we have for discounting some attitudes toward options do not generalize to all of them. Last (K3), I do think
the moral excellence of some can obligate others, and I doubt that
Kamm actually disagrees.

About several things we are in agreement. If there were a fundamental personal right to retributive justice (RJ), it would be difficult to justify its violation as a means to promote RJ, or a regime
of law in which RJ would eventually flourish. If the TRC is justified,
then either there was no violation of a right to RJ, or there was a
violation and it was justified, or RJ is not a fundamental personal
right. Whether anyone was obligated to accept the TRC is a further question, the answer to which is connected to our view of the
justificatory story for the TRC.

On my account, resolution of the question depends on four further facts. (1) After a long period of grave injustices perpetrated
by the state and its agents, victims' belief that extant institutions
of the criminal law could not provide "justice" were widespread
and not unreasonable, though not necessarily true. (2) Leaving
these crimes unanswered would undermine the legitimacy of any
future South African state. (3) Nelson Mandela's heroic (and public) transcendence of his own complaint in justice for the sake of
a future state inspired and made possible a novel quasi-judicial
model, the TRC, designed to manage the problems caused by (1)
and (2). (4) Whereas the system of criminal justice did not inspire
confidence or respect in the majority, the TRC, as a result of Mandela's heroic act, the inventiveness of the committee that wrote the
Postamble, and Bishop Tutu's charismatic compassion, did. The
challenge is to find a way to argue from these specific contextual
elements to a moral justification of the TRC.

The argument structure of "Contingency in Obligation" is dialectical and exploratory, its method experimental: some aspect of
the above account had to be revised or reconfigured, but it was
not clear ex ante which. One tack takes both the TRC and RJ to
be permissible options; then the permissibility of the TRC has to
be established in the face of complaints about lost rights. I examined two complaint-neutralizing strategies: Scanlon's Principle of
Established Practices and moral balancing. The Scanlon Principle
neutralizes complaints by taking the fact that a nonrejectable rule

is in place to be an independent source of obligation to it, in the face of burdens and other options. But it is a conservative principle that, in any case, depends on and cannot secure permissibility. Moral balancing is the wrong kind of response to rights violations (Kamm agrees that it is, but not about why). Taking a different tack, I argue that the majority's view of the TRC made a moral difference. By the majority's lights, the procedures of the TRC satisfied the need for justice. If they were right, the TRC would have to be equivalent to or a substitute for the institutions of retributive justice. But how could that be? If victims have a right that criminals "pay" for their crimes with some kind of hard time, the TRC offers no equivalent. The equivalence is possible only if what RJ is about is different: not about having criminals pay, but, say, about securing victims' status through public negative response to criminal acts directed at the law-breakers. This is something the TRC could do.[4]

The advantages of this route through the problem are threefold. First, it honors and further articulates the views of those trying to work out what to do. Second, the terms of justification are friendly (not necessarily congenial) to those addressed. A justification whose terms are alien to those acting is not for that reason faulty, but it is in principle less authoritative than one that engages with actual practice. (This is an instance where stability plays a moral role.) And third, running the investigating from the ground up encourages greater openness about interpretation of basic moral-theoretic notions: they are rarely transparent as we encounter and use them. But the advantages come with a cautionary demand that one be very careful about keeping the methodology in plain view. The argument is not that the TRC and RJ are equivalent permissible options, though it is important that they at first appear to be so. Under pressure from the ideas embedded in the TRC we are led to revise our understanding of RJ, and only with that revision the complaint "in justice" is no longer an obstacle to the TRC.

The more general picture is this: Suppose at t_1, P_1 is the moral principle we appropriately act on; at t_2 obligation-relative facts change and P_1 is no longer apt; P_2 and P_3 now capture whatever the moral value at issue is. But moral principles are life-shaping, not just of what we do, but of what we recognize and value and condemn. If P_2 requires us to construct institutions, while P_3 requires the inculcation of new virtues, the principles may in one sense be morally equivalent, but humanly they are hardly so. It is this feature that explains how moral front-runners or innovators can determine the structure of obligations for the rest of us by making some P_i that is generally not regarded as a real possibility appear viable or even compelling. The work of innovation is easier to notice when we attend to context and the way the moral situation in fact appears to deliberating agents.

This brings us to two nonstandard sources of obligation (or release from obligation) that I appeal to and that Kamm finds objectionable. The first is that exemplary acts of others can obligate us (or alter our obligations); and second, taking oneself to be unable to pursue a course of actions (that one may know others could take) can be a justifying reason for not taking it. The second, especially, is a delicate matter. It's one thing for someone not to want or feel like doing what she ought, another for someone to be so damaged that she cannot properly assess the moral features of her circumstances, and altogether another when, because of personal or shared history, persons cannot take individuals or institutions of authority at their word ("Fool me once . . ."). If a group has been abused by one or more of the arms of law enforcement, its members may not be in a position to assent to "justice being done." Asserting that this "cannot" is really a "will not" mistakes the nature of the liberty we assume agents have. A battered wife "can" leave her battering husband, but she does not and says she cannot. This is not a mere "predilection" she has; a battered wife can be caught in a web of fear and anxiety, self-doubt and mistrust, such that options that others could take are not real possibilities for her. The moral landscape such persons inhabit is differently configured from that of a normal moral agent. We may or may not view such persons as morally impaired; certainly their agency is not fully responsive to some facts.

With such considerations in mind it can be hard to say whether there really are, in a moral sense, multiple options available. In the spirit of Kamm's transformation principle one might want to say that in some cases the history of a situation so burdens the choice set of an individual or group that a pair of principles that would be on a par for many are not on a par for them: to choose one of the options would be sufficiently burdensome as to discount it from contention as a principle of obligation, given the (contingently) less burdensome alternative. This is not to say that whenever one of two contending principles is less burdensome the other cannot obligate: no general claim of that sort is being made. Rather, in some circumstances, for some agents, the burden of acting on some otherwise obligating P_i makes doing so supererogatory.[5] It is in this restricted environment that I offered the rhetorically intended "can implies ought." Many de facto disenfranchised communities simply suffer under political regimes whose laws and courts abuse them; their assent is a matter of indifference. The architects of the TRC saw that in their circumstances the practical impossibility of assent to the regime of courts and criminal law made the fact of possible assent to the TRC a source of obligation through which justice could be satisfied. (It is important in this regard not to focus overmuch on the amnesty—as if it were the substitute for criminal justice—but rather to attend to the opportunities the TRC afforded victims to give voice to the truth about what was done to them.) The TRC was the better means to a stable political regime, but its primary justification did not appeal to that.[6]

One reason Kamm is drawn to K1 is that she thinks the correct argument for the TRC to be that of transforming a morally superior permissible option into an obligation. In the argument that I make, the moral superiority of the TRC plays no role, at least not in the sense Kamm seems to have in mind. The disagreement here may be about the supererogatory in general.[7] I do not think that someone who knowingly does more than she has to, promotes some greater good, or bears some burden she morally need not, has thereby acted in a morally superior way, if "superior" is taken to mean "better." What she has done is morally good, but it is not morally better than actions that meet the moral mark. Morality neither recommends more, nor criticizes less. It permits more and can commend agents for going above and beyond duty. Mandela went above and beyond. The TRC, which is formed in the possibility space of Mandela's action, is not likewise a going above and beyond: accepting it is not a morally superior act or an act of civic benevolence, but a duty, perhaps a duty in justice.

Along with Kamm I resist any suggestion that, in general, where others do morally praiseworthy actions, we are thereby obligated to do what they do. (Nor do I think that being able to and wanting to do something exceptionally good makes one obligated to do it. How could it?) But I do claim that our obligations—the obligations we have and what we are obligated to do—can be affected by what heroic individuals choose to do. This can be quite ordinary. Suppose each member of our town would be obligated to give \$N for the local needy, but Rich Neighbor provides it all. The rest of us are then obligated to give less, and may now have an obligation in gratitude toward Rich Neighbor. In other cases, because of what some do that goes beyond duty, ordinary dutiful folk might have to do more. There's nothing here that Kamm should object to. Suppose the villagers of Le Chambon were not obligated to risk the lives of their families to protect Jews hiding from Nazis. And suppose some villagers decided to do so, taking on some considerable cost and risk.[8] Before the heroic acts, there was nothing short of heroism that ordinary villagers could do to save Jews. Now, given the heroism of some, there are things the non-heroic can do—namely, not report the heroic villagers to the Germans, not complain about minor transgressions (people walking across their land at night), tolerate minor food shortages, etc. By in effect lowering the bar for acts that contribute to saving Jews, the heroic acts of the few encumber many others. Where there was nothing they were obligated to do before, they are now obligated to act. This strikes me as an obvious interpersonal extension of K1—when the balance of burdens and risks is changed, so are the facts of obligation.

Part of the point of introducing the idea of "lived morality" with its virtue, stability, is to explain some of the intuitions we have about moral burdens. That a decent person should be able to live an ordinary moral life is not an extra-moral ambition. This is part of the explanation of the conservative nature of morality—that we manage some moral business *this* way is an additional reason for continuing to do it. And is part of the explanation for why one might have to bear being pinched for the sake of some greater good, but not have to give up one's limb or life, and why congruence and not mere compossibility is the appropriate standard for sets of principles, even though to realize congruence we might fall short of some morally best state of affairs. Independent considerations of sacrifice and supererogation do not do the work in setting standards here, since, I would hazard, it is the standards for these notions that are being set.

As part of this investigation, I looked at (and rejected) balancing arguments that might allow a right to be violated for the sake of some significant social good, in particular the good of having that very right not violated. Kamm argues that the correct explanation of this rejection is the inviolable moral status of persons (expressed in and the rights that articulate it): not violating fundamental rights takes precedence over protecting agents from suffering their violation. I don't disagree. Nonetheless, I couched my discussion of non-balancing in terms of the moral relations between agents. I did so because I think we cannot see everything that matters by attending to moral status. Let me say a little more about what's at stake here.

One of the deep ideas behind Kantian proscriptions is that some things sum, others don't. If a headache gives me a certain amount of pain, then in a day when I have two, I have had (at least) twice as much pain. By contrast, there is no amount of wrongness that comes with a killing per se, no summing where there are two—just one killing, and then another (deaths sum in the relevant sense; killings don't, though of course you can count them). It is true that if I could prevent more killings from occurring simply by going to island A instead of island B, then, other things equal, I should go to A. But that doesn't show that the wrongness of killings sum; rather, I am in the unusual position of doing many separate things (preventing this killing and that one) with a single action.[9] (If the wrongness summed it would add weight to the side of preventing five killings versus saving five from drowning; it doesn't do that.)

To see some of the point in offering moral explanation in terms of relations to others, I discussed lies instead of killings (different kinds of cases show different things). Lies don't engage inviolability in the direct way that killings do, but they too resist summing and exhibit the differing valences of doing and preventing. Suppose that the wrong in lies is a kind of insult. That insult occurs whether or not the act is completed (if while A lies to B, I whisper the truth in B's ear, I can avert some harm that the lie might have caused, but I do not make what A is doing less wrong). This suggests that if there is an obligation to prevent lies from occurring, it would have a different source than the obligation one has not to stand in lying relations to others. One might argue that if it were permissible to lie to prevent lies that would make persons less inviolable than they are, but (1) it is not plausible that inviolability extends to being lied to (though lying is a serious wrong),[10] and (2) it would be better if we had a common account of the no-summing feature across kinds of cases that also explains why doings and preventings come out differently.

Each of us has primary responsibility for what we do, and for the chain of effects that issue from our choices. Averting a harm, preventing a lie, is not just blocking the occurrence of a morally bad event (a canceling of it, as it were) but entering into a relationship with the parties affected, and different relationships, depending on the action, occasion, and cost. Suppose A would lie to B and the lie is (with or without A's intending it) beneficial to B. Perhaps the lie will give B a moment of calm in which she can complete an important task. If I have no special relationship to either A or B that would explain it, I see no reason to prevent (or correct) the lie. If I am asked to confirm the lie with one of my own, that is a different and more difficult matter.

One might think that if the moral difference between doing and preventing applies to lies, that is evidence that what we have here is a further articulation of persons' status—not now their inviolability, but some kind of respect-worthiness. In a sense, I would agree. The point of the approach I adopt lies elsewhere: by taking the first-order data to be the moral relations between persons we are more naturally led to a more finely grained articulation of what our moral status amounts to—an articulation which, after the fact, can be re-presented in principles of obligation. One enters into a moral relation to another through one's intentional actions—what one aims to do in acting and why. As before, although we can know in advance that certain kinds of relation are impermissible, agents' sincerely nuanced grasp of their circumstances and aims may produce unexpected results (that is, differing sets of permissions and obligations). There is thus reason to think that where conflict is resistant in the face of known principles, attending to the specific aims and understandings of creative individuals and groups can reveal moral complexity that might otherwise elude us. This is the work of what I called revisionary casuistry.

About the TRC the question was about the kind of insult, if any, those who would introduce the TRC were directing at others who had claims of RJ. This is a question about moral relations. If they saw themselves violating rights to RJ for a good cause, then they were wrong in proceeding. But if, as I think is a reasonable interpretation of what happened, they instead came to be aware that the terms in which the challenge was raised did not fully capture the moral values involved, then a justified route to the TRC might be available (including the suspension of access to RJ in its customary form for an historically specific set of grievances). There remain interesting counterfactuals: a different cast of characters would have seen the situation and the distribution of burdens differently. Whether their vision would have made other paths real possibilities is not a question we can answer a priori. In a different moral setting, similar crimes might have called forth a different moral outcome.[11] I do think this conclusion a radical one.

Morality is not a static system. Its most fundamental principles and values can enter lived morality in different forms. As our understanding of the moral bases of our institutions deepens, we may discover that we are in more challenging circumstances than we knew. The kind of practical conflict that led to the TRC show us not just the moral deficiencies of persons, but also the limits of the principles we have available to negotiate our shared circumstances. No remedy can erase wrongdoing; the right remedy can sometimes make the wrongdoing less able to damage the future. The TRC created the possibility of constituting a political community without altogether rejecting the wrongful history of apartheid as part of its past. The challenge was not to get the criminals to accept the new order (as if the legitimacy of postwar Germany depended on Nazi assent), but to make the state credible to the legions of surviving victims. It is true that the TRC created an opportunity for perpetrators to re-enter society through the public acknowledgment of the wrongs they had done (often face-to-face with their victims or their families). This accomplished one of the normal goals of a system of punishment. But the real work was in creating a venue in which victims could have standing to publicly identify actions against them as crimes (in this case, actions of the state itself). In a healthy polity, these two functions work together; that is partly why it can seem that the role of legal institutions is to negotiate victims' rights with respect to perpetrators (that they "pay for their crimes"). One of the insights of those who devised the TRC was that these two functions could be separated: the community has obligations to victims and different obligations with respect to perpetrators. If they were right, then it is in one sense true that the choice of the TRC did not introduce burdens that others were entitled not to bear. But there is another sense in which this does not capture the burdens involved. Where fundamental moral interests can be differently instantiated, the shift from one form to another requires a kind of justification that does not reject but rather reinterprets the forms forgone. It is exactly unlike the case where we discover that modes of action we took to be permissible, however you look at them, in fact violate fundamental rights.

To summarize: (1) Where Kamm and I agree is that the supererogatory actions of some can sometimes obligate others. It is, I agree, useful to think of this as an example of a moral transformation rule and an explanation of how some kinds of moral creativity may have an effect. Whether universal morality is structured by a few or many such rules is an open question. As a challenge to inquiry, I think actual practice has much to teach us, so long as we are open to seeing the effect of moral creativity as altering the terms of moral engagement. (2) There is considerable difference in how Kamm and I see the work of moral theory. I do not think its task is over with the articulation of sets of valid principles of action. Moral principles shape and are shaped by the way persons live. If we accept the idea that there is rarely only one way to instantiate a fundamental moral value, we enter a realm of contingency about how things work out in a time and place, and so also a set of questions about revision and reform. We should not expect a general account of the moral burdens that such transitional situations may involve. (3) Related to this is a difference in the way we regard the nature and moral impact of psychological possibility. A path that an agent or group cannot believe is available is in a morally relevant way not really available for them. It of course matters why they cannot see or accept a possibility: if their path-blindness is self-induced, or the result of negligence, their "cannot" may not count against moral possibility. But, if it is the product of their having suffered abuse or systematic injustice, there may be things they cannot do—their world may lack possibilities that ours contains. Correlatively, the mere fact that we see (or even welcome) a good path before us does not obligate us to take it: we need not do as much good as we can. What happened with the TRC was that Mandela's heroic act affected the moral imagination of others in a way that made the possibility of acting for *justice* real; and that possibility, I claimed, did obligate, at least if, as I also argued, rights were not thereby wrongfully compromised.

NOTES

1. I want to take this opportunity to thank my two commentators at the NOMOS session in 2004, Seyla Benhabib and Frank Michelman; responses to their thoughtful criticisms were worked into the final version of my paper. Since the completion of the paper, F. M. Kamm wrote an additional set of comments, included here as "Moral Improvisation and New Obligations." I am grateful to the editors of this volume for giving me the opportunity to reply to Kamm; engagement with her criticisms has prompted what I hope is helpful clarification some of the central positions of the original paper.

2. Fluency in more than one "moral language" is possible; it's an open question how wide-ranging this competence can be, or whether there are special obligations here.

3. Although universal values are constant, change at ground level affects our grasp of them.

4. What the state may permissibly use hard time for is no easy matter to say; the idea of "paying" for crimes through hard time equivalences strikes me as very hard to justify.

5. We would say none of this for someone who merely preferred not to act on P_i or objected to the smallest burden.

6. That is, had the TRC served justice and yet undermined the possibility of a unified state, it would have failed a secondary condition of justification.

7. I am doubtful that the supererogatory in general is best understood in terms of actions that would be duties if not for the burden of performing. Acts of kindness require a different account, as do acts of heroism. An agent who sees that she might do more than duty requires responds to moral reasons; it would be odd if it were entirely discretionary how she responds to them.

8. I am not here considering indirect risk to non-assenting others.

9. The same reasoning applies to forced choice situations or the case where the same agent initiates ten wrongful killings which he could then prevent by killing another.

10. One might think that some profoundly manipulative lies do threaten inviolability. Perhaps so. But I think this would tell us more about inviolability than about lies.

11. As Kamm rightly points out, in other circumstances those who were victims might insist on using the regular courts, despite (or because of) their skepticism, or they might make use of international tribunals. None of this is a conceptual matter.

5

THE IDEA OF POLITICAL PLURALISM

WILLIAM A. GALSTON

Introduction: A Sketch of Liberal Pluralism

We often use the phrase "liberal democracy," but we don't always think about it very carefully. The noun points to a particular *structure* of politics in which decisions are made, directly or indirectly, by the people as a whole; and more broadly, to an understanding of politics in which all legitimate power flows from the people. The adjective points to a particular understanding of the *scope* of politics, in which the domain of legitimate political decision-making is seen as inherently limited. Liberal governance acknowledges that important spheres of human life are wholly or partly outside the purview of political power. It stands as a barrier against all forms of total power, including the power of democratic majorities.

The question then arises, How are we to understand the nature and extent of limits on government? The signers of the U.S. Declaration of Independence appealed to the self-evidence of certain truths, among them the concept of individuals as bearers of rights that both orient and restrict governmental power. Today, individual rights represent an important (some would say dominant) part of our moral vocabulary. The question is whether they are sufficient to explain and justify the full range of constraints we may wish to impose on the exercise of public power—for example, limits on government's right to intervene in the internal affairs of civil associations and faith-based institutions.

In a recent book, *Liberal Pluralism*,[1] I argue that we must develop a more complex theory of the limits to government. In this endeavor, three concepts are of special importance. The first is political pluralism, an understanding of social life that comprises multiple sources of authority—individuals, parents, civil associations, faith-based institutions, and the state, among others—no one of which is dominant in all spheres, for all purposes, on all occasions. Because so many types of human association possess an identity not wholly derived from the state, pluralist politics does not presume that the inner structure and principles of every sphere must mirror those of basic political institutions. For example, in filling positions of religious authority, faith communities may use, without state interference, gender-based norms that would be forbidden in businesses and public accommodations.

The second key concept is *value pluralism*, made prominent by the late British philosopher Isaiah Berlin. This concept offers an account of the moral world we inhabit: while the distinction between good and bad is objective, there are multiple goods that differ qualitatively from one another and which cannot be ranked-ordered. If this is the case, there is no single way of life, based on a singular ordering of values, that is the highest and best for all individuals. This has important implications for politics. While states may legitimately act to prevent the great evils of human existence, they may not seek to force their citizens into one-size-fits-all patterns of desirable human lives. Any public policy that relies on, promotes, or commands a single conception of human good or excellence as equally valid for all individuals is on its face illegitimate.

The third key concept in my account of limited government is expressive liberty. Simply put, this is a presumption in favor of individuals and groups leading their lives as they see fit, within the broad range of legitimate variation defined by value pluralism, in accordance with their own understandings of what gives life meaning and value. Expressive liberty may be understood as an extension of the free exercise of religion, generalized to cover comprehensive conceptions of human life that rest on non-religious as well as religious claims. This extension applies to groups as well as individuals. Some shared cultural understandings go just as deep, define identity just as much, as do shared religious beliefs. They are equally entitled to deference—again, within limits.[2]

There is a presumption in favor of this expanded conception of free exercise, and a liberal pluralist state must discharge a burden of proof whenever it seeks to restrict it.

This standard for state action is demanding, but hardly impossible to meet. While expressive liberty is a very important good, it is not the only good, and it is not unlimited. In the first place, the social space within which differing visions of the good are pursued must be organized and sustained through the exercise of public power; to solve inevitable problems of coordination among divergent individuals and groups, the rules constituting this space will inevitably limit in some respects their ability to act as they see fit. Second, there are some core evils of the human condition that states have the right (indeed the duty) to prevent; to do this, they may rightly restrict the actions of individuals and groups. Third, the state cannot sustain a free social space if its very existence is jeopardized by internal or external threats, and within broad limits it may do what is necessary to defend itself against destruction, even if self-defense restricts valuable liberties of individuals and groups. A free society is not a suicide pact.

Liberal pluralists, then, endorse the essential conditions of public order, such as the rule of law and a public authority with the capacity to enforce it. They also endorse what may be called a "minimal universalism"—that is, the moral and practical necessity of organizing public life so as to ward off, to the greatest extent possible, the great evils of the human condition, such as tyranny, genocide, mass starvation, and deadly epidemics.[3] (I call the human condition characterized by the absence of the great evils as one of basic decency.) This minimal universalism overlaps with contemporary movements for universal human rights and provision of basic needs.

So understood, liberal pluralist government is robust within its appropriate sphere. In securing the cultural conditions of its survival and perpetuation, for example, it may legitimately engage in civic education, carefully restricted to the public essentials—the virtues and competences that citizens will need to fulfill diverse roles in a liberal pluralist economy, society, and polity. Nor do limits on the scope of democratic authority imply limits on the scope of democratic participation. Liberal pluralists may favor representative institutions or more direct self-government, strong executives or parliamentary supremacy. Democracy can be "strong" without being "total." Indeed, if the reasons in favor of liberal pluralism are compelling, then in practice self-government can be strong only if it does not strive to regulate every aspect of our lives.

One thing above all is clear: because the likely result of liberal pluralist institutions and practices will be a highly diverse society, the virtue of tolerance will be a core attribute of liberal pluralist citizenship. This type of tolerance does not mean wishy-washiness or the propensity to doubt one's own position, the sort of thing Robert Frost had in mind when he defined a liberal as someone who cannot take his own side in an argument. It does not imply, or require, an easy relativism about the human good; indeed, it is compatible with engaged moral criticism of those with whom one differs. Toleration rightly understood means the principled refusal to use coercive state power to impose one's views on others, and therefore a commitment to moral competition through recruitment and persuasion alone.

Liberal pluralism is (in the terms John Rawls made familiar) a "comprehensive" rather than "political" theory. It makes sense, I believe, to connect what one believes to be the best account of public life with comparably persuasive accounts of morality, human psychology, and the natural world. As a practical matter, of course, it makes sense to seek overlapping consensus. Politics as we know it would come to a halt if cooperation required agreement, not only on conclusions, but on premises as well. But philosophical argument, even concerning politics, need not mirror the structure of public life. A political philosopher may assert that X is true, and foundational for a particular understanding of a good, decent, or just society, without demanding that all citizens affirm the truth of X. Indeed, the founders of a political regime may publicly proclaim what they take to be moral, metaphysical, or religious truths as the basis of that regime without insisting that all citizens assent to those truths. In the United States, naturalizing citizens affirm their loyalty to the Constitution, not the Declaration of Independence, and all citizens pledge allegiance to the republic for which the flag stands, not Locke or Hutcheson. So I disagree with Martha Nussbaum when she suggests that making public claims about foundational truths somehow signals disrespect for those who dissent.[4] Disrespect requires something more—namely, the use of coercive state power to silence and repress dissenters. Respect requires, not parsimony in declaring truth, but rather restraint in the exercise of power. By limiting the scope of legitimate public power, liberal pluralism does all that is necessary to secure the theoretical and institutional bases of respect.

LIBERAL PLURALISM: INTERNAL RELATIONSHIPS

While it is not the purpose of this essay to dig deep into the foundations of liberal pluralism, some remarks about relations among its principal elements may at least ward off misunderstandings.

In the first place, I do not argue that value pluralism entails political pluralism, or vice versa. In that sense, they are independent claims about the basic structure of key domains. I do contend, however, that they fit together, in the sense that the conclusions toward which they point turn out to be logically and practically compatible. It is also the case that many arguments against political pluralism rest on the denial of value pluralism—that is, on the assertion of some dominant end or principle that it is task of political authorities to promote, come what may.

The modes of argument that lead me toward these two forms of pluralism are similar: an unblinkered inspection of the way each of these domains happens to be structured points toward basic plurality. It might have been otherwise (logically or metaphysically), but it isn't. When we attend to the way moral arguments go in specific cases, we reach a point where the assertion that value A dominates all others in all situations comes to appear forced and implausible—the sort of claim one would make only if one is determined to maintain one's position at all costs.[5] Likewise, at some point the contention that claims flowing from political ends or necessities trump all others goes against the grain of normal human responses. I shall argue, for example, the pressure from political authorities on children to betray their parents, or on sisters to ignore family ties and treat brothers simply as enemies of the state, runs against the grain of our intuitive humanity. Again, it might have been otherwise, but it isn't. I'm not trying to do political or moral philosophy valid for "all rational beings" (whatever that might mean) but rather for the kind of beings we are, in the circumstances in which we are placed.

At first glance, the relation between expressive liberty and value pluralism may seem more difficult. Haven't I elevated expressive liberty above other values, and isn't that inconsistent with the basic structure of value pluralism? Not so. Value pluralists need not (and in my view should not) assert that all goods and principles are on a par, arranged purely horizontally. There may be good reasons for giving some greater weight than others or for ascribing presumptive force to a subset of values.[6] Value pluralists need only deny that one or more values override all others, without regard to circumstances or the magnitudes of the tradeoffs and sacrifices that the once-and-for-all elevation of some values over others may entail.

Why a presumption in favor of expressive liberty? Answer: having a vision of the way you want your life to go is not a theoretical matter. Having that vision, as we all do, means wanting to live in one way rather than others. So expressive liberty is a value the implementation of which enables individuals to realize a wide range of other values. To restrict individuals' expressive liberty is to deprive them of what they cannot help regarding as a very great good. There may be reasons to do so, but these reasons must be weighty; whence the presumption.

WHY POLITICAL PLURALISM?

I turn now to the main focus of this essay—political pluralism, understood as a distinctive empirical account of human society that also supports a specific normative account of political authority.

A liberal democracy is (among other things) an invitation to struggle over the control of civil associations. State/society debates have recurred over the past century of U.S. history, frequently generating landmark Supreme Court cases. While the specific issues vary, the general form is the same. On one side are general public principles that the state seeks to enforce; on the other are specific beliefs and practices that the association seeks to protect. *Boy Scouts of America v. Dale*[7] is the latest chapter in what will no doubt be a continuing saga.

Within the U.S. constitutional context, these issues are often debated in terms such as free exercise of religion, freedom of association, or the individual liberty broadly protected under the Fourteenth Amendment. Rich and illuminating as it is, this constitutional discourse does not go deep enough. It is necessary to reconsider the understanding of politics that pervades much contemporary discussion, especially among political theorists, an understanding that tacitly views public institutions as plenipotentiary and civil society as a political construction possessing only those liberties that the polity chooses to grant and modify or revoke at will. This understanding of politics makes it all but impossible to give serious weight to the "liberal" dimension of liberal democracy.

The most useful point of departure for the reconsideration of politics I am urging is found in the writings of the British political pluralists and pluralist thinkers working in the Calvinist tradition.[8] This pluralist movement began to take shape in the 19th century as a reaction to the growing tendency to see state institutions as plenipotentiary. This tendency took various practical forms in different countries: French anticlerical republicanism, British parliamentary supremacy, the drive for national unification in Germany and Italy against subordinate political and social powers. Following Stephen Macedo (though disagreeing with him in other respects), I shall call this idea of the plenipotentiary state "civic totalism."[9]

Historically, one can discern at least three distinct secular-theoretical arguments for civic totalism. (Theological arguments, which raise a different set of issues, are beyond the scope of these comments.) The first is the idea, traced back to Aristotle, that politics enjoys general authority over subordinate activities and institutions because it aims at the highest and most comprehensive good for human beings. The *Politics* virtually begins with the proposition that "all partnerships aim at some good, and . . . the partnership that is most authoritative of all and embraces all the others does so particularly, and aims at the most authoritative good of all. That is what is called . . . the political partnership."[10] (For present purposes, whether this statement is an adequate representation of Aristotle's full view is a matter we may set aside.)

Hobbes offered a second kind of justification for civic totalism: any less robust form of politics would in practice countenance divided sovereignty—the dreaded imperium in imperio, an open invitation to civic conflict and war. Sovereignty cannot be divided, even between civil and spiritual authorities.[11] In Hobbes's view, undivided sovereign authority has unlimited power to decide whether, and under what conditions, individuals and associations would enjoy liberty of action. No entity, individual or collective, can assert rights against the public authority. Indeed, civil law may rightfully prohibit even the teaching of truth, if it is contrary to the requirements of civil peace.[12] A third argument for civic totalism was inspired by Rousseau: civic health and morality cannot be achieved without citizens' wholehearted devotion to the common good. Loyalties divided between the republic and other ties, whether to civil associations or to revealed religious truth, are bound to dilute civic spirit. And the liberal appeal to private life as against public life will only legitimate selfishness at the expense of the spirit of contribution and sacrifice without which the polity cannot endure. Representing this tradition, Emile Combes, a turn-of-the-century premier in the French Third Republic, declared that "there are, there can be no rights except the right of the State, and there [is], and there can be no other authority than the authority of the Republic."[13]

I do not wish to suggest that these three traditions converge on precisely the same account of civic totalism. A chasm divides Hobbes and Rousseau from Aristotle. To oversimplify drastically: Greek religion was civil, offering support for the institutions of the polis. The post-classical rise of revealed religion—especially Christianity—ruptured the unity of the political order. Much renaissance and early modern theory sought to overcome this diremption and restore the unity of public authority. Hobbes and Rousseau wrote in this "theological-political" tradition and tried in different ways to subordinate religious claims to the sovereignty of politics.

For this reason, among others, Hobbes and Rousseau were less willing than was Aristotle to acknowledge the independent and legitimate existence of intermediate associations. They were drawn instead to a doctrine, originating in Roman law and transmitted to modernity through Bodin among others, according to which intermediate associations existed solely as revocable "concessions" of power from the sovereign political authority. Individuals possessed no inherent right of association, and associations enjoyed no rights other than those politically defined and granted. In short, intermediate associations were political constructions, to be tolerated only to the extent that they served the interests of the state. This Roman-law stance may be contrasted to the view of early Calvinists that a civil association required no special fiat from the state for its existence. As Frederick Carney puts it, "Its own purposes, both natural and volitional, constitute its raison d'etre, not its convenience to the state."[14]

These three traditions may seem far removed from the mainstream of contemporary views. Doesn't the liberal strand of "liberal democracy" qualify and limit the legitimate power of the state? Isn't this the entering wedge for a set of fundamental freedoms that can stand against the claims of state power?

The standard history of liberalism lends support to this view. The rise of revealed religion created a diremption of authority and challenged the comprehensive primacy of politics. The early modern wars of religion sparked new understandings of the relation between religion and politics, between individual conscience and public order, between unity and diversity. As politics came to be understood as limited rather than total, the possibility emerged that the principles constituting individual lives and civil associations might not be congruent with the principles constituting public institutions. The point of liberal constitutionalism, and of liberal statesmanship, was not to abolish these differences but rather, so far as possible, to help them serve the cause of ordered liberty.

THE TOTALIST TEMPTATION

Despite this history, many contemporary theorists, including some who think of themselves as working within the liberal tradition, embrace propositions that draw them away from the idea of limited government and toward civic totalism, perhaps against their intention. Some come close to arguing that if state power is exercised properly—that is, democratically—it need not be limited by any considerations other than those required by democratic processes.

Jürgen Habermas offers the clearest example of this tendency. He insists that once obsolete metaphysical doctrines are set aside, "There is no longer any fixed point outside the democratic procedure itself." But this is no cause for worry or regret: whatever is normatively defensible in liberal rights is contained in the discourse-rights of "sovereign [democratic] citizens."[15] The residual rights not so contained constitute, not bulwarks against oppression, but rather the illegitimate insulation of "private" practices from public scrutiny.

An eminent American democratic theorist, Robert Dahl, is tempted by Habermas's stance. He characterizes as "reasonable" and "attractive" the view that members of political communities have no fundamental interests, rights, or claims other than those integral to the democratic process or needed for its preservation. The only limits to the legitimate scope of democratic power are the requisites of democracy itself. Put simply: a demos that observes the norms of democratic decision-making may do what it wants.[16]

Unlike Habermas, Dahl is not entirely comfortable with restricting the domain of rights to the conditions of democracy. He concedes that this proposal raises a "disturbing" question: What about interests, rights, and claims that cannot be adequately understood as aspects of the democratic process but which nonetheless seem important and defensible? What about fair trials, or freedom of religion and conscience? Without definitively answering this question, Dahl examines the various ways in which the defense of rights may be institutionalized, concluding that those who would temper democratic majorities with "guardian" structures such as courts bear a heavy burden of proof that they rarely if ever discharge successfully. The most reliable cure for the ills of democracy is more democracy; the resort to non-majoritarian protections risks undermining the people's capacity to govern itself.[17]

John Rawls presents the most complex case of the phenomenon I call the totalist temptation. He asserts that "the values of the special domain of the political . . . normally outweigh whatever values may conflict with them."[18] Why is this the case? Rawls offers two reasons. First, political values are very important; they determine social life and make fair cooperation possible. Second, conflict between political and nonpolitical values can usually be avoided, so long as political values are appropriately understood.[19]

Rawls famously maintains that justice is the preeminent political value, the "first virtue of social institutions" and that "laws and institutions no matter how efficient and well-arranged must be reformed or abolished if they are unjust."[20] Nonetheless, he asserts, consistent with the liberal tradition, that the principles of justice do not directly regulate institutions and associations—such as churches and families—within society.[21] (Principles of justice do affect these institutions indirectly, via the influence of just background institutions.)

The difficulty is to explain why, within the structure of Rawls's theory, the principles regulating the basic structure of society should not be applied directly to institutions such as churches and the family. Taken literally, many of these background principles would seem to warrant such interventions. For example, imbalances in parenting responsibilities can affect women's "fair equality of opportunity." Does this mean, as Rawls seems to suggest, that "special provisions of family law" should prevent or rectify this imbalance?[22] If the family is part of the basic structure of society, as Rawls now claims, why does he judge it "hardly sensible" that parents be required to treat their children in accordance with the principles directly governing the basic structure?[23]

The ambiguous status of the family reflects a deeper structural problem in Rawls's account. At one point he offers a formulation that seems promising: we distinguish between the point of view of citizens and of members of associations. As citizens, we endorse the constraints of principles of justice; as association members, we want to limit those constraints so that the inner life of associations can flourish. This generates a "division of labor" that treats the basic structure and civil association as being, so to speak, on a par with one another.[24]

But on closer inspection, it turns out that there's a hierarchical relation after all, with the principles of justice serving as trumps. Otherwise put, the basic structure constitutes the end, and the various associations are in part means to that end. So, for example, "The treatment of children must be such as to support the family's role in upholding a constitutional regime."[25] But what if (say) religious free exercise includes teachings and practices that don't do this? (Imagine a religious group that has no intention of altering the public structure of equal political rights for women but teaches its own members that women shouldn't participate in public life.)

Rawls is certain (quite sensibly in my view) that "we wouldn't want political principles of justice to apply directly to the internal life of the family."[26] The reasoning appears to be that various associations have inner lives that differ qualitatively from that of the political realm, so that political principles would be "out of place."

This then raises a question: Why aren't political and nonpolitical associations understood as related horizontally rather than vertically? Why can't nonpolitical associations be seen as limiting the scope of politics at the same time that the basic structure of politics constrains associations?

Rawls's apparent answer runs as follows: the domain of the nonpolitical has no independent existence or definition but is simply the result (or residuum) of how the principles of justice are applied directly and indirectly. In particular, the principle of equal citizenship applies everywhere.

In one sense, this is clearly true. If an association uses coercion to prevent some of its members from exercising their equal political rights, the state must step in to enforce them. But the more usual case is that the association organizes itself according to norms (of membership or activity) that are inconsistent with principles of equal citizenship. What is the state's legitimate power in the face of these dissenting practices? Is it so obvious that the legitimate activities of nonpolitical associations should be defined relative, not to the inner life of those associations, but rather to the principles of the public sphere? Can't we say something important about the distinctive natures of individual conscience, friendship, families, communities of faith or inquiry, and shouldn't those primary features of our social life have an effect on the scope of political principles, not just vice versa? Even if justice is the "first virtue" of public institutions and enjoys lexical priority over other goods of the public realm (a debatable proposition), does it follow that the public realm enjoys comprehensive lexical priority over the other forms of human activity and association?[27]

THE PLURALIST ALTERNATIVE

It is in the context of questions such as these that political pluralism emerges as an alternative to all forms of civic totalism. Political pluralism, to begin, rejects efforts to understand individuals, families, and associations simply as parts within and of a political whole. Relatedly, pluralism rejects the instrumental/teleological argument that individuals, families, and associations are adequately understood as "for the sake of" some political purpose. For example, religion is not (only) civil and in some circumstances may be in tension with civil requirements. This is *not* to say that political communities must be understood as without common purposes. The political order is not simply a framework within which individuals, families, and associations may pursue their own purposes. As we have seen, there are core evils that only decent politics can minimize, and core goods that only sensible politics can promote. But civic purposes are not comprehensive and do not necessary trump the purposes of individuals and groups.

Political pluralism understands human life as consisting in multiplicity of spheres, some overlapping, with distinct natures and/ or inner norms. Each sphere enjoys a limited but real autonomy. It rejects any account of political community that creates a unidimensional hierarchical ordering among these spheres of life. Rather, different forms of association and activity are complexly interrelated. There may be local or partial hierarchies among subsets of spheres in specific context, but there are no comprehensive lexical orderings among categories of human life.

For these reasons, among others, political pluralism does not seek to overcome, but rather endorses, the post-pagan diremption of human loyalty and political authority created by the rise of revealed religion. That this creates problems of practical governance cannot be denied. But pluralists refuse to resolve these problems by allowing public authorities to determine the substance and scope of allowable belief (Hobbes) or by reducing faith to civil religion and elevating devotion to the common civic good as the highest human value (Rousseau). Fundamental tensions rooted in the deep structure of human existence cannot be abolished in a stroke but must rather be acknowledged, negotiated, and adjudicated with due regard to the contours of specific cases and controversies.

Pluralist politics is a politics of recognition rather than of construction. It respects the diverse spheres of human activity; it does not understand itself as creating or constituting those activities ex nihilo. Families are shaped by public law, but that does not mean that they are "socially constructed." There are complex relations of mutual impact between public law and faith communities, but it is preposterous to claim that the public sphere creates these communities. Do environmental laws create air and water?

A pluralist politics is however responsible for coordinating other spheres of activity, and especially for adjudicating the inevitable overlaps and disputes among them. This form of politics evidently requires the mutual limitation of some freedoms, individual and associational. It monopolizes the legitimate use of force, except in cases of self-defense when the polity cannot or does not protect us. It understands that group tyranny is possible and therefore protects individual against some associational abuses. But pluralist politics presumes that the enforcement of basic rights of citizenship and of exit rights, suitably understood, will usually suffice. Associational integrity requires a broad though not unlimited right of groups to define their own membership, to exclude as well as include, and a pluralist polity will respect that right.[28]

VARIETIES OF ARGUMENTS FOR POLITICAL PLURALISM

The core of my thesis is that different forms of human activity and association generate different kinds of claims, both to liberty and authority, and that no single ensemble of claims dominates the rest for all purposes or in all circumstances. As a distinctive form of activity and association, politics both makes claims and is limited in various ways by claims deriving from other sources. The question is how to justify this thesis.

Joseph Raz offers an argument for limited political authority based on two premises: the idea of responsibility as the core of human agency; and an understanding of political authority as derived from the consent of individual agents. Raz contends that while individuals can legitimately transfer responsibility for some aspects of their lives to others, they cannot abandon responsibility altogether without undermining agency. Thus, he concludes, "Only limited government can be legitimate."[29]

Limited how, exactly? Raz argues that a doctrine specifying the content of limited government would have two parts. The first is instrumental: delegating responsibility to government lacks a rationale in areas where individuals can act for themselves as efficiently and effectively as others can act for them. The second principle of limitation is avowedly non-instrumental: it consists of all those matters regarding which "it is more important to act independently than to succeed in doing the best." Raz remarks, laconically, that he "feel[s] the need for a substantive account of this category," an account he does not provide.[30] Any effort to do so would quickly encounter, inter alia, well-worn debates about the justification of paternalism—that is, the category of interventions in which considerations of an agent's well-being trump those of responsibility or autonomy.

Much liberal thought grounds limits to government on some conception of individual rights. While this line of argument has considerable merit, it is also incomplete. It is not easy to move from the concept of rights to a specific conception. Most Americans can recite the Declaration's famous litany of life, liberty, and the pursuit of happiness; few realize that the words "among which are" precede this triad, raising but not answering the question concerning the content of these unnamed additional rights. Similarly, the Ninth Amendment cautions that "the enumeration in the Constitution of certain rights shall not be construed to deny or disparage others retained by the people." But what exactly are these retained rights?

The language of individual rights goes astray, moreover, not when it claims to be *a* source of limits on governmental authority, but when it presents itself as the *sole* source. I take seriously the idea of individual inviolability, rightly understand, and I shall defend in detail one aspect of inviolability—namely, freedom of conscience. But I want to suggest that we may do better to proceed more empirically, by considering the diverse forms of human sociability and association.

For example, family obligations can limit the scope of political authority. Sophocles' *Antigone* revolves around primordial imperatives of kinship that stand opposed to the imperatives of patriotic loyalty. The fact that one of Antigone's brothers was slain in battle against his own city does not per se justify Creon's effort to prevent her from burying him. To be sure, Antigone is as deaf to Creon's legitimate concerns for his city as he was to her family ties. One might (just) make out a case for Creon's stance. Still, the playwright presents the disaster that befalls Creon as the result of his extension of political authority beyond its rightful limits. Whether we ultimately agree with Sophocles or not, the basic point is that political leaders cannot rightly assign a weight of zero to nonpolitical values.

American constitutional law endorses the proposition that family ties limit political authority because the status of parenthood generates a sphere of authority. For example, in the famous case of *Pierce v. Society of Sisters*, the Supreme Court rejected the right of a public authority (in this case, the state of Oregon) to require all parents within its jurisdiction to send their children to public schools. In justifying its stance, the Court declared that "the fundamental theory of liberty upon which all governments in this Union repose excludes any general power of the State to standardize its children by forcing them to accept instruction for public school teachers only. The child is not the mere creature of the State; those who nurture him and direct his destiny have the right, coupled with the high duty, to recognize and prepare him for additional obligations."[31] This does not mean, of course, that family activities are immunized from political regulation. The *Pierce* court explicitly recognized a substantial degree of legitimate governmental regulation of the family, including its educational decisions. For example, the deep theory of liberty on which the court relied allows the state to require "that all children of proper age attend some school."[32] It is the task of what might be called pluralist casuistry to distinguish legitimate from illegitimate assertions of political authority over families.

Consider another example. U.S. law and jurisprudence limit the sway of public authority over religious associations. I have always made reference to the commonplace that these associations may establish their own criteria for their religious offices, general public norms of nondiscrimination to the contrary notwithstanding. But these limits go even deeper. As Laurence Tribe observes, courts and other agencies of the U.S. government "may not inquire into pervasively religious issues."[33] The rationale for this restriction goes beyond prudential fears of entanglement and political divisiveness. It reflects, as well, the belief that doctrinal and scriptural interpretation are beyond the competence and rightful authority of political power.

Democratic polities have not always acknowledged these limits. Well into the 20th century, the British House of Lords operated on the premise that property was contributed to religious bodies pursuant to an "implied trust" framed by the doctrines and practices of those bodies prevailing at the time of the donation. When doctrinal disputes and schisms occurred, the Lords did not hesitate to adjudicate property claims on the basis of their own interpretation of the litigants' fidelity to those doctrines and practices, an intrusion against which British pluralists such as Figgis protested bitterly but to no avail.

As early as 1872, however, U.S. courts abandoned the implied trust doctrine in favor of the rule that whenever the ordinary principles of contract and property law did not resolve disputes within religious association, courts should defer either to the majority in congregational churches or to the highest authority in hierarchical churches. The Court's argument for this position was rooted in principle as well as prudence:

> The law knows no heresy, and is committed to the support of no dogma, the establishment of no sect. The right to organize voluntary religious associations to assist in the expression and dissemination of any religious doctrine, and to create tribunals for the decision of controverted questions of faith within the association, and for the ecclesiastical government of the individual members, congregations, and officers within the general association, is unquestioned. All who unite themselves to such a body do so with an implied consent to this government, and are bound to submit to it. But it would be a vain consent and would lead to the total subversion of such religious bodies, if any one aggrieved by one of their decisions could appeal to the secular courts and have them reversed. It is of the essence of these religious unions, and of their right to establish tribunals for the decisions of questions among themselves, that those decisions should be binding in all cases of ecclesiastical cognizance, subject only to the appeals as the organism itself provides for.[34]

There is, in short, a sphere of religious authority distinct from, and limiting, the scope of rightful political authority.[35]

This is not exactly a new idea. In the familiar New Testament story of the silver coin, Jesus responds to a politically charged inquiry about paying taxes to Rome with the maxim, "Pay Caesar what is due to Caesar, and pay God what is due to God."[36] The task of tracing the line between God's realm and Caesar's has challenged political thought, secular and theological, for two millennia. But the difficulty of this task does not obviate its necessity, once we acknowledge the independent force of religious claims.

This line of argument is bound to leave many readers unsatisfied. No, religious communities may not engage in human sacrifice, and if they try, political authorities have the right and duty to stop them. Yes, religious communities may assign positions of religious authority on grounds that would not be permitted in the public domain, and it would be wrong for political authorities to prevent them. But isn't there a broad middle ground of issues between these extremes, which liberal pluralist theory doesn't help us resolve?

This is a fair objection, as far as it goes, but it doesn't go as far as those who urge it think it does. It reflects, I would suggest, more of a disagreement about the possibilities of theory than a critique of liberal pluralism in particular. In my view, theory mostly provides a template of considerations that the sound exercise of practical reason must take into account. It will yield very few bright lines that neatly resolve entire categories of controversies. Rather, it structures the productive conduct of the form of practical reason known as casuistry. It yields results that look much more like common law than the clear rules of law that many students of jurisprudence crave. Broader patterns are inductive and emergent, not laid down in advance.

This common-law approach does not mean that liberal pluralism cannot reach clear conclusions in specific cases. On the contrary: I have argued that, for example, it vindicates famous decisions of the U.S. Supreme Court such as *Pierce v. Society of Sisters* and *Wisconsin v. Yoder*[37] and that it warrants far more accommodation to the plaintiff parents than the courts ultimately accorded them in *Mozert v. Hawkins County Board of Education.*[38] But liberal pluralists must always remain open to the possibility that circumstances will override presumptions. It is impossible to expunge the need for the exercise of judgment that cannot be reduced to rules.

FREEDOM OF CONSCIENCE

I now turn, in detail, to the idea of individual conscience as an important source of pluralist limits on state authority. To frame this inquiry, I begin by recalling an important but largely forgotten episode in U.S. constitutional history: a rapid and almost unprecedented turnabout by the Supreme Court on a matter of fundamental importance. I begin my tale in the late 1930s.

Acting under the authority of the state government, the school board of Minersville, Pennsylvania, had required both students and teachers to participate in a daily pledge of allegiance to the flag. In the 1940 case of *Minersville v. Gobitis,*[39] the Supreme Court decided against a handful of Jehovah's Witnesses who sought to have their children exempted on the grounds that this exercise amounted to a form of idolatry strictly forbidden by their faith. With but a single dissenting vote, the Court ruled that it was permissible for a school board to make participation in saluting the American flag a condition for attending public school, regardless of the conscientious objections of parents and students. Relying on this holding and quoting liberally from the majority's decision, the West Virginia State Board of Education issued a regulation making the flag salute mandatory statewide. When a challenge to this action arose barely three years after *Gobitis,* the Court reversed itself by a vote of 6 to 3.[40] To be sure, during the brief interval separating these cases, the lone dissenter in *Gobitis* had been elevated to Chief Justice and two new voices, both favoring reversal, had joined the Court, while two supporters of the original decision had departed. But of the seven justices who heard both cases, three saw fit to reverse themselves and to set forth their reasons for the change.

This kind of abrupt, explicit reversal is very rare in the annals of the Court, and it calls for some explanation. A clue is to be found, I believe, in the deservedly well-known peroration of Justice Jackson's majority decision overturning compulsory flag salutes: "If there is any fixed star in our constitutional constellation, it is that no official, high or petty, can prescribe what shall be orthodox in politics, nationalism, religion, or other matters of opinion or force citizens to confess by word or act their faith therein. If there are any circumstances which permit an exception, they do not now occur to us. We think the action of the local authorities in compelling the flag salute and pledge transcends constitutional limitation on their power and invades the sphere of intellect and spirit which it is the purpose of the First Amendment to our Constitution to reserve from all official control."[41]

Justice Frankfurter, the author of the majority opinion in *Gobitis,* penned a lengthy dissent, a personal apologia whose tone of injured dignity was set by its opening sentence: "One who belongs to the most vilified and persecuted minority in history is not likely to be insensible to the freedoms guaranteed by our

Constitution."[42] But he declared that what was at stake was not a constitutional question but rather a policy judgment. In this arena, courts should override legislatures only if reasonable legislators could not have chosen to employ the contested means in furtherance of legitimate ends. As a general proposition, there is a presumption in favor of legislatures, and legislation must be considered valid if there exists some rational basis for connecting it to a valid public purpose.[43]

Exceptions to this presumption arise when the state employs constitutionally prohibited means. But the mandatory flag salute was not of this character. The state action at issue, Frankfurter asserted, was not intended to promote or discourage religion, which was clearly forbidden. Rather, it was "a general non-discriminatory civil regulation [that] in fact [but not as a matter of intended effect] touches conscientious scruples or religious beliefs of an individual or a group."[44] In such cases, it is the legislature's role to make accommodations, not the Court's. Frankfurter argued that

> Jefferson and those who followed him wrote guarantees of religious freedom into our constitutions. Religious minorities as well as religious majorities were to be equal in the eyes of the political state. But Jefferson and the others also knew that minorities may disrupt society. It never would have occurred to them to write into the Constitution the subordination of the general civil authority of the state to sectarian scruples. . . . The constitutional protection of religious freedom terminated disabilities, it did not create new privileges. It gave religious equality, not civil immunity. Its essence is freedom from conformity to religious dogma, not freedom from conformity to law because of religious dogma. . . . The essence of the religious freedom guaranteed by our Constitution is this: no religion shall either receive the state's support or incur its hostility. Religion is outside the sphere of political government. This does not mean that all matters on which religious organizations or beliefs may pronounce are outside the sphere of government.[45]

Many other laws (e.g., compulsory medical measures) have employed compulsion against religious scruples, but courts have not struck them down: "Law is concerned with external behavior and not with the inner life of man. It rests in large measure upon compulsion. . . . The consent on which free government rests in the consent that comes from sharing in the process of making and unmaking laws. The state is not shut out from a domain because the individual conscience may deny the state's claim."[46]

Indeed, Frankfurter asserted, it was wrong to describe the mandatory flag salute as compelled belief: "Compelling belief implies denial of opportunity to combat it and to assert dissident views. Such compulsion is one thing. Quite another matter is submission to conformity of action while denying its wisdom or virtue with ample opportunity for seeking its change or abrogation."[47] Frankfurter concluded his dissent with a profession of political faith. Liberal democracy is more a matter of active, self-governing citizens than of protective or tutelary courts: "Of course patriotism cannot be enforced by the flag salute. But neither can the liberal spirit be enforced by judicial invalidation of illiberal legislation. . . . Only a persistent positive translation of the faith of a free society into the convictions and habits and actions of a community is the ultimate reliance against unabated temptations to fetter the human spirit."[48]

JURISPRUDENCE, MORAL INTUITION, AND POLITICAL THEORY

I am not a legal historian. I offer this case, not for its own sake, but with moral intent. I want to use these materials as a basis for testing our judgments about two questions. First: Looking at the judicial bottom-line—the "holding"—are we more inclined to favor the outcome in *Gobitis* or in *Barnette*? Second: What kinds of broader principles underlie our judgment concerning these specific cases?

It is easy to sympathize with Frankfurter's dismay at the deployment of judicial review to immunize concentrated economic power against public scrutiny; with his belief that democratic majorities should enjoy wide latitude to pursue the common good as they see it; with his belief that the requirements of social order and unity may sometimes override the claims, however worthy, of individuals, parents, civil associations, and religious faith; and with his conviction that the systematic substitution of judicial review for democratic self-correction can end by weakening citizenship itself. Nonetheless, I believe (and I am far from alone) that Frankfurter's reasoning in *Gobitis* was unsound, and his holding unacceptable. There are certain goods and liberties that enjoy a preferred position and are supposed to be lifted above everyday policy debate.

If liberty of conscience is a fundamental good, as Frankfurter acknowledges, then it follows that state action interfering with it bears a substantial burden of proof. A distant harm, loosely linked to the contested policy, is not enough to meet that burden. The harm must be a real threat; it must be causally linked to the policy in question; and the proposed remedy must do the least possible damage to the fundamental liberty, consistent with the abatement of the threat. The state's mandatory pledge of allegiance failed all three of these tests. *Gobitis* was wrongly decided; the ensuing uproar was a public indication that the Court had gone astray; and the quick reversal in *Barnette*, with fully half the justices in the new six-member majority switching sides, was a clear indication of the moral force of the objections.

We now reach my second question: Is our judgment on these cases a particularized moral intuition, or does it reflect some broader principles? The latter, I think. What Justice Jackson termed the "sphere of intellect and spirit" is at or near the heart of what makes us human. The protection of that sphere against unwarranted intrusion represents the most fundamental of all human liberties. There is a strong presumption against state policies that prevent individuals from the free exercise of intellect and spirit. There is an even stronger presumption against compelling individuals to make affirmations contrary to their convictions. This does not mean that compulsory speech is always wrong; courts and legislatures may rightly compel unwilling witnesses to give testimony and may rightly punish any failure to do so that does not invoke a well-established principle of immunity, such as the bar against coerced self-incrimination. Even here, the point of the compulsion is to induce individuals to tell the truth as they see it, not to betray their innermost convictions in the name of a state-administered orthodoxy.

It is easy for polities—even stable constitutional democracies—to violate these principles. In that obvious empirical sense, fundamental liberties are political constructions. But that democratic majorities can deprive minorities of liberty, often with impunity, does not make it right. Like all politics, democratic politics is legitimate to the extent that it recognizes and observes the principled limits to the exercise of democratic power. The liberties that individuals and the associations they constitute should enjoy in all but the most desperate circumstances go well beyond the political rights that democratic politics requires. We cannot rightly assess the importance of politics without acknowledging the limits of politics. The claims that political institutions can make in the name of the common good coexist with claims of at least equal importance that individuals and civil associations make, based on particular visions of the good for themselves or for humankind. This political pluralism may be messy and conflictual; it may lead to confrontations not conducive to maximizing public unity and order. But if political pluralism, thus understood, reflects the complex truth of the human condition, then the practice of politics must do its best to honor the principles that limit the scope of politics. There is an ambiguity that I must now address. My announced topic in this section is freedom of conscience. But what is "conscience," anyway? For James Madison and other 18th century thinkers, the term clearly pointed toward religious conviction. Although Justice Jackson's sphere of intellect and spirit includes religion, it encompasses much else besides. So is conscience to be understood narrowly or expansively?

We may approach this question from two standpoints, the constitutional and the philosophical. Within constitutional law, both the narrow and expansive views have found proponents among able interpreters of the First Amendment. On the narrow side, Laurence Tribe argues that "the Framers . . . clearly envisioned religion as something special; they enacted that vision into law by guaranteeing the free exercise of religion but not, say, of philosophy or science."[49] Christopher Eisgruber and Lawrence Sager object that "to single out one of the ways that persons come to understand what is important in life, and grant those who choose that way a license to disregard legal norms that the rest of us are obliged to obey, is to defeat rather than fulfill our commitment to toleration."[50] In effect, they argue that we must read the religion clauses of the First Amendment in light of the Equal Protection Clause of the Fourteenth.

We see this debate playing out in a fascinating way in the evolution of the jurisprudence of conscience-based exemptions from the military draft. Section 6(j) of the World War II–era Universal Military Training and Service Act made exemptions available to those who were conscientiously opposed to military service by reason of "religious training and belief." The required religious conviction was defined as "an individual's belief in a relation to a Supreme Being involving duties superior to those arising from any human relation, but [not including] essentially political, sociological, or philosophical views or a merely personal moral code."

In the case of *United States v. Seeger* (1965), however, the Court broadened the definition of religion by interpreting the statue to include a "sincere and meaningful belief which occupies in the life of its possessor a place parallel to that filled by the God of those admittedly qualifying for the exemption."[51] Five years later, in *Welsh v. United States,* a Court plurality further broadened the reach of the statute to include explicitly secular beliefs that "play the role of a religion and function as a religion in life." Thus, draft exemptions could be extended to "those whose consciences, spurred by deeply held moral, ethical, or religious beliefs, would give them no rest or peace if they allowed themselves to become a part of an instrument of war."[52]

For our purposes, the real action takes place in the penumbra of the plurality's opinion. Justice Harlan, who provided the fifth vote for the expansive reading of conscientious exemption, argued in a concurring opinion that while the plurality's interpretation of the statutory language was indefensible, the Court could and should save the statute by engaging in an explicit act of reconstruction. The reason: it would be a violation of both the Establishment and Equal Protection clauses for Congress to differentiate between religious and non-religious conscientious objectors.[53] This is the judicial precursor of the Eisgruber/Sager position.

For their part, the three dissenters argued that while Harlan was right as a matter of statutory construction, he was wrong as a matter of constitutional interpretation. They wrote that "neither support nor hostility, but neutrality, is the goal of the religion clauses of the First Amendment. 'Neutrality,' however, is not self-defining. If it is 'favoritism' and not neutrality to exempt religious believers from the draft, is it 'neutrality' and not 'inhibition' of religion to compel religious believers to fight when they have special reasons for not doing so, reasons to which the Constitution gives particular recognition? It cannot be denied [the dissenters concluded] that the First Amendment itself contains a religious classification."[54] This is Lawrence Tribe's point exactly.

To shed light on this dispute, it is useful to move outside the realm of constitutional adjudication and raise more general considerations. There are, I suggest, two features of religion that figure centrally in the debate about religiously based exemptions from otherwise valid laws. First, believers understand the requirements of religious beliefs and actions as central rather than peripheral to their identity; and second, they experience these requirements as authoritative commands. So understood, religion is more than a mode of human flourishing. Regardless of whether an individual experiences religious requirements as promoting or rather thwarting self-development, their power is compelling. (In this connection, recall the number of Hebrew prophets—starting with Moses—who experience the divine call to prophetic mission as destructive of their prior lives and identities).

My suggestion is that at least in modern times, some individuals and groups who are not religious come to embrace ensembles of belief and action that share these two features of religious experience—namely, identity-formation and compulsory power. It does not seem an abuse of speech to apply the term conscience to this experience, whether religious or non-religious. My concept of expressive liberty functions, in part, to support the claim that conscience in this extended sense enjoys a rebuttable presumption to prevail in the face of public law. In this respect, though not others, I find myself in agreement with Rogers Smith when he writes that "the only approach that is genuinely compatible with equal treatment, equal protection, and equal respect for all citizens is treating claims of religious and secular moral consciences the same. Fully recognizing the historical, philosophical, and moral force of claims for deference to sincere conscientious beliefs and practices whenever possible, I would place all such claims in a 'preferred position' as defined by modern constitutional doctrines: governmental infringements upon such conscientious claims would be sustainable in court only if it were shown that they were necessary for compelling government interests."[55]

What are the kinds of collective interests that suffice to rebut the presumption in favor of individual conscience? I can think of at least two. First, the state cannot avoid attending to the content of conscience. Deep convictions may express identity with compulsory power and nonetheless be deeply mistaken in ways that the state may rightly resist through the force of law. And second, even if the content of an individual's conscientious claim is not unacceptable in itself, its social or civic consequences may expose it to justified regulation or even probibition.

It may well be possible to add other categories of considerations that rebut the presumptions of conscience. In practice, the combined force of these considerations may warrant more restriction than accommodation. My point is only that the assertion of a conscience-based claim imposes a burden on the state to justify its proposed interference. There are many ways in which the state may discharge that burden, but if my position is correct, Justice Frankfurter's argument in *Gobitis* is not one of them. It is not enough to say that whenever a state pursues a general good within its legitimate purview, the resulting abridgement of conscience may represent unfortunate collateral damage but gives affected individuals and groups not legitimate grievance or cause of action. Claims of conscience are not trumps, but they matter far more than Frankfurter and his modern followers—democratic civic totalists—are willing to admit.

The ultimate reason is this: in a liberal democracy, the state is not an end in itself but rather a means to certain ends that enjoy an elevated status. The ability of individuals and groups to live in ways consistent with their understanding of what gives meaning and purpose to life (which I call expressive liberty) is one of those ends. This kind of liberty may rightly be limited to the extent necessary to secure the institutional conditions for its exercise. Beyond that point, the rightful relation of ends and means is turned on its head. That is the line a liberal democratic state ought not cross.

Conclusion

As I have defined it, political pluralism is the thesis that human life, individual and associational, consists in a heterogeneous variety of activities, each of which generates a distinctive ensemble with claims to respect and authority. Politics is but one of these activities. While it possesses distinctive competences and advances distinctive claims, its authority does not dominate every other type of activity.

I do not mean to suggest that there are neatly separated, hermetically sealed spheres, each of which is dominated by a single set of claims. For example, we have seen that parents and public institutions each exercise rightful authority over decisions concerning the education of children. (For some purposes, children share this authority as well.) We have also seen that the line between religious and political authority over social life can prove exceedingly difficult to draw. While there are many instances in which it appears reasonably clear which set of claims is to take priority, there are many others (perhaps the majority) in which claims qualitatively different in their content and source will vie for control, with no obvious principles for resolving the conflict. Indeed, part of the point of politics is to deal with such controversies, through bargaining, voting, and attending to particular circumstances. It is inevitable that these political decisions will reflect not only path dependency but also differences of natural endowment and social power. (Republican government, however perfect, is no exception; Hobbes called democracy the "aristocracy of orators."[56]) My point is only that once we recognize the diversity of authority claims, it becomes impossible to sustain the theory of civic totalism.

Must we acknowledge this diversity? My argument is that once we attend to some basic features of social life, it becomes far more plausible to affirm than to deny this diversity; the idea of a single dominant authority appears procrustean, even counterfactual. Political pluralism is an empirical social theory with normative force.

NOTES

1. William A. Galston, *Liberal Pluralism: The Implications of Value Pluralism for Political Theory and Practice* (New York: Cambridge University Press, 2002).

2. For a detailed account of what taking culture seriously means, see my discussion of Brian Barry's "Culture and Equality" in Galston, *The Practice of Liberal Pluralism* (New York: Cambridge, 2004), 176-182.

3. For a development of this point, see Stuart Hampshire, *Justice Is Conflict* (Princeton, NJ: Princeton University Press, 2000).

4. Martha Nussbaum, "Political Objectivity," *New Literary History* 32, no. 4 (2000): 883-906.

5. For more on this, see Galston, *The Practice of Liberal Pluralism*, ch. 2.

6. For more on how presumptions operate within value pluralism, see Galston, *Liberal Pluralism*, 69-78.

7. 530 U.S. 640 (2000).

8. For the British tradition, see Paul Q. Hirst, ed., *The Pluralist Theory of the State: Selected Writings of G. D. H. Cole, J. N. Figgis, and H. J. Laski* (London: Routledge, 1989). For the Calvinist tradition, see James W. Skillen and Rockne M. McCarthy, eds., *Political Order and the Plural Structure of Society* (Atlanta: Scholars Press, 1991).

9. For the full account of our agreement and (mainly) disagreement, see my review of Macedo's latest book, *Diversity and Distrust: Civic Education in a Multicultural Society* (Cambridge, MA: Harvard University Press, 2000), recently published in *Ethics* 112, no. 2 (2002): 386-391.

10. Aristotle, *Politics*, book 1, ch. 1, 1252a1-a6, in *The Politics*, trans. Carnes Lord (Chicago: University of Chicago Press, 1984), 35.

11. Thomas Hobbes, "Of Commonwealth," ch. 29, in *Leviathan*, ed. Richard Tuck (Cambridge: Cambridge University Press, 1996), 221-230.

12. Hobbes, *Leviathan*, "Of the Kingdom of Darkness," ch. 46; cf. "Of Commonwealth," ch. 17.

13. Quoted by J.N. Figgis in Hirst, *The Pluralist Theory of the State*, 112.

14. Frederick Carney, "Associational Thought in Early Calvinism," in *Voluntary Associations: A Study of Groups in Free Societies*, ed. D. B. Robertson (Richmond, VA: John Knox Press, 1966), 46.

15. Quoted and discussed in John Rawls, *Political Liberalism* (New York: Columbia University Press, 1996), 379.

16. Robert Dahl, *Democracy and Its Critics* (New Haven: Yale University Press, 1989), 182, 183.

17. Ibid., 183-192.

18. Rawls, *Political Liberalism*, 139, 157.

19. Ibid., 139-140.

20. John Rawls, *A Theory of Justice* (Cambridge, MA: Harvard University Press, 1971), 3.

21. John Rawls, *Justice as Fairness: A Restatement*, ed. Erin Kelly (Cambridge, MA: Harvard University Press, 2001), 10.

22. Ibid., 11.

23. Ibid., 165. To complicate matters further, on one and the same page (10), Rawls seems to characterize the family both as part of the basic structure of society and as an institution within the basic structure. I don't see how it can be both, and it makes a huge difference which it is.

24. Ibid., 165.

25. Ibid.

26. Ibid.

27. For much more on civic totalism, see Galston, *The Practice of Liberal Pluralism*, ch. 3.

28. Granted, "exit rights" is a general concept that admits of a range of possible specifications. I have defended a relatively robust conception, one that warrants a greater measure of state interference in religious and cultural communities than many dyed-in-the-wool pluralists can accept. (See Galston, *Liberal Pluralism*, 122-123.) That has not prevented fervent egalitarians from attacking my conception as insufficiently attentive to the plight of vulnerable minorities within minority communities. For my response to Susan Okin on this point, see *The Practice of Liberal Pluralism*, 182-185.

29. Joseph Raz, ed., *Authority* (New York: New York University Press, 1990), 12.

30. Ibid., 13.

31. 268 U.S. 510 (1925), at 535.

32. Ibid., at 534; emphasis mine.

33. Laurence Tribe, *American Constitutional Law*, 2nd. ed. (Mineola, NY: Foundation Press, 1988), 1227.

34. *Watson v. Jones*, 80 U.S. 679 (1872), at 728-29. While this case was decided on the basis of common law, 80 years later the Court rendered a parallel decision based on the First Amendment. See *Kedroff v. Saint Nicholas Cathedral*, 344 U.S. 94 (1952).

35. For a parallel discussion, see Nancy L. Rosenblum, *Membership and Morals: The Personal Uses of Pluralism in America* (Princeton, NJ: Princeton University Press, 1998), 80-83.

36. Matthew 22:15-22; Mark 12:13-17; Luke 20:20-26.

37. 406 U.S. 205 (1972).

38. 827 F.2d 1058 (1987).

39. 310 U.S. 586 (1940).

40. *West Virginia v. Barnette*, 319 U.S. 624 (1943).

41. 319 U.S. 642.

42. 319 U.S. 646.

43. 319 U.S. 646-651.

44. 319 U.S. 651.

45. 319 U.S. 653-654.

46. 319 U.S. 655.

47. 319 U.S. 656.

48. 319 U.S. 670-671.

49. Tribe, 1189.

50. Christopher L. Eisgruber and Lawrence G. Sager, "The Vulnerability of Conscience: The Constitutional Basis for Protecting Religious Conduct," *University of Chicago Law Review* 61 (1994): 1315.

51. 380 U.S. 163 (1965), at 176.
52. 398 U.S. 333 (1970), at 339, 344.
53. 398 U.S. 345, 356-357.
54. 398 U.S. 372.
55. Rogers M. Smith, "'Equal' Treatment? A Liberal Separationist View," in *Equal Treatment of Religion in a Pluralistic Society*, eds. Stephen V. Monsma and J. Christopher Soper (Grand Rapids, MI: Eerdman's, 1998), 193.
56. Thomas Hobbes, *The Elements of Law Natural and Politic* (1640), ch. 21 (4), in the Liberty Library of Constitutional Classics, http://www.constitution.org/th/elements.htm (accessed June 20, 2007).

6

VALUE PLURALISM, AUTONOMY, AND TOLERATION

DANIEL M. WEINSTOCK

A number of political theorists have in the past few years argued that once the truth of value pluralism is established, the rejection of autonomy liberalism (AL) follows almost automatically.[1] For some theorists, such as William Galston, the alternative is a form of toleration liberalism (TL).[2] For others, such as John Gray, the conclusion to be drawn from value pluralism is even more radical. Liberalism must on his view be rejected outright, as it instantiates a particular set of values that rules even liberal toleration out of court.[3] My intention in this paper is to show that the philosophical distance that must be traveled by these theorists in order to make good their rejection of AL is in fact much greater than they seem to think. My argument will proceed in three steps. First, I will propose some conceptual ground-clearing which will establish the terms of the debate between proponents of AL and TL. The core of the argument will be delivered in the second and third parts of the paper, in which I will show that at least some degree of autonomous decision-making is a necessary ingredient of the moral psychology most naturally affirmed by value pluralists, and that value pluralism is at most causally related to the type of social pluralism that a politics of toleration is designed to resolve.

I will end with some reflections suggesting that the distance between AL and TL may at the end of the day not be quite as great as might initially seem. In order to avoid crippling objections, both need to make concessions to the other, the net result of which might be to blur the distinction between them altogether.

I

I take liberalism to be a body of doctrine and practice principally concerned with the rights that the state ought to guarantee against the possible encroachment of democratic decision-making, market forces, and individual malfeasance. Disagreements among liberals often have to do with the question of why we have these rights.[4] These disagreements as to the grounds of rights inevitably give rise to disputes concerning their content. Autonomy liberals believe that the rights of citizens should promote autonomous choice and decision-making. They are motivated by an ideal according to which people should be able to reflectively endorse the ways of life around which they organize their existences. They should be able to articulate, and when necessary to revise, their conceptions of the good life, or at the very least to give uncoerced assent to the conceptions that have been handed down to them by tradition.[5] Toleration liberals on the other hand believe that autonomy is just one value among others. Some ways of life are non-individualist, based on deference to established authority and respect for traditions, but they are just as valuable as those that emphasize the individual's authorship or reflective endorsement of her own conception of the good.[6]

Defenders of these two ways of defining liberalism disagree about the rights that the state should uphold. For example, in the area of education AL will tend to be skeptical, and TL will tend to support, an extensive parental right to educate children according to parents' conceptions of the good, and to withdraw children from state-sponsored education that they see as inimical to these conceptions. They will tend therefore to be on opposite sides of the debates on cases such as *Yoder*.[7] AL will be more inclined than TL to support measures aimed at defending the rights of "internal minorities." It holds that conceptions of the good that limit the educational and professional opportunities of women, or that discriminate on the basis of sexual orientation, are not just "different," but wrong, and that, ceteris paribus, the state should step in to uphold what defenders of AL view as rights that would otherwise be denied. Proponents of TL will tend to think that as long as people have the ability to exit a way of life in which their rights are limited, there is no wrong that the state ought to make right.[8]

Examples illustrating the differences between AL and TL could be multiplied. What is important is that we be clear on what lies at the basis of these examples. AL is committed to the realization of the human capacity for autonomous choice-making, whereas TL wants liberal society to be as open as possible to different ways of imagining and of trying to live according to different conceptions of the good, and both sets of theories organize the schedule of rights for which they think the state is to be held ultimately responsible accordingly.

It is important to note that there are other debates over the point of rights within which AL and TL might line up together. For example, they will both tend to oppose the view that democratic rights enjoy a kind of normative primacy, and that the content of other rights ought to be up for grabs within the democratic political process. They ascribe great importance to some practice of judicial review of legislation to protect individual and minority rights.[9]

We must now get a clearer handle on the idea of value pluralism, which seems to lie at the heart of the debate between AL and TL. Value pluralists hold that there exists a range of values that are all appropriate objects of human aspiration, and that there exists no metric according to which these values can be rank-ordered. Value pluralism is not relativism. It does not hold that *anything* goes. But it recognizes that humans are complex, multi-dimensional beings, and that there exists a concomitantly varied set of acceptable conceptions of human flourishing.

Proponents of TL argue that AL is based on the denial of value pluralism. On their view, it gives pride of place to one particular value, namely autonomy. Now, sophisticated defenders of TL recognize that autonomous decision-making can end up affirming a range of values. I can after all autonomously choose to live a life of observance of authoritative religious dictates, for example. Their opposition to AL is not based on the caricature according to which the latter recognize only the life of the antinomian maverick as valuable. Rather, it revolves around the more subtle point that AL sees autonomy as imposing a limit-condition on acceptable ways of life. They see autonomy liberals as claiming that any way of life can be valuable, provided that two conditions are satisfied. First, they insist on the condition that these ways of life instantiate values, rather than pseudo-values. Second, they insist on the choice of these ways of life being made autonomously. The first condition constitutes common ground between AL and TL, and distinguishes both from the relativist. The disagreement between them has to do with the second condition. Defenders of TL and AL agree that substantively non-autonomous ways of life can be valuable. But AL holds, whereas TL denies, that in order for these ways of life to be valuable they have to be procedurally autonomous, that is, they have to have been chosen by their adherents in circumstances that can fairly be taken to ensure autonomy.[10]

I want to claim in what follows that the connection between these two conditions is actually much tighter than TL thinks. That is, I want to show that an endorsement of some degree of autonomous decision-making must be affirmed by the value pluralist both to make out the cognitivist distinction between values and pseudo-values, and to account for the motivational hold that particular values can have in a context of value pluralism. Both the rejection of monism and of anti-cognitivism, which is central to the value pluralist position, requires the recognition of the importance of choice.

II

Value pluralism is a philosophical thesis about how matters stand in the axiological domain. It is committed to some species of cognitivism, either realist or anti-realist. Cognitivism is a condition of value-pluralism being distinguishable from relativism, as it claims that there is a way of distinguishing sham and genuine values. And it claims that no metric exists that can reduce the plurality of values.[11]

Does value pluralism tell us anything about moral psychology? Does it tell us anything about the beliefs and dispositions that people ought to have?

Value pluralists clearly think, or at least are committed to believing, that people who do not affirm value pluralism are *mistaken*. Monists hold that there is one supreme value, to which all other values can be reduced. Relativists believe that there is no fact of the matter in the area of value, and that what people believe in this area is a function of what their preferences happen to be, or of how they happen to have been brought up. Their existence represents a problem for value pluralists. All we have to do is ascribe to them a preference for people living in the light of the truth rather than in the shadow of error, and we reach the conclusion that value pluralists should naturally prefer that monists and relativists change their views to bring them into line with the truth about value.

This would be a troubling result for toleration liberals who want to construct an argument for toleration on the basis of value pluralism. For the kinds of groups that they argue liberals ought to be tolerant of do not look or behave like pluralists. As we have seen above, the paradigm case for toleration liberals like Galston and Spinner-Halev are tightly knit religious groups, such as the Amish, who go to significant lengths to ensure that their members do not learn to appreciate the value of other ways of life, and to see them as real options. On the face of it, the groups on behalf of which they plead for toleration seem like monists rather than pluralists.

So it looks at first glance as if value pluralists are committed to wanting groups like the Amish to change. They view them as in some important way benighted, and as needing to change their views about value. Now, the changes that value pluralists are committed to envisaging are not at first glance the same as those that autonomists would recommend. Those who believe that autonomous affirmation is a limit-condition on acceptable ways of life would urge not so much a change of belief on the part of members of Amish-like groups, but rather a change in the manner of commitment. They would tend to view a certain degree of reflexivity as desirable, a relation of the individual to her conception of the good life that affords some place to *choice*. But to the degree that the change desired by autonomist liberals warrants the charge that they are intolerant of such groups, so, it would seem, is the kind of change that value pluralists seem committed to.

There are various responses available to the toleration liberal who wants to derive an argument for toleration from value pluralism. One would remind us of the fact that there are other areas of philosophy where a divide between philosophical truth and the beliefs that people ought to hold given that truth is viewed as unproblematic, even as desirable. Stephen Stich for example has argued that it is not always in people's interests to hold true beliefs. Error can to some degree be pragmatically justifiable.[12] And some consequentialists, such as Sidgwick, have argued that consequentialist ends may very well best be achieved by moral agents holding non-consequentialist moral views.[13] Why couldn't value pluralism be realized unwittingly as it were by a range of monists all affirming different values or rank-orderings of value?

This response is unavailable to value pluralists however because value pluralism, unlike pragmatism and consequentialism, is not a normative theory. It is descriptive, geared at accounting for the way things actually stand in the area of value. Consequentialists are happy for people to have whatever beliefs best conduce to the production of morally desirable outcomes. Pragmatists are similarly interested in people having whatever beliefs will allow them to do well. Value pluralists of the kind that political philosophers like Galston claims to be do not analogously hold that people should have whatever views about value leads to the maximization of the range of values held by people. They claim to describe rather than to prescribe, and so they cannot help themselves to the view that it would be a good thing for people to be monists (or relativists) because this would increase the number of realized values. Now, such a normative theory is imaginable. One can imagine someone holding that increasing the number of realized values would be a good thing even if it required that no one actually believed values other than the ones that they affirm *are* values. Perhaps they think that this would be aesthetically valuable, or that it would please God. Whatever the warrant for such a hypothetical value pluralist consequentialism, it is clearly not a position held by toleration liberals.

A variant of this response has recently been put forward by Galston in response to my initial formulation of the argument.[14] Galston argues that it does not follow from the fact that value pluralism is true that truth should be reckoned a dominant value within the domain of value. He writes that "there are some genuine goods whose instantiation in ways of life allows or even requires illusion."[15] Therefore people who have rather monistic beliefs about values may very well be mistaken, but given the value of error within in a particular schedule of values, we should not wish to align their beliefs with the truth about the domain of value.

This argument trades on a confusion. Let's distinguish between two perspectives, that of the theorist reflecting on the domain of value, and that of the practitioner of a particular schedule of goods, whose way of life instantiates value. Now it could be that from the former perspective, some of what the practitioner does seems to be premised upon error. But the error is apparent only from the perspective of the theorist. The practitioner does not shrug his shoulders at the thought that his beliefs might be mistaken, satisfied in the thought that his way of life instantiates values of such importance that he can continue to adhere to them while all the while acknowledging their error, he actively denies it. I would have thought that there are very few Rortyan ironists among the members of those religious and ethno-cultural groups whose practices pose the problem of tolerance to begin with. They value truth just as much as anyone, and would probably be offended at Galston's suggestion that truth does not loom as large for them as it does for those who cleave to the "classic Enlightenment value of public truth."[16]

So it isn't the case that truth is valued less by practitioners than it is by theorists, but that theorists can see the utility in people having false views. As Galston puts it, "It is impossible for contradictory religious creeds to be equally true, but many help undergird important individual and social virtues".[17] As Moses well understood, ascribing divine authorship to moral prescriptions can contribute to their acquiring motivational purchase.

I think that this plausible-sounding claim is actually more problematic than it might seem. First, Galston is undoubtedly right that the factual claims made by different religions cannot all obtain. Either Jesus was the son of God, as Christians claim, or he was not, as everyone else (most notably Jews and Muslims) believes. Now, though this disagreement is about a question of fact, it is not one about which we are likely to acquire decisive evidence any time soon. So though it is true that, in principle, different religious narratives are incompossible, their faithful can actually live as if they were not. What's more, the theorist is not in a position decisively to say where the balance of illusion lies.

Second, though some individual and social virtues are in fact undergirded by what may end up to be illusions, it may be the case that they would be better and more robustly supported by truth and reason. When one's allegiance to a virtue or a moral practice is contingent upon revelation, it is vulnerable to crises of faith. Grounding morality rationally might take away some of the motivational hold that religious grounding affords when it works, but it may produce more secure uptake than religion.

What's more, if the usefulness of illusion is to be measured by the virtues that it grounds, then the vices and ills that it produces should also be part of the equation. Monism, whether grounded religiously or not, has certainly underpinned moral fervor, but it has given rise to rather more unsavory passions as well. Feeling as if one is possessed of the truth has given rise historically to one or the other of a pair of antisocial motivations—either missionary zeal or moral autarky.

Finally, it seems clear to me that the practitioner of monistic faiths only has beliefs within the domain of value. Clearly, he also has views *about* the domain of value. It is well-nigh impossible to live in modern societies, or even alongside modern societies, without coming at some point or other to occupy the standpoint of the "theorist." One cannot avoid comparing one's way of life to that of others, and assessing the rival claims that they might make about the values that are most worth pursuing. It is one thing for one's conception of the good life to be based upon illusory beliefs, it is quite another to have mistaken views about conceptions of the good life and the relations that obtain among them. Monists have beliefs of both kinds. Some of them are on all fours with the beliefs of theorists. I cannot see how the pluralist theorist can be as sanguine as Galston seems to be about the errors that monists make about the domain of value.

Another response a toleration liberal who wants to lean on value pluralism might make would be to question whether the members of Amish-like groups need deny pluralism. Though they sometimes seem to behave as which they do, we can imagine them holding something like the following view about the relationship between those practices, in the area of education for example, that would seem to betoken a commitment to some kind of monism, and a belief in value pluralism. "We do not deny that there is any number of valuable ways of life, instantiating views about the good life quite different from ours. We can imagine other people being able to lead fully valuable lives, but those lives would not be right for us, given who we are. We have no choice but to affirm Amish values." We could thus imagine a position that would reconcile a full appreciation of the truth of value pluralism with the claim that not all people can access all values.

(I now want to flag an unargued simplifying assumption made by toleration liberals. I have dealt with it extensively elsewhere,[18] and I will return to it in section III of this paper. It is what I take to be the mistaken view that social groups embody ways of life, and that different ways of life in turn embody distinct values of rank-orderings of values.[19] This would allow us to see social pluralism as the realization of value pluralism. It also allows the view that I have just ascribed to my hypothetical Amish-like person to gain prima facie plausibility. After all, it is inconceivable for me to make the life of a monk of a Shinto temple a real option for me. But if we see that way of life as instantiating a value such as "contemplation," then it is presumably one that I can access, as it is presumably multiply realizable. Much rides here on metaphysical questions to do with the individuation of values, which I cannot consider in the context of this short paper. For the sake of the argument in this section, I will arguendo grant the toleration liberal the claim that social groups embody and realize different values.)

Now there are various ways in which the story I have just adumbrated can be completed. They all turn on various ways of understanding the crucial phrase "no choice" in the statement I have ascribed to my hypothetical Amish-like person.

A first reading would take the story literally, and claim that values are somehow hardwired. Who we are somehow determines the values that we hold. There would on this view be as little room for an individual to determine his values autonomously as there would be for him to determine his height or the color of his skin. Call this the *determinist* view.

The determinist view is implausible on its face. Indeed, it would rule out the admittedly dramatic but not uncommon phenomenon of value conversion. But the point that I want to insist on here is that it is also difficult to square with the value pluralist's commitment to cognitivism. As we have seen, the pluralist wants to distinguish her position from that of the relativist, who holds that there is no way to distinguish real from ersatz values, and that the values that we hold are simply a function of the preferences we happen to have or of the social locations we happen to inhabit. A determinist view of value would leave the kind of pluralist we are presently trying to describe no critical distance with which to assess the value-claims of others, and to distinguish real from sham values among these claims. Worse, it would give him no way to claim with any confidence that what he ascribes meaning and importance to within his way of life actually *is* valuable. He is saddled with his values, willy nilly, and though he experiences them as valuable, he does not possess the critical purchase to determine whether his own claim can be vindicated.

A second, more plausible reading of the "no choice" phrase would see it as a façon de parler. When the claim is made that one has no choice but to affirm a certain set of values given (say) the way one has been brought up, it should really be read as claiming that one's upbringing strongly inclines an agent to affirming these values. An illustration and a discussion of this view of one's relationship to the values of one's community of origin are provided in a recent book by G. A. Cohen. Cohen has noted the troubling fact that though he, as a philosopher, is strongly committed to the view that his values should be those that have the most rational warrant, he cannot help but to observe that he has as a matter of fact spent his entire philosophical career defending values that are quite closely related to those that he encountered growing up as the son of parents deeply involved in the Labour Movement in Montreal in the 1950s.[20] A plausible way to interpret the datum reported by Cohen (and which probably conforms with the experience of a great many people) is that the views we have grown up with are possessed of a certain robustness. By robustness I mean that the amount of evidence and countervailing information it will take to defeat the value commitment one inherits will be quite great, at any rate greater than the amount of evidence that would be sufficient to unseat our beliefs about value were we starting from a standpoint of axiological neutrality. Call this the "strong inclination" view.

That one's value commitments are possessed of considerable robustness, especially when they have served one well, strikes me as an entirely plausible claim. Note that it does not rule out, and in fact it positively requires that agents can achieve a certain critical distance relative to these initial commitments. Indeed, if one's initial social location inclines rather than determines, it follows that one is monitoring one's environment for evidence of one's value commitments' warrant (or lack thereof).

A third interpretation of what might plausibly be meant in claiming that one has "no choice" but to affirm the values with which one has been brought up would view it as affirming a second-order normative commitment. It can be taken as a way of affirming the authority of one particular source of value (in this case tradition) and of rhetorically pinning oneself to the mast. The speaker can be taken as fully recognizing the variety of values and ways of life that are in fact available to him, and as committed to living his life *as if* they were not real options for him. (This is an at least plausible way of reading Luther's oft-quoted phrase: "Hier stehe Ich. Ich kann nicht anders.") Call this the *second-order* view.

This is surely an accurate description of the moral psychology of some moral agents. The point I want to make about it is that though it is a commitment to being bound by tradition, it is very much an exercise in self-binding, and thus a manifestation of procedural, though not of substantive, autonomy. One can choose to limit one's range of choice, and enact any number of strategies, both practical and psychological, to commit oneself to this second-order choice.[21] Though the end-result of this type of process might very well be that the agent is convinced that he has "no choice," his finding himself in that situation results from a creative use of autonomous agency.

From the point of view of the pluralist who wants to distance himself from a non-cognitivist position such as relativism, the best way of understanding the practitioner of a monistic moral creed who claims to have no choice but to affirm the values that she does is thus not to view her as determined to affirm these values in a way that precludes the exercise of choice. Minimally, he should view her as holding these values robustly but defeasibly. She does not actively cast around looking for new values to affirm and corresponding new ways of life to take up. Her capacity for choice is exercised in a more subtle, less readily apparent manner. She appreciates the value of other ways of life, but does not weight them in the same way as she does the way of life that she was born into. She recognizes that there is independent value in being true to a way of life that one has been able to live a good and decent life in, and that there are transition costs to attempting to adopt another set of values that might be deemed preferable from some notional "view from nowhere." Her capacity for choice manifests itself both by her *not* revising her conception unless a substantial burden of proof is met, and by her revising it if and when the threshold for continued adherence is passed. The point I want to insist on for present purposes is that abiding by what might appear to be a suboptimal set of values is an exercise of autonomous agency. It is both an independently plausible conception of moral agency, one that accounts both for the difficulty and for the reality of moral conversion, and one that squares better than does the determinist one with cognitivism about value.

What of the person who binds herself to a set of values and a corresponding way of life in a manner that makes that threshold disappear? She also clearly exercises autonomous agency. The psychological and institutional mechanisms through which individuals bind themselves to conceptions of the good and ways of life that they fear they might otherwise be tempted to quit are of the utmost ingenuity, and they are often quite consciously adopted. (Though even when they are adopted unconsciously, this cannot be taken as evidence of a lack of agency. There are a panoply of means adopted by human agents to fit their behavior to their values, and it is an overly rationalistic one that rules out of the court of autonomous agency all those that do not rise to the level of consciousness.[22]) That they might struck many as self-defeating does not take away from the fact that they are the work of agents.

The pluralist who wants to deny that autonomy is a necessary ingredient of all conceptions of the good life might at this point want to object that I have in essence equated autonomy with agency. Can one really say of an individual who lives her entire life within a conception of the good within which she has been raised, and who is never prompted by circumstances to activate her capacity for revision of her conception of the good by the monitoring capacity, in any significant sense autonomous?

I am less concerned with the way in which we use a particular term such as autonomy than I am with what that usage reveals and occludes. As I will show at greater length in the final section of this paper, though liberals and autonomy theorists have succeeded in making the distinction between "procedural" and "substantive" autonomy fairly common currency, they have been less careful at articulating precisely what is involved in the procedural conception. Conscious adoption and revision have come for many to seem criterial of procedural autonomy. But surely the capacity to abide and remain true to a set of values in a range of circumstances that might put pressure on them, but that one would have a second-order preference to withstand, is part of the total package of dispositions that are pointed to by the very etymology of the concept. The insistence of many theorists that one manifests one's autonomy by endorsing and when needed, by revising, in other words by living according to *one's own* lights has occluded the fact that the notion of *lawfulness* is also implicated in the concept, that part of what having values *means* is that they exercise some authority over the agent. (I will return to this point at greater length in the final section of this paper.) The important point for present purposes is that agency is exercised by faithfulness and commitment as much as it is by adoption and revision, and that there are reasons etymological, conceptual, and (I would argue) historical for claiming that these capacities are components of a complete picture of what autonomous agency involves. An individual "strongly inclined" in the sense defined here to adhere to the values that she has been raised in is thus not heteronomous. She can therefore not be claimed as evidence for the view that good lives can fail to instantiate autonomy.

Let me take a step back to survey the argument. We began by considering ways in which to pull the sting of the argument according to which the pluralist cannot but find regrettable that the monist or the relativist have erroneous beliefs about value. The move we have been considering would have the person who lives as a monist acknowledge the truth of value pluralism, but deny that it makes any practical difference to the way he lives his life, because his social location gives him no choice as to what values to affirm. We have seen that the "determinist view" offers the only interpretation of this claim that immunizes the pluralist against the claim that he must admit the procedural autonomist's claim that autonomy constitutes a limit condition on valuing, that one cannot really *value* without in some sense *choosing*, but that this determinist view is implausible on its face, and that it fails to square with the pluralist's commitment to cognitivism. Determinism about value is actually more compatible with relativism, which can be taken to claim that what one values is determined by what one's preference or location happens to be.

Both the strong inclination and the second-order views provide more plausible interpretations of the "no choice" thesis, but each assumes the exercise of autonomy. The former can be cashed out as claiming that one's present views are fairly robust with respect to countervailing evidence, which means that the agent will only change her views given that a fairly high burden is met. The latter can be interpreted as the view that the agent chooses to treat her views as non-negotiable. In neither case can it really be claimed that the other values that make up the universe of value do not constitute accessible options for the agent. There is a strong, but not indefeasible presumption against them in the case of the individual whose moral psychology is best captured by the strong inclination view; and they are ruled out by the agent in the case of the agent characterized by the second-order view, which means that, at a cost which will depend on the kind of self-binding mechanism which the agent has chosen to enact, they can be ruled back in.

I conclude that the unavoidable acknowledgement on the part of the value pluralist that the monist and the relativist are wrong about value is corrosive for the toleration liberal who wants to distinguish himself from the autonomy liberal who affirms a procedural conception of autonomy as a limit condition on valuing. Initial appearances to the contrary, the epistemic acknowledgement of value pluralism brings recognition of choice as a condition of valuing in its train.

III

The foregoing argument has been developed under a simplifying assumption that I now want to put in question. The simplifying assumption, which is crucial to the case of theorists who argue from value pluralism to liberal toleration, is that there is a fairly simple mapping that can be carried out between the plural values that there are, and the social groups whose presence gives rise to the need for a politics of liberal toleration. For value pluralism to be relevant to the political problem of group pluralism, that is, it would have to be the case that the pluralism of groups represents the this-worldly instantiation of the pluralism of values.

We have seen that even if we grant this assumption, the inference from value pluralism to TL does not go through. But the assumption should not be granted. It is simply implausible to suppose that the best way to account for the social groups that raise the issue of pluralism is in terms of divergent values.

The advocates of a politics of tolerance tend to think that social groups that realize different values to those of the majority should be granted some degree of autonomy to organize their communal existence according to these different values. This is what the toleration that they request from the broader community often amounts to. For example, they argue that they should be exempted from laws applying to members of the majority, when these laws are contrary to their distinctive schedule of values.

To show that if there is a case for toleration, it is not best understood in terms of recognition of the legitimacy of plural schedules of values, consider the following fable. Imagine a society, call it *Homogenea*, whose members all come from the same ethnic stock. Their island nation was uninhabited until a few hundred years ago, and all present-day Homogeneans descend from a handful of original colonists. Homogenea is isolated, and its climate and terrain are harsh. So Homogenea has not had any immigration. All Homogeneans speak the same language, Homish. Homonogea is also religiously homogeneous. Its members all worship the deity, Sam, and all are members of the Church of Sam.

Despite its ethnocultural and religious homogeneity, Homogenea is in the throes of a moral debate that has reached crisis proportions. Roughly half of Homogenea's citizenry believe that male Homogeneans should always wear the traditional headdress of Sam faithfuls when they appear in public. Others believe that religious dress should be restricted to places of worship, and to certain major religious festivals. The disagreement, let us suppose, is over the right way in which to weight piety and civic-mindedness.

Homogeneans understand that there are really only two possible outcomes of this debate. Either the Homogenean legislature votes to ban the wearing of the headdress for all Homogeneans, or it allows it for all. There are no politically salient subgroups within this highly homogeneous society which might be singled out as warranting an exemption. What we have here is a true debate on questions of value within one unitary political community, of the same order as debates that within a community often oppose free marketeers to proponents of the welfare state, or pro-choice and pro-life movements on the issue of abortion.

What is important to note here is that if the practice is allowed, it will be allowed for all Homogeneans who wish to avail themselves of it. Those individuals whose value schedule inclines them to wearing religious headdress in public places will be permitted to do so. Individual values, rather than any antecedent group identity, are what is at issue here.

My story continues. The Homogenean legislature decides to ban the wearing of Samean headdress in schools, and a constitutional challenge fails, the Court deciding that the banning of the headdress does not constitute a serious enough obstacle to the practice of Samism to warrant overturning a democratically arrived at decision. Some pietists toe the line, and over time give up their claim. Others, however, do not, and continue to press their claim against the state. Over time, some partisans of piety splinter from Samism, and start their own religion, Orthosamism. Their liturgy and iconography, though related to that of Samists, comes to differ more and more from that of their spiritual forebears.

A hundred years after the initial legal challenge, a group of Orthosamists brings a new suit. This time, the Court finds in favor of the would-be headdress wearers, claiming that the ban constitutes an unjustifiable burden upon the Orthosamists' freedom of religion, given the centrality of the headdress to the religion. They exercise an option that did not exist in Homogenea's earlier history, which is to invoke a sub-group identity and set of associated practice as grounds for exemption-seeking. Remember that at the earlier stage of historical development, the available options for legislatures and courts was either to prohibit the practice for all Homogeneans, or to allow it for those Homogeneans who value the affirmation of religious over civic values. The possibility that is opened up by the emergence within Homogenean society of religious pluralism is that a practice be countenanced for the members of some groups but not for others. Orthosamists are exempted from a prohibition that applies to the members of the majority. It is at this stage, therefore, that we can speak of a politics of toleration.

What is the point of this little fable? It is to suggest that a politics of tolerance, in which a group is exempted from a law applying to the rest of the population, only comes in at this second historical stage. But the value disagreement between pietists and proponents of a more civic ethics was already present at the first. This suggests that what calls for a politics of tolerance has not so much to do with differences in value as it does with differences in culture and identity. Value differences are, at best, a necessary, but not a sufficient condition for the demand for tolerance to make sense. (I would argue that it is not even a necessary condition: imagine a further stage in my fable, a thousand years in the future, where the origins of the sartorial disagreement in a debate about the appropriate way in which to rank civic and religious values has receded from memory. Orthosamists engage in the practice, and other Homogeneans refrain from it, not because they affirm particular rank-orderings of values, but rather out of a sense of tradition. The different sartorial practices are in other words central to group identities, but they are not rooted in value differences. Those who feel that a politics of toleration is still apposite here out of respect for distinct traditions and identities are in effect claiming that value pluralism is not even a necessary condition for a politics of toleration.)

It is a mistake to view the pluralism of groups as the worldly realization of value pluralism. As the fable of Homogenea has made plain, we can well imagine situations in which a politics of toleration among groups makes sense, but in which differences in value have receded from view. And I would argue that the fable is not so far removed from our world. The kind of group memberships that raises the problem of toleration is driven not by different value choices, but by identification with a historical tradition, with a religious narrative, with a set of cultural or liturgical practices. The problems of group pluralism and of value pluralism are, in other words, largely independent.

IV

I have been operating thus far on the hypothesis that the conceptual distance between AL and TL is actually as great as the protagonists to the debate take it to be. I think that this hypothesis is mistaken, however, and I want to suggest in these concluding remarks that when each side acknowledges a potentially fatal flaw in their position and attempts to repair it, the result will be that we will end up with positions that differ in emphasis rather than in substance.

As has been noted by a number of theorists, including Brian Barry[23] and Susan Okin, the toleration liberal must avoid sacrificing "internal minorities,"[24] mostly women and children, to pluralism. Toleration liberals think that social groups whose mores and practices do not align squarely with those of the (presumably liberal) majority should be accommodated to some significant degree to live their lives as they see fit, even when this involves ways of raising children and of enacting gender roles that members of the majority find morally problematic. The objection made by liberals is that this may end up cutting loose from any form of protection those members of the group who are singled out for treatment that may seem harsh and unfair.

The response of many toleration liberals has been to advocate exit rights for such individuals. Toleration would on this view be evidenced by the liberal state not intervening in the affairs of groups organized around practices and beliefs that may prima facie be seen as violating the rights of some members. Respect for the interest of these members would be manifested by the state's enforcement of secure exit rights. The state would on this view bear the responsibility of ensuring that no obstacle lies in the way of individuals who decide to quit their membership in these groups. Where exit rights exist, and those who might be thought to have reason to leave choose to stay, it can be assumed that they do so voluntarily, and that the liberal state must respect their decision.

Exit rights would like most rights be a sham if they were thought of in a purely formal way. The enforcement of exit rights thus cannot mean simply the prohibition of physical coercion. It must go to at least some lengths to ensure that individuals possess the agency required to make use of their exit rights.

Some theorists, such as Chandran Kukathas and Jeff Spinner-Halev, envisage rather minimal exit rights.[25] I would argue that they do not take seriously enough the moral claims that might be made on behalf of women, and perhaps especially on behalf of children for whom issues of exit and consent are emphatically beside the point.

Others, like William Galston, are more committed to making exit a real option for individual members. In Galston's view, four sets of conditions must be in place in order for an individual to be possessed of a "meaningful" right of exit. Individuals must be aware of other life-options that are available to them in the broader society; they must be able to assess them as to their desirability, and to be psychologically able to access them as real alternatives for them, and they must be possessed of aptitudes and capacities that enable them "to participate effectively in at least some ways of life other than the ones they wish to leave."[26]

This set of strictures strikes me as entirely plausible. The problem for toleration is that they look for all the world like core ingredients of a perfectionist political program aiming at inculcating autonomy to all members of society, and that they would involve the kind of state intervention that one would have thought the toleration liberal would condemn.[27]

Now, we can assume that the knowledge conditions of which Galston writes will almost automatically be in place for all but the most isolated minority groups living in the context of modern societies. Orthodox Jews, Mennonites, Amish, and others live cheek by jowl with people leading all kinds of lives and pursuing myriad conceptions of the good.

But the other conditions will doubtless require substantial intervention. Precisely because they cannot shelter their young from an *awareness* of the options that lie close at hand within the broader society, minority communities often enact all kinds of material, epistemic and psychological barriers designed to prevent them from being able to *access* them. They sometimes attempt to present these options as debased and immoral (think of many communities' strictures against intermarriage, or against women entering the workplace), thus contravening the condition that Galston sees as central to exit rights, according to which individuals must be able to assess options on their merits.

My principal claim in this context is this: were the state systematically to see to it that all citizens had secure rights of exit from whatever groups and associations they happen to belong to, it would have to counteract the epistemic and motivational obstacles that groups routinely, and quite rationally put in place to retain membership. This would involve intrusions much more far-reaching than the disallowing of legal and financial obstacles that many other theorists have seen as marking the limits of the state's reach with respect to associational life. It would have to put in place a compulsory educational program with an avowedly perfectionist agenda, aimed at counterbalancing many of the teachings and ethical dispositions inculcated by teachers and parents within the community in question.

Imagine a community whose norms were structured around a clear division of gender roles between men and women. According to this community's norms, the role of women is to raise children and to take care of the household. In order to reinforce these gender roles, this division of labor is sanctioned by an ethical code that ascribes great value to the virtues of domesticity and childrearing, and that shrouds any departure by women from these virtues in the aura of vice. It also tailors the education of girls to their taking on of these roles. Capacities and aptitudes that might be of service in the economic and professional arenas are simply not inculcated, as they are seen as useless for the roles that women will be called on to perform. Through a variety of subtle and not-so-subtle mechanisms, moreover, the identities of members are "policed" in ways that make it unlikely that they will defect even if they come to perceive the norms and practices of the community as painful and oppressive.

According to the conception of exit rights that Galston affirms, the liberal-democratic state would have to observe that the community in question fails to provide its members with meaningful exit rights. It would be duty-bound to counteract this tendency. The most obvious lever that the state disposes of to do so is the educational system. In order to ensure that members of the community possessed full exit rights, it would have to require attendance by the children of the community in public schools, or impose a curriculum on the community's private school. That curriculum would have to go further than simply juxtaposing the conception of gender roles put forward by the community with one that does not constrain the prospects of women as severely. It would have to present the community's vision of the proper role of women as false. And it would have to put in place mechanisms whereby the psychological and motivational hold of the community on children is lessened, else the psychological conditions that Galston sees as central to exit rights not be satisfied.

Toleration liberals are thus saddled with a dilemma. They can either put forward a minimalist conception of exit rights and lay themselves open to the objection that they fail to take seriously the interests of (among others) women and children. Or they can enforce more stringent conditions upon these rights, and end up affirming a position that does not differ markedly in the practical prescriptions it makes from autonomy liberalism.

Does this signal a victory for the autonomy liberal? Not really. Because autonomy liberalism must respond to a concern, articulated most cogently by Eamonn Callan, to the effect that autonomy liberalism as it is most commonly construed, gives only a partial account of the aptitudes and dispositions that a truly autonomous individual would possess. Callan's argument is that the traditional argument for autonomy "emphasizes the value of autonomous revision to conceptions of the good without registering the symmetrical value of autonomous adherence."[28] Autonomy liberals are at this stage fairly used to the distinction, invoked above, between procedural and substantive conceptions of autonomy. But they have had a tendency to equate the procedure involved in the procedural account with choice and revision. At least part of what autonomy involves is the ability to be guided by a stable set of values, and not to throw that set of values into question on a whim.

My discussion of exit rights led to the conclusion that people should be able to revise their allegiances should they want to. A conclusion which might be taken to flow by a serious engagement with arguments such as Callan's is that while education should provide children with the wherewithal required to entertain different ways of life from the ones in which they have been brought up, and to exercise the options that seem more attractive to them, they should also be taught the importance of faithfulness and commitment. This has educational implications: we should avoid placing independent value on revision as such, and eliding the difference between substantive and procedural autonomy by surreptitiously introducing a preference for the life of the maverick over that of the pillar of the community.

But it also has social and political implications. As many theorists have noted, modern consumer culture exercises disproportionate attraction on members of modern societies, and especially on the young. The satisfactions that it offers are relatively easy and immediate, whereas those that are afforded by commitment and faithfulness are longer-term and perhaps less immediately appreciable. Are there any measures that can be taken, compatible with a broadly liberal political ethics, and sensitive to the concerns about the possibility of exit that have just been discussed, that might right the balance between market goods and other kinds of goods in the eyes of individuals? This strikes me as a worthwhile area of investigation, one that is made necessary for the autonomist liberal sensitive to Callan's complaint that procedural autonomists have been unduly fixated on revision, and insufficiently on adherence.[29]

It is beginning to look as if the chasm with which we began between autonomy and toleration liberals is not as unbridgeable as may initially have been thought. Toleration liberals cannot be so tolerant as to preclude individuals from acquiring the competences required to question their memberships when they no longer suit their interests. And autonomy liberals cannot be so enamored of autonomy that they forget to think about the conditions that are required for choosers to be presented with the worth of lives of commitment and faithfulness fairly. The breaking down of dichotomies is usually a mark of philosophical progress. I hope that the foregoing suggestions will not prove an exception to that rule.

NOTES

1. This paper is a distant relative of a paper delivered at a NOMOS session in Boston in December 2004. Thanks to participants for helpful comments. I would like to thank Rob Merrill for some useful discussion thereafter.

2. William Galston, "Two Concepts of Liberalism," in *Liberal Pluralism: The Implications of Value Pluralism for Political Theory and Practice* (Cambridge: Cambridge University Press, 2002), 15-27.

3. John Gray, *Two Faces of Liberalism* (New York: The New Press, 2000).

4. One central line of debate on this issue opposes theorists who view rights as grounded in the human capacity for choice, and those who view it as rooted in the need to protect the fundamental interests of persons. See for example Matthew H. Kramer, N. E. Simmonds, and Hillel Steiner, *A Debate over Rights* (Oxford: Oxford University Press, 1998).

5. Prominent autonomy liberals include Will Kymlicka and Rob Reich. See Will Kymlicka, *Multicultural Citizenship* (Oxford: Oxford University Press, 1995) and Rob Reich, *Bridging Liberalism and Multiculturalism in American Education* (Chicago: University Of Chicago Press, 2002).

6. Other toleration liberals include Jeff Spinner-Halev and Chandran Kukathas. See the former's *Surviving Diversity: Religion and Democratic Citizenship* (Baltimore: Johns Hopkins University Press, 2000) and the latter's *The Liberal Archipelago: A Theory of Diversity and Freedom* (Oxford: Oxford University Press, 2003).

7. For a parent's rights approach, see Shelly Burtt, "In Defense of *Yoder*: Parental Authority and the Public Schools," in *NOMOS XXXVIII: Political Order*, eds. Ian Shapiro and Russell Hardin (New York: New York University Press, 1996), 412-437.

8. For a toleration-liberal approach to the problem of internal minorities, see Jeff Spinner-Halev, "Autonomy, Association, and Liberalism," and for an autonomy-liberal see Rob Reich, "Minors within Minorities: A Problem for Liberal Multiculturalists," both in *Minorities Within Minorities: Equality, Rights, and Diversity*, eds. Avigail Eisenberg and Jeff Spinner-Halev (Cambridge: Cambridge University Press, 2005), 157-172 and 209-226, respectively.

9. One author who the autonomy and the toleration liberal might both line up against is thus Jeremy Waldron, *Law and Disagreement* (Oxford: Oxford University Press, 1999).

10. To the best of my knowledge, the distinction between procedural and substantive conceptions of autonomy originates in Gerald Dworkin, *The Theory and Practice of Autonomy* (Cambridge: Cambridge University Press, 1988).

11. A paradigmatic value pluralist is John Griffin. See his *Well-Being: Its Meaning, Measurement, and Moral Importance* (Oxford: Oxford University Press, 1986), esp. 89-92. For a clear statement of the distinction between pluralism and relativism, see Robert B. Louden, *Morality and Moral Theory: A Reappraisal and Reaffirmation* (Oxford: Oxford University Press, 1992), esp. 89-90.

12. Stephen Stich, *The Fragmentation of Reason* (Cambridge, MA: MIT Press, 1990).

13. Henry Sidgwick, *The Methods of Ethics* (Indianapolis: Hackett, 1981), esp. book IV.

14. In my "The Graying of Berlin," *Critical Review* 11, no. 4 (1997): 481-501.

15. William Galston, *Liberal Pluralism*, 53.

16. Ibid.

17. Ibid.

18. Daniel M. Weinstock, "Fausse route: le chemin vers le pluralisme politique passe-t-il par le pluralisme axiologique?" *Archives de philosophie du droit* 49 (2006): 185-197.

19. For an uncritical equation of different "ways of life" and divergent values, see John Kekes, *The Morality of Pluralism* (Princeton, NJ: Princeton University Press, 1993), 11.

20. G. A. Cohen, *If You're an Egalitarian, How Come You're So Rich?* (Cambridge, MA: Harvard University Press, 2000), ch. 2.

21. A variety of such mechanisms is explored in Jon Elster, *Ulysses Unbound* (Cambridge: Cambridge University Press, 2000).

22. On this point see Owen Flanagan, "Identity and Strong and Weak Evaluation", in *Identity, Character, and Morality*, eds. O. Flanagan and A. Rorty (Cambridge, MA: Harvard University Press, 1990), 37-65.

23. Brian Barry, *Culture and Equality* (Cambridge, MA: Harvard University Press, 2001); Susan Moller Okin, *Is Multiculturalism Bad for Women?* (Princeton, NJ: Princeton University Press, 1999).

24. A recent collection of essays has been entirely devoted to the set of issues that arise when the interests of internal minorities are taken into account. Avigail Eisenberg and Jeff Spinner-Halev, eds., *Minorities within Minorities: Equality, Rights, and Diversity* (Cambridge: Cambridge University Press, 2005).

25. Jeff Spinner-Halev, "Autonomy, Association, and Pluralism" in *Minorities Within Minorities*, 157-171; Chandran Kukathas, *The Liberal Archipelago*, 103-114.

26. William Galston, *Liberal Pluralism*, 122-123.

27. Cf. George Crowder, "Galston's Liberal Pluralism" (paper presented at the Australasian Political Studies Association Conference, University of Adelaide, Adelaide, Australia, 29 September–1 October 2004).

28. Eamonn Callan, "Autonomy, Child-Rearing, and Good Lives," in *The Moral and Political Status of Children*, eds. David Archard and Colin Macleod (Oxford: Oxford University Press, 2002), 118.

29. The only philosophical paper I am aware of that investigates this terrain in any depth is Joseph Heath, "Liberal Autonomy and Consumer Sovereignty," in *Autonomy and the Challenges to Liberalism*, eds. John Christman and Joel Anderson (Cambridge: Cambridge University Press, 2005), 204-225.

7

THE LIMITS OF LIBERAL PLURALISM

A COMMENT ON WILLIAM GALSTON

ROBIN WEST

Professor Galston means by "liberal pluralism" a sort of mid-course correction of political liberalism, the central idea being that the liberal state and its constitutional actors all ought to recognize the multiple sources of moral authority in our lives, the different norms of governance those authorities generate, the communities they create, and the surplus social value they bestow on us all. His two primary examples of such non-state moral authorities, and the rules and communities they create, although he alludes to others, are the various "authorities" that govern religious and family life—not just divine authority and the authority of conscience, presumably, but also the all-too-human authority of priests, ministers, bishops, popes, husbands, fathers, and patriarchs. Those authorities, in turn, generate rules—such as, for example, gender conformity and exclusion from positions of spiritual leadership, in the case of Catholicism, or gender subordination, marked by expectations of wifely obedience, passivity, and submissiveness, in the case of some fundamentalist Protestant households. Those authorities, and those rules, in turn, facilitate not only ways of life, but also very material communities of faith and family—communities that are vitally important to the lives of many citizens within liberalism's empire.

Obviously, not all of the authorities that govern these intermediary associations, and certainly not all of the rules they generate,
are consistent with fundamental commitments of political liberalism. To give an example outside of family or faith, neighborhood
organizations often exert moral authority in the forms of restric-
tive covenants, dictating aesthetic and associational limits on the
architectural styles and numbers of unrelated individuals permitted to each household, within the neighborhood's confines. These
covenants, which not so long ago often explicitly precluded the
sale of one's home to racial and religious minorities, interfere
quite markedly with individual exercises of expression as well as
with traditionally liberal free market forces. To take another example beyond faith and family, the authoritative voices of college fraternities, sports organizations, and the colleges that sponsor both,
with their multi-textured authorization and delegation of powers,
constitute independent "moral authorities" within the playgrounds
of academe: they get a lot of deference from the state to organize
various matters typically within the control of public rather than
private authorities. The social and political structures those organizations create are often profoundly (and notoriously) illiberal.
Similarly, a wide assortment of private schools, private clubs, and
civic associations, from military academies, to the Boy Scouts, to
Kiwanis Clubs, to private Golf Courses, exert authority and create
communities in part through membership rules that include and
exclude quite explicitly by reference to gender, religious affiliation,
sexual orientation, or class. The rules they generate to effectuate
those exclusions, and the communities in turn created by those
rules, stand in stark contrast to norms of equality that otherwise
characterize the liberal state in which they are embedded.

Nevertheless, Galston argues, despite their illiberality, we are all
richer for the existence of these non-state authorities, from church,
to family, to college fraternities, private clubs, and neighborhood
associations. And who is the "we" so enriched? Not only those of
us within those communities, Galston urges—although, one might
interlineate, the less privileged members of those communities are
perhaps not quite as enriched as the more privileged—but also,
he argues, those of us who are relatively indifferent toward them
are also enriched—those of us happy to have bowlers either bowl
alone or together, so long as we are never required to set foot in a

bowling alley. That is the "we," including liberals as well as outsiders and community members, who are enriched by the existence of illiberal communities. And why? Life is better, not only for the members of these groups, but for all of us, by virtue of the diversity, and the moral competition, that these illiberal intermediate associations contribute to our common life. Furthermore, and perhaps most important, these groups, not despite of, but by virtue of their illiberality, stand as a bulwark against a sort of totalistic secular liberalism. They stand as a counter, therefore, against the danger of a particular kind of majoritarian tyranny, but not a majority defined by mediocrity or passion, as Mill may have feared, but rather, a liberal majority over-enthralled with liberal norms of justice. That danger, Galston thinks, is a grave one: totalistic liberal secularism carries with it the risk of becoming a sort of unchecked political power. And liberalism, at its heart, is all about preventing the amassment or concentration of power and authority in one source. So, it is in the best interest of liberalism, ultimately, to see that these groups thrive. They provide life its meaning, for many who participate in them, and although on first blush it may seem paradoxical, they actually ensure basic conditions of liberal life for the rest of us.

Yet, Galston worries, these groups are clearly disfavored—and even endangered—by political liberalism, as most of us now understand and to some degree practice that political faith. Political liberalism, for almost a half century now, has been committed to the eradication of not only state-sponsored unjust discrimination or subordination, but also, to the eradication in private life as well, surely in associational life, of habits of discriminatory and subordinating modes of thought and action. There is a tension, at best, and a collision course, at worst, between liberalism, as theory and constitutional guidelight, on the one hand, and these illiberal intermediate associational groups, or authorities, on the other, which, despite their internal illiberality, are an essential component of liberal life. How, then, to ensure the survival of these groups within liberalism—groups that enrich life in liberal societies, are even necessary for liberalism to thrive, yet espouse ways of life so antithetical to basic liberal commitments?

This is not a new question within liberal theory or practice. Political liberalism has a quite rich answer, but it is one William Galston has rejected for twenty years now: don't protect (or even "recognize") the groups themselves, but rather, protect the rights and liberties of individuals to enter into illiberal associations, no matter how inegalitarian their internal structure.[1] For Galston, however, and many others now as well, and for reasons that go well beyond the current project, this answer is insufficient: liberalism cannot ultimately protect the existence of these groups solely through the protection of the individual rights of the members within them— whether those rights be understood as rights of privacy, of associational liberty, of speech, of thought, or of religious belief. It won't do, in other words, to respond to the conflict between the liberal state and the illiberal associations it must protect, in the relatively well-worn way of strengthening the liberties of some individuals, so they are brought into better balance with the equality rights of others.

Rather, Galston argues, what needs changing is neither the illiberality of the groups themselves, nor the mix of rights and liberties of the individuals within them or affected by them, but rather liberalism itself. Political liberals need to change our ways of thinking, if we are to recognize the existence, appreciate the value, and then protect these illiberal intermediary institutions. Mostly, we need to acknowledge that what is required here is not simply a regard for individual rights—the rights of the occasional dissenter, the non-conformist, the Millian eccentric, and the like—but rather, a regard for the separateness and legitimacy of illiberal non-state *authorities,* and the often-times conformist, traditional, non-eccentric lives to which those authorities give meaning. A truly liberal state must recognize the authority that governs these associations, and grant them their due sphere of sovereignty, including the space and freedom to generate their rules of illiberal internal self-governance. And, second, American liberals in particular must look anew at our constitutional history, in order to appreciate the considerable degree to which our own history reflects liberal pluralism, rather than liberal individualism. Only by so doing, can we see in our history, as well as in our aspirations, a commitment to pluralism, and thereby (presumably) discover the constitutional wherewithal to act on it.

I think that Galston is right descriptively, and, although its only done in very broad strokes, historically as well. The nature of our political lives cannot be fully captured by positing only the existence of states, individuals, and individual rights. We live within these intermediate associations he is describing, and although they are undoubtedly impacted on they are not created by the state: the state is not everywhere already, at least for those of us not in prison. These associations have moral meaning the state should recognize; they are not simply the consequence of impenetrable bubbles of rights around individuals, within which the individual can be weird, arbitrary, rational, irrational, social, or antisocial, without fear of state interference. The shared life of the parishioners in St. David's Episcopal Church, down the street from my house, for example, is not "like" the solitary life of the Unabomber or the Millian eccentric or the political dissident preaching revolution or the performance artist smearing herself with butter. Casting the similarities between the parishioners and these nonconforming individualists all in terms of rights, overstates the commonality and clearly misdescribes both. The associational communities that concern Galston are not the spheres of autonomy that permit individual eccentricity, but rather, the social worlds within which shared lives of conforming participants are governed, ordered, conscribed, and sometimes oppressed, but through systems of interest, lines of authority, and sometimes within bonds of love. Rights discourse, as construed within political individualist liberalism, doesn't come close to even describing much less protecting their interest.

Galston is also right, I believe, to suggest a re-characterization of our history of constitutional rights protection. Although it is too long a story for these comments, that history has indeed been at least in part about state deference to other spheres of authority—particularly the patriarchal family—rather than either state recognition or creation of individual rights.[2] This story is still largely untold, and it is good to see this forthrightly acknowledged.

I disagree with Galston, then, not in his description of this expansive understanding of what liberalism requires, or even what our constitution requires of us, but rather, in his normative conclusions regarding the proper relation between the liberal state and these illiberal associations. I think he is far too sanguine about the harms these groups do to their disadvantaged members, the threats they pose to the rest of us, and most important, the complicity of the state in perpetuating those harms. I will focus on just three particular harms, all of which are present in all forms of liberalism, but which might be worsened rather than bettered by the particular modification Galston seeks.

First, liberal pluralism risks an increase, rather than a decrease, in the sufferance and infliction of private violence, and particularly domestic and sexual violence. Galston needs to attend to this directly, as do liberals of all stripes. As is now at least on occasion recognized, political, liberal constitutionalism, at least in the United States, has not done a good job of delivering a state that is true to Hobbes's central promise for the liberal state: that it will monopolize a society's legitimated levers of violence. The individualist liberal state, traditionally understood, has not managed to follow through on this promise: pockets of unchecked violence, ignored or marginalized by the state ostensibly charged with the duty to police against it, persist. Liberal pluralism, I am afraid, might do even worse: out of an undue regard for the authority of private spheres of political sovereignty, it doesn't even squarely make the promise.

The second harm I will characterize, roughly, as the problem of "capture." Administrative agencies, as anyone interested in pain medication knows, can be captured by the interests they are intended to regulate. Likewise, the liberal state itself can be captured by the association interests it is supposed to be policing, regulating, or at least holding at bay. This is a danger the risk of which is worsened (quite intentionally so, as far as I can tell) by liberal pluralism, as opposed to liberal individualism: the liberal pluralist, unlike the liberal individualist state, sees itself as, at most, coordinating these separate spheres of civic sovereignty, rather than holding them at bay.

The third harm is simply of misdirection. If the essence of liberalism is to fight concentrations of power, in Galston's reformulation, then we need to think about where the greatest danger of concentrated power currently lies. It does not lie with an unduly individualistic or egalitarian liberal state. Nor, though, in my view, does it lie with a pluralistic liberal state overly solicitous of right wing Christian sensitivities. It does not lie with any nation state. Rather, the greatest danger of concentrated power, likely for the next decade and perhaps the next century, that liberals must confront, is the multinational corporation—an association, no longer intermediate, but primary, increasingly beyond the reach of any nation, any state, any law, or any legal ideal, liberal, egalitarian, or otherwise. It is the multinational corporation, not the state, the church, or the family, that is the authority that increasingly dominates, authorizes, constrains, and threatens the lives of the world's inhabitants, and that is increasingly beyond the reach of liberal, or just nationalist, state, civil control. If liberals, with their commitment to state sponsored equality, and social conservatives, with their commitment to tradition and social value, could find a way to join forces, there might be hope that neither will be eclipsed, if not eradicated, by the transnational reach of reckless and profit-seeking corporate life.

I raise all three *potential* harms as warning flags to which I think Galston and other liberal pluralists must attend. These are not intended to derail the project of Liberal Pluralism, which I think is a worthy project of some importance. I am quite sure that Liberal Pluralism can be defined so as to address them. My suggestion is that its architects ought to do so, and explicitly. I'll elaborate very briefly on each.

First, then, on private, and particularly familial, violence. How do the "authorities" within these private, intermediate associations that Galston lauds, such as the family, actually maintain their authoritative power? Perhaps, on occasion, through moral persuasion, force of example, excellent child-raising, role modeling, and the like. Too often, though, that authority, particularly in the nuclear family, has been maintained through calibrated, measured, violence—what used to be called, in the domestic home, "chastisement."[3] This is not just an historical curiosity—a good deal of contemporary familial authority comes as well from the hidden fist within the glove of family privacy. Galston does not, of course, argue that the liberal pluralist state should tolerate domestic violence. Quite the contrary, according to Galston, the authorities within families and other associations as well must maintain themselves "non-coercively." Thus, while the liberal state might and perhaps ought to tolerate a little animal sacrifice in the name of pluralism, no one, Galston opines, would think that the state would tolerate, in the name of religious or associational freedom, the sacrifice of human beings.[4] But this sounds like definitional wishful thinking. We have, in this country, a thoroughly disgraceful history of tolerating the sacrifice of human beings in the name of associational freedoms of intermediary organizations, or put differently, we have a long history of state non-involvement with certain forms, but only certain forms, of private violence, much of it quite explicitly intended to maintain the lines of private, "moral," non-state authority. Galston's essay in fact inadvertently provides a good way to describe the phenomenon: the various states, historically, have under-policed certain sorts of violence, precisely because they defer to private power. They have done so, explicitly or implicitly, toward the end of protecting the various moral "authorities" of intermediate associational life: church, culture, family, or conscience. Consider the fifty-year history of lynchings, abetted by the states' non-involvement with these murders, that maintained racial subordination after the Civil War.[5] Likewise, if less lethally, consider the hidden battery, chastisement, or discipline of women, that maintained the "separate sphere" of domesticity,[6] also abetted by state non-involvement. Notice the largely unchecked violence of "bullies" on their victims on schoolyards, and the still under-policed rapes in college dormitories. Or, consider the inadequately policed-against violence of urban gangs,[7] the arguably constitutionally protected right to gun ownership, and the proliferation of weapons of individual destruction in this culture;[8] the unchecked and until recently unnoticed sexual aggressions of the clergy; the too-often ignored male-on-male violence perpetrated against vulnerable sexual minorities;[9] the sexual and sexualized violence against prostitutes, to say nothing of the sex traffic itself, and so on, and so on, and so on. Where, one wonders, in the midst of this carnage, has the so-called nanny state, so notoriously over-involved with our private lives, so "always already" present, been? What it has been, is always already not there—absent, during the lynchings, absent during the domestic beatings, absent during the school fights, absent during the sexual abuse of altar boys, absent during the rapes and murders of prostitutes, drag queens, and other despised sexual minorities.

So, the first worry I have regarding Galston's essay is simply that I'm not sure whether or how the shift from liberal individualism to liberal pluralism is going to address this problem. The danger is that it will worsen it (albeit only rhetorically): arguably, it takes the worst inclinations of individualist liberalism, so to speak, with regard to private violence, and then magnifies them. Let me explain. The liberal, American-styled constitutional state's disgraceful under-involvement in doing anything about private violence, and particularly, for these purposes, domestic violence and sexual violence, is not some sort of weird oversight—a failure to notice that those are human beings and not animals being sacrificed in satanic rituals. Nor has it been, at least for most of that history, a side product of an otherwise commendable urge to protect individual "rights" of privacy, speech, religion, or the like. Rather, the liberal state's under-involvement—its persistent refusal to police against certain forms of private violence—has been all about deferring to the authorities within this separate sphere of sovereignty. It is deference to authority, not respect for rights that, for most of our family law history, drove the state's decision to stay out of these private hells, often with lethal consequences. The legal scope, and breadth, and depth, of the liberal state's deference to familial authority, and the fist and sword required to maintain it, in fact, has been nothing short of breathtaking. That deference to private authority—rather than respect for individual rights—was the impulse and norm behind this under-policing and non-involvement, was explicitly recognized in the coverture doctrines of the 17th, 18th, and 19th centuries.[10] It was also, though, the impulse behind the 18th and 19th century rules of chastisement, authorizing the husband to exercise moderate corporal discipline upon disobedient wives.[11] More recently, it was reflected in modern law in the husband's explicit legal entitlement to force sex on his wife—the so-called "marital rape exemption"—that persisted through most of the 20th century, much of which is still good law, and which is still the suggested legal rule promulgated by the American Law Institute in their so-called Model Penal Code.[12] It is reflected, only slightly more obliquely, in the various immunity doctrines in tort law, only recently dismantled, protecting both charities and families against civil suits for violent wrongs.[13] It is explicitly referenced today in various "cultural defenses" in criminal law, according to which if an act of violence against a disobedient wife is legitimate in the culture of origin of a newly arrived immigrant, that somehow mitigates the severity of the crime within our own state.[14] It appears in various mitigation rules regarding "crimes of passion" that have the effect of legitimating sometimes lethal violence against adulterous wives.[15]

Most important, though, the shall-we-say dark side of deference to non-state authority is reflected in the current state of our constitutional law. The individual citizen, the Supreme Court told us twenty years ago in *DeShaney v. County of Winnebago Social Services*,[16] whether that citizen be an abused wife, a four-year-old child beaten into permanent severe mental retardation by an abusive parent, a citizen of a poor and under-policed neighborhood, or any one else, does not have a constitutional right to a police force.[17] There is no constitutional right to be protected against private violence, nor does the state have a constitutional duty to provide such protection. The state might protect you against violence, if it chooses to, but it doesn't have to. So, the individual on the receiving end of the violence that is sometimes used to effectuate the authority and the discipline in these private sovereignties applauded and recognized by liberal pluralism, has no constitutional right to state redress, or protection, against the harms that violence inflicts. Put this unfortunate dicta together with a more modern case: not long ago, we learned from the Supreme Court that the core component of the most far-reaching federal legislative attempt to correct for the states' failures, or inabilities, to police against domestic violence—the civil remedy created by the Violence Against Women Act—is unconstitutional.[18] Criminal violence, the court held, particularly familial criminal violence, as well as the state's non-response to it, are matters of state law and control, the explicit directive of the Fourteenth Amendment's Section Five—that Congress must act, if the states fail to provide equal protection of the law—notwithstanding. So—putting these together—according to our constitutional structure, the federal government defers to the authority of states, on matters of private violence, and according to state law, states may if they choose defer to private authorities on such matters, and this is all precisely how it ought to be. There is no constitutional right on the part of the individual to be protected by states against private violence, and there is correlatively no constitutional duty on the part of the state to ensure that the sort of authority Galston lauds is not the sort of authority that comes at the end of a fist or a shotgun. And there is no power, on the part of Congress, to correct this, and to act, should it deem it wise to do so, in the event that the states, for whatever reason, have failed to police against all of that private violence, and the dubious moral authority that violence engenders.

So, in light of this settled constitutional authority, we ought to push the familiar question back one step. The question is not, why all this violence in this too-violent country, but rather, why this history of state deference? Why has the American liberal state so consistently failed to police against so many forms of private violence, and why has American constitutionalism so utterly failed to impose on the state a duty to do so? I would argue that in the case of U.S. liberalism, the state's deference to patriarchal authority in the domestic sphere, and then the Court's and the Constitution's deference to that state deference, has not stemmed, for most of our history, from a solicitude for the "privacy rights" of individuals—that's a modern invention. Nor is it the result of unfortunate but inevitable under-funding of police and social welfare services. That under-funding is a consequence, not a cause, of the pattern I'm describing. Rather, state under-involvement in private domestic violence, and federal, judicial, and constitutional deference to that state under-involvement, for most of our history, has stemmed from a willful deference to the separate political sovereignty of familial patriarchs. We are most assuredly no longer in the thick of that history of deference. But we are still suffering the aftermath; our constitutional doctrine, in particular, still bears the mark of it. The consequence of all of that deference, for our spiritual and physical wellbeing, has not been terribly uplifting. Pluralistic liberalism does not confront it, and it threatens to worsen it, albeit only rhetorically.

Much more briefly, on the second of my three harms. Galston worries about the creep of secular totalism, and discusses at some length two famous cases from the 1940s involving the Pledge of Allegiance to make his point.[19] In our complicated lives we pledge allegiance, Galston argues, not only to the flag and to the republic for which it stands, but to other authorities as well, and Justice Frankfurter was tragically wrong, in 1941, to view this split loyalty as worrisome.[20] The Supreme Court in 1943 agreed.[21] In what we might view as the high-water mark of the Court's explicit embrace of liberal pluralism, the Court ultimately held, over Frankfurter's dissent, and reversing course from its position on the same issue from just two years prior, that it is an unconstitutional abridgment of First Amendment rights for states to require school children to recite the Pledge of Allegiance.[22] Such mandatory declarations of devotion to the state, Justice Jackson opined, impermissibly infringe on the sphere of authority governed by conscience—and therefore on our First Amendment rights, properly understood.[23] To reframe this in Galston's vocabulary: what had happened in 1940 in West Virginia was that secular civic totalism had impermissibly crept into public consciousness, in the guise of this mandated public vow of secular patriotism, and the Court was right to strike down that law, in the name of the authority of individual conscience.

The red flag I want to raise, suggested by Galston's discussion of this famous case, is that this "seepage" of the authority of the state into the realm of private conscience is not the only kind of "seepage" that ought to concern the liberal pluralist. Indeed, the most recent case involving the Pledge of Allegiance raises precisely the opposite problem of the one that concerns Galston, and is in fact an eerie sort of vindication of the very concerns Justice Frankfurter raised in his famous dissent from Justice Jackson's paean to pluralism: and that is the creep of religiosity into the fiber of the secular state, whether or not the "creep" was initially motivated by a desire to avoid the danger of civic totalism. In *Newdow*,[24] decided just prior to the last election, a good sixty years after *Barnette*,[25] as you may recall, a citizen of Washington State objected to the inclusion of the phrase "One Nation Under God" in his daughter's school's Pledge of Allegiance, claiming it violated both her Free Exercise rights, and the Establishment Clause of the First Amendment. He won that argument in the Ninth Circuit[26]—a victory that created an uproar, including the spectacle of a unified House of Representatives, reciting the pledge authored for schoolchildren, and while so reciting (apparently) spontaneously yelling for emphasis, the phrase "Under God." The Supreme Court reversed the Ninth Circuit, on standing grounds.

I think the case sounds a warning bell. A number of the concurring Justices would have reached the merits, and what they penned is not heartening for future men or women of conscience who might want to object to either the patriotic or religious content of the schoolchildren's pledge.[27] Most noteworthy, perhaps, is Justice O'Connor's concurring opinion. (Justice Thomas's is too bizarre.) Again, the case involved not the pledge in its entirety—to which Newdow had no objection—but rather, the inclusion of the modifier "Under God" following "One Nation." "Under God," it should be noted, was added to the original pledge sometime after Jackson and Frankfurter's debate, and at the height of the red scare in the 1950s—the original pledge having been penned in the late 19th century by a socialist seeking to solidify ceremonially the "One Nation" outcome of the Civil War. But back to the present: O'Connor opined in *Newdow* that the phrase "Under God" in the otherwise rigorously secular pledge is a form of "secular, ceremonial deism" so ubiquitous as to be innocuous, and therefore, constitutional.[28] Thus, she offered, for our constitutional edification, the "ubiquitousness" test of undue establishment: if state declarations of religiosity are just white noise—if they are nowhere because they are everywhere—then they are constitutionally permissible. White noise is harmless noise, and, particularly in a rights-based culture, harmlessness is everything—no harm, no foul.

But look at where the ubiquitousness requirement, plus the rights focus, leads, at least in O'Connor's analysis: the constitutionality of innocuous, ubiquitous religiosity, in the form of a vow of patriotism repeated daily for twelve years over a childhood, that asserts the nation's subordination not to the Constitution, but to God. This goes well beyond liberal pluralism. A Nation Under God, presumably, is a rather different thing than a Nation that respects the sometimes-conflicting duties of those of its citizens who place *themselves* under God. The unfortunate unintended consequence, then, of Newdow's suit, is the constitutional legitimation of the literal subordination of the nation-state to divine authority—so long as that subordination is so ubiquitous that no one really notices, at least most of the time.

The contrast with *Barnette* could not be more striking, although O'Connor does not mention it, and Galston does not discuss it. In *Barnette*, in the 1940s, a religious dissenter complained of his obligation to utter a nationalist and secular vow of patriotism. He won. In *Newdow*, sixty years later, an atheist was denied the right to even have heard his claim that what had originally been a secular and nationalist vow of patriotism—which he found unobjectionable—by virtue of the added clause "Under God," unconstitutionally subordinated the nation to religious authority. That outcome, I believe, should strike us, whether individualist or pluralist liberals, as alarming. The Constitution, the First Amendment, the Supreme Court, the Establishment Clause all, are supposed to protect *against* the state's subordination to religious authority. We should worry if the Constitution and the Court charged with the task of interpreting it, not unlike an agency charged with the task of regulating industry, is captured by the authorities it is charged with the duty of regulating.

Lastly, the harm of misdirection. Galston's modification of liberalism is driven by a worry that the liberal egalitarian state might become totalistic, amassing for itself too much unchecked power. Liberalism, he reminds us, is all about reducing the risk of amassed, unchecked power. But if Galston is right that that is the danger at which liberalism is rightly poised, then it need not target itself. Egalitarian nation-states are hardly the greatest source of unchecked contemporary power. Liberals concerned about unchecked power, whether pluralists or individualists, would do better to direct their attentions to the unchecked power of corporations, rather than set their sights on the excesses of one another. The modern corporation is much like the intermediate association Galston describes, but without any moral purpose: its purpose, unchecked and unregulated by the state, is to maximize profit. The corporation has now achieved "personhood" in American jurisprudence, and as such, is the beneficiary of all sorts of constitutional protections against legal sovereignty. It has rights to be free of harsh punishment; it enjoys rights of equality, property, and liberty. It exercises all of these rights, domestically, so as to be freed of the legal constraint of an overly egalitarian sovereign. It is also, increasingly, freed from the burden of legal process: it is allowed the prerogative of authoring its own "alternative" conflict-resolution procedures. To the extent that it does so, the abuse of individuals, workers, consumers, and laborers that occurs under its auspices are increasingly invisible to the state: governed by private contract, beyond the reach of tort, and all protected by a bubble of economic privacy. It is becoming an authority to reckon with. The state defers to its powers, increasingly, habitually. If unchecked, profit-seeking will soon eclipse equality and morality both, within its own sphere of sovereignty. If it is to be checked, it will require more than an active national state, it may require an active international one. Given all of this, there is no doubt, in my mind, that the challenge for liberalism in the next decade, and possibly the next century, will be to do precisely that—to somehow check this currently growing, and seemingly unbridled, source of concentrated power. From that task—call it the "corporate wars"—the cultural wars, as well as this intramural dispute between individualist-egalitarian and pluralist liberals that the cultural wars have now engendered, among much else, is one mighty distraction.

CONCLUSION

In light of the above reservations, I would suggest the following friendly amendments to Galston's liberal pluralism. (1) The state has a moral duty, and ought to have a legal and constitutional duty as well, to police against the violence that is sometimes the vehicle for the conveyance of authority in private sovereignties. Correlatively, the individual has a right to that protection. Both the duty to protect against private violence and the correlative right on the part of the individual to that protection should be regarded as foundational, and therefore a part of our constitutional structure. (2) The state is more than just a neutral arbiter between competing religious views. It must maintain itself as a non-religious forum for the articulation and construction of competing political visions. (3) Corporations are sources of private authority, but the source of that authority is their accumulation of private property, not the conveyance of moral vision. It is therefore no part of liberal pluralism to promote their interests. Because liberal pluralism is a kind of liberalism, it ought to be a part of liberal pluralism to resist their alarming and growing usurpation of traditional state, individual, and community functions.

So amended, liberal pluralism strikes me as a welcome counterweight to the excessively individualistic thrust of our contemporary interpretations of the liberal tradition. Without these amendments, though, I'm not sure the flame is worth the candle consumed to produce it. Liberal individualism has been, whatever its many flaws, the vehicle by which the moral authority of private violent hierarchies have been dismantled. Without question, individualism carries costs of its own—costs that Galston and others have gone to great lengths to uncover. Before tossing the baby out with the bath water, though, we need to be careful to preserve liberalism's gifts. There are, I think, three. The first gift, I think, has been the suggestion—rarely followed in practice, but right at the center of the liberal vision—that the state, and only the state, should monopolize violent force, when exercising moral authority. It follows from this quite basic Hobbesian ideal that the state has a duty to insure that other private authorities do not wield violence when exercising authority. The second gift of liberalism to the world, I think, has been the suggestion that the state itself should be rigorously non-religious, while also allowing religious life to flourish. It's a difficult balancing act, but the first half of this promise is at least as important as the second. The third gift of liberalism has been its insistence that the state exists so as to further, to promote, the very human interests of all, and equally so. Whatever else this requires, it seemingly requires a state that actively resists the accumulation of wealth and power, and increasingly the usurpation of state functions, in the hands of transnational corporate entities, that seek not human betterment but profit maximization.

Liberal pluralism needs to commit to these classically and foundationally liberal pillars: the monopolization of violence in the state; the non-religiosity of the state, and the idea of human wellbeing, rather than corporate profit, as the raison d'etre of political organization. Without such an explicit underscoring of the ground it shares with both individual and classical liberalism, I fear that liberal pluralism could become, whatever the intentions of its founders, a source for the rhetorical legitimation of countless small and large acts of profoundly illiberal injustice.

NOTES

1. Individuals have broad First Amendment rights to enter into private associations that discriminate on the basis of sex, race, religion, and so forth. The Fourteenth Amendment does not prohibit the discrimination that may occur within those groups, so long as they are truly private. *See, e.g., Boy Scouts of America v. Dale,* 530 U.S. 640 (2000); *Pierce v. Society of the Sisters of the Holy Names of Jesus and Mary,* 268 U.S. 510 (1925); *Kiwanis Int'l v. Ridgewood Kiwanis Club,* 806 F.2d 468 (3d Cir. 1986), *cert denied,* 483 U.S. 1050 (1987).

2. Thus, the line of decisions culminating in *Roe v. Wade,* and arguably *Roe v. Wade* itself, had as much, if not more, to do with protecting the separate moral autonomy and authority of the family, than with

protecting anyone's individual rights. *See, e.g., Roe v. Wade,* 410 U.S. 959 (1973) (protecting a woman's right to abortion, but primarily through recognizing the independent autonomy of both the doctor-patient relationship and the husband-wife relation); *Griswold v. Connecticut,* 381 U.S. 479 (1965) (striking anti-contraception laws so as to protect the autonomy of the marital unit); *Pierce v. Society of the Sisters of the Holy Names of Jesus and Mary,* 268 U.S. 510 (1925); *Meyer v. Nebraska,* 262 U.S. 390 (1923) (protecting the rights of parents to dictate the terms of their children's educations). The exception to this pattern was *Eisenstadt v. Baird,* 405 U.S. 438 (1972), which extended Griswold, without discussion, to unmarried individuals.

3. For histories of legal violence within family life, and its role in maintaining the moral and political authority of fathers and husbands, see Reva Siegel, "The Rule of Love: Wife Beating as Prerogative and Privacy," *Yale Law Journal* 105, no. 8 (1996): 2117-2207; Jill Hasday, "Contest and Consent: A Legal History of Marital Rape," *California Law Review* 88, no. 5 (2000): 1373-1505.

4. William A. Galston, this volume, pp. 111–112.

5. See Emma Jordan, *Lynching: The Dark Metaphor of American Law* (New York: Basic Books, 1999).

6. Siegel, "The Rule of Love"; Hasday, "Contest and Consent."

7. *United States v. Lopez,* 514 U.S. 549 (1995) (finding a law prohibiting guns within a certain range of school districts unconstitutional because it was outside the commerce clause).

8. *United States v. Broussard,* 80 F.3d 1025 (5th Cir. 1996) (finding a Second Amendment right to gun ownership).

9. Marc Spindelman, "Homosexuality's Horizon," *Emory Law Journal* 54, no. 3 (2005).

10. See Sir William Blackstone, *Commentaries on the Laws of England* (1765) (stating that, upon being married, a woman's legal existence is either suspended or consolidated into that of her husband). For an historical account of coverture, see Hendrik Hartog, *Man and Wife in America: A History* (Cambridge, MA: Harvard University Press, 2000).

11. See Siegel, "The Rule of Love."

12. See Hasday, "Contest and Consent"; Robin West, "Equality Theory, Marital Rape, and the Promise of the Fourteenth Amendment," *Florida Law Review* 42 (1990): 45-79.

13. See generally Dan B. Dobbs and Paul T. Hayden, *Torts and Compensation: Personal Accountability and Social Responsibility for Injury,* 4th ed. (St. Paul, MN: West, 2001), 386-389.

14. See generally Rui Kaneya, "At Any Price: Marriage and Battered Immigrant Women," *The Chicago Reporter,* March 2002; "Democrats Introduce

Comprehensive Reauthorization of Violence Against Women Act," *U.S. Federal News*, Press Release, June 30, 2005.

15. See Victoria Nourse, "Passion's Progress: Modern Law Reform and the Provocation Defense," *Yale Law Journal* 106, no. 5 (1997): 1331-1449.

16. 489 U.S. 189 (1989).

17. Ibid., 196.

18. 529 U.S. 598, 619-20 (2000).

19. Galston, this volume, pp. 113–116.

20. Ibid., p. 115.

21. *West Virginia State Bd. of Educ. v. Barnette*, 319 U.S. 624 (1943).

22. Ibid., 642-43.

23. Ibid.

24. Elk Grove Unified Sch. Dist. v. Newdow, 124 S.Ct. 2301 (2004).

25. 319 U.S. 624 (1943).

26. *Newdow v. United States Congress*, 328 F.3d 466 (9th Cir. 2003).

27. Elk Grove Unified Sch. Dist. v. Newdow, 124 S.Ct. 2301, 2312-33 (2004) (O'Connor, J., Rehnquist, J., Thomas, J., concurring).

28. *Newdow*, 124 S.Ct at 2323.

8

INTERNATIONAL LAW AS
INTER-PUBLIC LAW

BENEDICT KINGSBURY

I. Introduction

In this essay, I seek to take some steps toward the development of a theory of international law that is an alternative—I hope a better alternative—to the standard account of international law simply as *jus inter gentes*, the law established between governments of states to regulate relations between states as juridical entities. I do not here present anything approximating a full alternative theory, but I try to indicate some features such an alternative theory could have. I argue that international law should be theorized as the law between public entities outside a single state, these public entities being subject to public law and to requirements of publicness. I focus in this paper on the entities whose practice counts in making international law, on the processes whereby these entities make international law, and some implications about the content of international law. My account incorporates most of the substance and institutions of the established *jus inter gentes*: much international law is indeed made by the agreements or the practices of national governments among themselves. But I offer a different view of the reasons for treating that as international law, a broader view of the entities responsible for making international law, and a more demanding view of what is needed to make international law. My project is concerned with the generation and modification *of* international law. I do not in this essay propose any different view to the prevailing one on the question of who is or could be regulated *by* international law: states, corporations, individuals, inter-state organizations, private standard-setting organizations, and so forth.

A. *Problems Calling for an Alternative Theory*

I begin by highlighting three features of the contemporary world which pose deep puzzles for the prevailing *jus inter gentes* model of international law. First, the concept of the state as a juridical unit, a central concept in the model of international law as *jus inter gentes*, does not adequately reflect the quality of states as public law entities, a quality that distinguishes them from mere "rational actors." Second, the *jus inter gentes* model of international law does not account adequately for the burgeoning activities of regulatory entities that are neither states nor simple delegates of states. Third, efforts to get beyond the obvious limitations of the *jus inter gentes* model of international law (e.g., proposals to refer instead to transnational law, or global law) have had the quixotic effect of buttressing that model: this is because these alternative ideas are generally not framed conceptually, and so do not set meaningful conceptual limits to what they include, making them unconvincing catchalls. In the next few paragraphs, I will elaborate on each of these three puzzles, and argue that they impel the effort to develop a viable alternative theory of international law, of the sort this paper seeks to advance.

1. States and Other Public Law Entities

Traditional *jus inter gentes* theories of international law (of the type represented by Lassa Oppenheim's 1905–1906 treatise on international law) embrace a coarse but robust statism, which analyzes the state as a legal personality with a single directing mind.[1] Such theories, however, do not take account of the fact states are producers of national rules which are increasingly required to meet conditions for law which go beyond those of command backed by sanction: these national rules have a quality of publicness in their orientation. When states—as public law entities and committed to publicness in law—come together with each other in an international legal rule-making and decision-making normative process, the results are not identical in form or meaning to what would result from a comparable process among unitary rational non-public actors.

This idea makes more space to meet democratic demands by institutions and groups within the state to have greater influence on and roles in global regulation. It offers scope to encompass legal governance forms adopted in inter-societal relations (e.g., cross-border governance institutions of co-religionists), in transnational relations among elements of states (e.g., networks of government regulators, such as the Basel Committee of central bankers), and in the jurisgenerative work of bodies that do not depend on states. Rather than treat the entities that act in such legal contexts as if they were externalized Hobbesian sovereigns-*manqué*, or as if they were simply delegates of such sovereigns under a statist theory, I propose treating them as public entities. These entities, along with the states that are the archetypical public entities, are the actors in an inter-public order that is, I suggest, the basis for a concept of international law preferable to the prevailing statist one.

2. Transnational Normative Governance That Is Not Traditional Inter-State Law

A vast amount of normatively framed regulatory practice does not fit within the standard model of international law as the law between states. Patterns of transnational regulation and its administration in global governance now range from regulation-by-non-regulation (laissez-faire), through formal self-regulation (such as by some industry associations), hybrid private-private regulation (for example, business-NGO partnerships in the Fair Labor Association), hybrid public-private regulation (for instance, in mutual recognition arrangements where a private agency in one country tests products to certify compliance with governmental standards of another country), network governance by state officials (as in the work of the Organization for Economic Cooperation and Development [OECD] on environmental policies to be followed by national export credit agencies), inter-governmental organizations with significant but indirect regulatory powers (for example, regulation of ozone depleting substances under the Montreal Protocol), and inter-governmental organizations with direct governance powers (as with determinations by the Office of the UN High

Commissioner for Refugees of individuals' refugee status). Instead of neatly separated levels of regulation, a congeries of different actors and different layers together form a variegated "global administrative space" that includes international institutions and transnational networks as well as domestic administrative bodies that operate within international regimes or cause transboundary regulatory effects.[2]

A theorist informed about all of this practice might answer simply by stipulation: international law is *jus inter gentes,* and any other norms and practices are not international law but something else. This has the merit of delimiting the field. More important, adherence to a positivist conception of international law sourced in the will and consent of states may be the best way to maintain legal predictability and to sustain rule of law values in international relations.[3] It may be preferable to retain a unified view of an international legal system than to countenance the deformalization and the mosaic pattern that some of the likely alternative approaches may entail. But I will argue that a theory of international law must be concerned with the normative production and the regulatory activities of such entities, at least when they exercise governing powers.

3. Limits to an International Law That Is Not
Confined to *Jus Inter Gentes*

Any theory of international law that accounts for more than just traditional inter-state law must be coherent and set cogent limits to the concept of international law. Herbert Hart pointed to the problem of treating international law simply as morality (in the way Austin does): the result is that morality becomes "a conceptual wastepaper basket into which go the rules of games, clubs, etiquette, the fundamental provisions of constitutional law and international law, together with rules and principles which we ordinarily think of as moral ones."[4] Treating every normative assertion in transnational governance as international law, on condition only that it is made with a claim to authority and establishes a sense of obligation, seems certain to lose many of the useful distinctions that the concept of international law presently helps to draw. I share Hart's view that a theory of international law, like a theory of law in general, should distinguish law from coercion (or, more generally, from the expression of coercive power), and should distinguish law from morality. Thus it is to be expected that there will be rules and principles of political order that are not legal rules and principles. (Indeed, the rules and principles of political order can handle some international issues better than legal rules and principles could.) Likewise, many moral rules are not rules of international law and many international law rules are not in themselves moral.

Yet while Hart directs attention to the right problem, the approach he takes to international law in chapter 10 of *The Concept of Law* does not seem to provide the basis for a solution. It was perhaps tenable to say in 1961 that a set of rules, not unified by any rule of recognition and hence not a "system" in his sense, might nevertheless be a bounded set, given that the rules he addressed were associated with perhaps 100 states and a small number of significant inter-state organizations. The dominant line among international lawyers now is to update chapter 10 by proposing a rule of recognition to render international law a unified system, rather than the mere set of rules Hart concluded it was. One retort is that for practical purposes "international law" is rightly divided into different substantive areas, or different clusters of institutional practices, or different sets of participants, and no grand unity is needed. But I doubt it is possible over a long period to sustain such fragmentation. Some reasons for this are political and social—recurrent war and violence in high politics spill into low politics, the gross illegitimacy or injustice of one part of an institution colors the work of its other parts. Others are to do with the understandings of international lawyers that their subject is general—it is a unified formation, with common resources of method and authority, not flints lying in a pile. In an environment with weak institutions and little organized coercive power, law's claim to authority is acutely difficult to sustain without some colorable claim to a unity or system of law.[5] Thus I agree that the unity of international law calls for a unity of understanding and of justification (this leads me to put my claim in this paper in general terms). But a convincing rule of recognition for a legal system that is not simply the inter-state system has not been formulated, so far as I am aware. Even if a convincing formulation could be devised, the updated Hartian concept of international law would probably still be too austere. Hart's jurisprudential critics have not, for the most part, focused on the applicability of their criticisms to problems of international law. This is much to be regretted, as international law, although in many ways a special case, is also in some respects a limiting case. In my view, more is needed for an adequate concept of international law than chapter 10 can provide. I try to sketch some further elements in this paper, without returning much to Hart's Concept of Law and the body of work connected to this, but acknowledging the considerable influence of that corpus on the argument that follows.

B. Framing the Argument

The aspiration of this project is to build, eventually and imperfectly, a theoretical account of international law which is both normatively attractive and practically operable. The normative and the practical possibilities are acutely constrained by the heterogeneity of interest, beliefs, aspirations, and life possibilities among the vast array of actors who have a stake in any such global project. A further constraint is that a theory of international law ought to make reasonable sense of the actually existing rules, institutions, and practices of transnational governance and international politics, including the aspirations and possibilities that lie within these. Such a theory must speak in the language, and encompass the patterns of thought and argument that international lawyers share or recognize, else it will not recruit them to the enterprise embodied in such a theory. The theorist must thus look at once to normative theory and positive practice, blurring putative separations between these, a technique which is both a comparative advantage of international law and a comparative oddity.

Thus such a project is immediately confronted with a set of problems about how to build a theory of international law given the conflicting pulls toward moral universalism and pluralism. One approach begins at the pluralist end, with independent actors constrained by no external law, and envisages the building of law by their acts of will. Such an approach might begin with a dyadic analysis of the legal relations between every pair of actors in the system (an approach emphasizing the bilaterality of legal relations, the applicable rules depending on what each particular pair of states have agreed), then look at the gradual construction of dense lattices of bilateral obligations (particularly treaties) treaties that are tied to each other (e.g., through most-favored nation provisions, and through replication and reliance) so that extrication of a single one from the structure is scarcely tenable, then at the eventual sedimentation of these into a fused mass of general international law.[6] Another approach begins at the universalist end, deriving general legal norms from core moral requirements, then attenuating these to make them operable in practical contexts, including not only the accommodation of institutional and informational shortfalls and situation-specific problems, but also the resolution of apparent conflicts between different moral imperatives or with different religious and cultural understandings. I am going to argue for a model of international law that envisages universalist engagement but amongst normative sites each embedded in their own specific moral and legal-institutional contexts. This emergent inter-public model is cosmopolitan and universalist in its normative community, and local and pluralist in specific decisions, but is neither strongly universalist nor radically pluralist in the authoritative derivation of norms or in their application. The key point is that the normative content of law arises not in its derivation from or consonance with universal moral principles, nor in the self-governing power of each and every politically organized community, but in the public nature of law itself.

A second set of problems concern the normativity of international law, which I will explicate and defend on the basis of a three-part typology: distinguishing between realist regularity and Grotian normativity on the one hand, and between Grotian normativity and cosmopolitan morality on the other hand. I will present a view of international society and its law as a structure of "inter-public" public law, an alternative both to realist understandings of international law and institutions as the mutable product of interactions between rational actors based largely on the pursuit of their different interests under the existing distribution of power, and to a cosmopolitan universalism which aspires to a global constitutional order. In contrast to the realist model of unitary rational egoistic interest-maximizing states, in which international law is an epiphenomenal summary of the configuration of power among states at any particular moment, I argue that international law does have a normative dimension that shapes its content and that pulls and constrains states and other actors—it thus helps constitute and embody a modest international society. In contrast to cosmopolitanist accounts of international law, which define the ideal content of international law by reference to free-standing universal moral principles (sometimes formulated as principles on which agents reasonably could agree or could not reasonably reject), and then formulate principles for the non-ideal world of international law in terms of the approximation or facilitation or non-obstruction of eventual attainment of this ideal, I argue that the normative content of international law is immanent in the public quality of law in general and in the inter-public quality of international law. It emerges through the practice of seeking law-governed relationships rather than as a deduction from a priori principles of morality. The content that emerges through this repeated practice has general and recognizable features that function to constrain actors in their myriad interactions with one another. These regulative norms are identifiably present in multiplying sites of international and transnational decision-making. They appear whenever there is a felt demand for presenting decisions as non-arbitrary, as more than the result of power-inflected bargains between parties in a contractual arrangement.[7]

The paper makes two major arguments. The first argument is that law—especially public law—has a distinct quality of publicness, which refers to the claim of law to stand in the name of the whole society and to speak to that whole society even when any particular rule may in fact be addressed to narrower groups. I argue that this quality is increasingly part of the concept of international law, and that this quality is having a transformative effect on the sources of international law, reducing the significance of voluntarism, bilaterality, and opposability, and increasing the significance of generality, solidarity, and the integration of international law into a conception of world public order. The second argument is that international law is shaped by the inter-public nature of the various processes in which states and certain other public entities come together to establish rules and institutions. My intuition is that states, being themselves creatures of public law, and being producers of national rules which have a quality of publicness in their orientation, come together with each other in an international legal rule-making and decision-making normative process that is not identical to a comparable process among unitary rational non-public actors. This intuition runs against standard rational-actor bargaining models of international lawmaking. Whether it also runs against contemporary cosmopolitan universalism is more complex. My argument is not inconsistent with a public of publics, or a society of societies, or even (to use John Rawls's phrase) a community of communities. But proponents of these formulations generally envisage a greater unity in international society than I do—in my discussion I will emphasize the irreducible pluralism of publics, and international law as a form of *relationship* between them rather than an overarching order, something that lies between publics while at the same time integrating them through the relational quality integral to law. This inter-public law consists, in part, of the internationalization of public law, and in part of an international law dimension of public law. In both cases the relevant normative practices are conducted at multiple sites, each site subject to local considerations as to legal principles, institutional meshing, and sources of authority, so that there is neither a simple unified global hierarchy on the internationalist model, nor a complete disjunction between different sites of law.

After this introduction, the next two sections of the paper present the two arguments noted in the previous paragraph. A further section distinguishes the view I am espousing from a commitment to democracy in international law. The conclusion returns briefly to the implications of my view for universalism and pluralism.

II. Publicness as a Necessary Quality of Law: International Law Issues

A. *Publicness in the Legal Theory of Modern Democracies*

I begin here with a core jurisprudential idea: "publicness" is a necessary element in the concept of law under modern democratic conditions. The claim is that the quality of publicness, and the related quality of generality, are necessary to the concept of law in an era of democratic jurisprudence.[8] By publicness is meant the claim made for law that it has been wrought by the whole society, by the public, and the connected claim that law addresses matters of concern to the society as such.[9] This quality of aspiration to publicness is, as Jeremy Waldron has observed, what Weber misses in his means-oriented definition of the state (as the monopolist of legitimate violence), and what analytical jurisprudence misses in its formal analysis of legal systems.

Publicness might be simply another way of referring to the specific attributes of law that Lon Fuller enumerated: generality, publicity, non-retroactivity, clarity or intelligibility, non-contradiction, non-impossibility of compliance, constancy through time, and congruence between declared rule and official action.[10] Clearly they overlap. But the idea of publicness as used here goes beyond these largely procedural attributes. It goes to the way law speaks to those it addresses, and to the orientation and amplitude society expects of its law. These are relational qualities. I will turn shortly to elaborate on the meaning of the requirement of publicness.

Before doing that, a brief note on the legal theory problems I am not going to address here. Lon Fuller regarded the attributes in his list as representing an "inner morality" of law—whereas Joseph Raz has argued that these attributes are not moral, but are simply instrumental, making law effective for whatever purposes it is being used for.[11] A broader conception of publicness may raise more challenges than this for theories of law. Such a quality of publicness is not, of course, sufficient for law—many theorists would argue that it must be supplemented by (inter alia) an efficacy condition. Efficacy is difficult to achieve or sustain without the subjects of law feeling a sense of obligation that is not mere compulsion, or self-interest, and the quality of publicness described here may be incorporated into legal theory as part of the way in which law generates this sense of obligation.[12] This kind of "publicness" may also be incorporated into the kind of rule of recognition proposed by H. L. A. Hart.[13] But the fit is not exact.[14]

B. Public Law as a Special Case of the Requirement of Publicness in Law

"Public law" may be subject to different requirements as to publicness than other kinds of law.[15] The reasons for this are both functional and normative. Public law, like the organization of politics, is concerned above all with managing problems of deep disagreement. Public law is also centrally concerned with the organization and delivery of security, services, education, religion or religious opportunities, and welfare—the modern equivalents of Cicero's salus populi.[16] These concerns can be framed in Hobbesian terms by reference to the self-interests of the citizenry. But modern states play a further role in enabling citizens to discharge some of their moral duties toward others, or to achieve their aspirations of altruism. Legal structures for benevolent services typically have both interest-based and altruistic strands woven through them[17]—welfare is understood as both social insurance and charity. Public law, and politics, are also concerned with varieties of liberty: libertarian freedom from unnecessary constraint and intrusion, freedom to make and live out choices that might be described as autonomy and measured in terms of capabilities, freedom to participate and to shape the public sphere that might be described as republican citizenship. These concerns of public law provide special functional as well as normative reasons for requirements for publicness in national public law. These requirements could be to better advance the wider public interest by in some ways mobilizing, and in others channeling and restricting, state power for public purposes. Or they might be requirements giving effect to what many public lawyers in common law systems argue is a distinct set of public law values, that may give special meaning to "publicness" in this context. Demands for similar requirements of publicness are increasingly evident in public international law, although the realization of such demands is presently very uneven, and will not become prevalent without considerable further development.

C. *Components of Publicness: General Principles of Public Law*

General principles of public law combine formal qualities with normative commitments in the enterprise of channeling, managing, shaping, and constraining political power. These principles provide some content and specificity to abstract requirements of publicness in law. Principles potentially applicable within any system of public law, and in relations between different systems of public law, may include to different degrees some of the following. This is merely an indicative list, without any comparative or doctrinal analysis, but it is sufficient to suggest that the principles embodied in such a conception of public law are significant.[18] These are normative principles, that do real work, yet they are not principles of substantive justice in the Dworkinian sense. In accepting the idea of the rule law, of the unity of basic normative principles rather than the rule of arbitrary power or the rule of the philosopher, this is the kind of list one gets:

(i) The Principle of Legality. One major function of public law is the channeling and organizing of power. This is accomplished in part through a principle of legality—actors within the power system are constrained to act in accordance with the rules of the system. This principle of legality enables rule-makers to control rule-administrators. The agent is constrained to adhere to the terms of the delegation made by the principal. In a complex system of delegation, it is often preferable to empower third parties to control the agent in accordance with criteria set by the principal, creating the basis for a third-party rights dynamic even in this principal-agent model. In the case of inter-state institutions, the states establishing the institution often style themselves as principals (severally or collectively), with the institution as agent, but their direct control of the agent may be attenuated, a problem they typically mitigate both by legal controls and by limiting the operational capacity of the agent. Thus international institutions usually depend on individual states to act as agents in operational implementation.

(ii) The Principle of Rationality. The culture of justification has been accompanied by pressure on decision-makers (and in some countries, on rule-makers) to give reasons for their decisions, and to produce a factual record supporting the decision where necessary. This is part of both political and legal culture. In both contexts it leads those institutions with review power into continuous debates about whether and on what standard to review the substantive rationality of the decision: manifestly unreasonable, incorrect, etc.

(iii) The Principle of Proportionality. The requirement of a relationship of proportionality between means and ends has become a powerful procedural tool in European public law, and increasingly in international public law, although some national courts (e.g., in the United Kingdom) have balked at unfamiliar arguments based on it.

(iv) Rule of Law. The demand for rule of law can mean many things. The dominant approach is proceduralist,[19] meaning a general acceptance among officials (and in the society) of particular deliberative and decisional procedures. This is prima facie in tension with a conception of the rule of law as simply a structure of clear rules, reliably and fairly enforced, without regard to their substantive content (the "rule book" conception), and with "the ideal of rule by an accurate public conception of individual rights" (the "rights conception").[20] Proceduralists argue for adhering to procedures even at the price of unsatisfactory outcomes—but face problems in explaining why any decision taken in accordance with prescribed procedures should not then be part of the law which adherents of the rule of law must uphold.[21] David Dyzenhaus has argued for an approach which shifts the focus of rule of law from law (and rules), to the element of ruling—so a breach of procedural requirements is not unthinkable, but involves a compromise of legality that must be carefully weighed.[22]

(v) Human Rights. I mean here the basic rights the protection of which by the legal system is almost intrinsic (or natural) to a modern public legal system. This category overlaps a lot with the previous four categories, but I list it separately to leave scope for arguments that some human rights (perhaps of bodily integrity, privacy, personality) are likely to be protected by public law as an intrinsic matter (without textual authority), yet without being subsumed into "rule of law".

D. Publicness in International Law

How does the requirement of publicness operate in relation to international law?

If publicness were simply publicity—openness to all to know—we might easily trace a liberal (Benthamite) project to make international law knowable to all, and in making it knowable, to increase accountability of particular makers of international law to others who have some claim on them. When Woodrow Wilson called for an end to "secret diplomacy" and a new order of "open covenants, openly arrived at" (a norm still embodied in the UN Charter requirement that treaties be registered with the UN Secretary-General for publication in the UN Treaty Series), he had in mind that this publicity, in causing leaders to take more account of public sentiment and to defend their international commitments in public debates, would democratize foreign policy and dampen diplomatic tendencies to bellicosity. Almost every intergovernmental institution currently faces demands to increase the openness of its decision processes: the Basel Committee of central bankers now publishes drafts of its proposals to receive comments from interested private-sector groups before adoption, NAFTA arbitral tribunals now accept amicus briefs from third parties, and so on.[23] This political commitment to publicity as an element going to the legitimacy of governance is often expressed as a requirement that legal rules and decisions be made publicly accessible if they are to qualify as law. This claim has not completely dominated the field, but it has had the effect of raising doubts about the law quality of much secret or unpublicized state practice which a century ago would probably have satisfied the sources test for international law pedigree.[24] Many inter-state agreements and understandings on security matters and intelligence are kept secret, but much of this practice—e.g., the silent transfers of suspects without extradition processes, or promises to share intelligence information—is not generally analyzed as making international law or generating international legal obligation, in the way that other state practice is thought to do. The IMF keeps not only the deliberations of its own board secret, but also many pieces of "advice" to, and understandings with, borrowing countries. It seems to accept that doing this means these materials cannot easily be jurisgenerative. A different kind of case is the WTO Appellate Body, which issues important rule-based opinions employing legal reasoning just as a court does, but has had to resist characterization as a court issuing judgments, not only for WTO structural reasons, but also because it is constrained to hold almost all of its hearings behind closed doors, and is thus debarred from modern requirements of openness to the public in legal courts.[25]

Yet publicness is not simply (nor does it always entail) publicity. Publicness is a way of describing that quality of law which entails law claiming both to stand in the name of the whole society, and to speak to that whole society. The idea of international law standing in the name of a wider society has long animated internationalist writers and legal scholar-practitioners. Many participants see international law as having an expressive function for the realities of international society, or the hopes for it. The language of international law is used not only to conduct international politics (although international law certainly is a language of politics), but also to express a degree of commonality in some sort of world order system,[26] perhaps a human social system for general purposes,[27] or perhaps a series of social sub-systems for regulating specific issues in which participants in that sub-system are interested. Many people, particularly activist groups, seek to use international law as a means of articulating moral positions, in the absence of other universal languages for international affairs. Some of these moral commitments—in particular, non-discrimination—have become almost immanent in the way international law is understood.

The idea that international law should speak to the whole of society is evident in the continuous efforts to nudge the field beyond states-will theories of sources, beyond bilaterality and opposability, toward community norms, beyond a focus on managing disputes and adversarial proceedings, toward a deeper structure of normative enunciation and claims arising from neighborhood and impact rather than contract and technical legal interest. It appears in the idea of *jus cogens*—peremptory norms applicable to all, which no group of states can contract out of—and in other modern natural law ideas. It appears in the frequent resort to "general international law" rather than simply the specific agreement made by the parties in a dispute—for example, when the WTO Appellate Body applies principles of general international law such as proportionality, or a version of the precautionary principle, or a general principle about treaty interpretation. It appears in the 20th century quest for universality of participation and for equality among participants.[28] This idea is one of the main obstacles to the use of "club" models in international relations—the struggle between diplomatic-club and legalist-universal models has been a major theme in the WTO and several other institutions.[29]

Practical examples of the operation of these two elements of publicness in international law are difficult to elucidate sharply in the flurry of pragmatics. I will offer two, while acknowledging that I am simplifying each rather drastically.

The first example is the law of foreign state immunity. International law requires that a forum state (say Canada) grant immunity to a foreign state (say Argentina) if anybody tries to sue Argentina in Canadian courts, provided that the acts for which Argentina is being sued were public, rather than being commercial acts which a private actor might equally well have undertaken.[30] This often involves examination of the public law of the state being sued, as well as examination of the nature of the acts themselves. Thus the United States was immune from suit in Canada over employment on a military base in Canada, Saudi Arabia was immune from suit in the United States over police brutality toward an American there, and Germany was immune from suit in the United States by an American over World War II reparations. But each of those decisions, despite showing respect for foreign public law actions, was criticized on grounds that this grant of immunity did not speak fairly for the whole society of the forum state, nor did the legal actions of the foreign state comply with the requirement of being fairly addressed to all those affected.[31] The European Court of Human Rights, in very cautiously floating possibilities that forum states should override foreign sovereign immunity where necessary to allow individuals to pursue claims for violations of their human rights by foreign states acting in their public capacities,[32] raises concerns about human rights and the minimum requirements of publicness of law which are both heightened and blurred by the principles of respect for the autonomy and political character of foreign public law.

The second example is the *Shrimp-Turtle* case.[33] The United States prohibited import of shrimp from India, asserting that Indian shrimp vessels did not meet U.S. statutory requirements concerning protection of turtles. The WTO Appellate Body did not hold that the United States acted contrary to GATT in refusing to treat Indian shrimp in the same way as identical shrimp from elsewhere, even though the text of GATT seemed to call for this. The Appellate Body deferred to a U.S. public law decision that demand from U.S. markets for shrimp was not going to be permitted to more grievously threaten turtles. But the Appellate Body held that the way in which the U.S. authorities took their legal decision was arbitrary or unjustifiable, in so far as the United States did not provide India with proper notice of its plans to find Indian vessels non-compliant, an opportunity to contest these proposed findings in advance, or a reasoned written decision it could challenge. In effect, the U.S. process did not meet some of the requirements for publicness in law, as these requirements were not limited to a public composed of U.S. citizens, but included affected Indian interests as well.

In giving these as examples, I do not mean to suggest that international lawyers have been uniformly committed to the view that publicness is necessary to international law. One branch of the grand tradition of the jurisconsult locates the international law adviser inside the Foreign Ministry, moving seamlessly between legal advice and diplomacy but placing the national interest above all.[34] However, even among the jurisconsults a different tradition holds the Foreign Ministry legal adviser as committed to basic values of the general applicability of international legal rules and the need for ministers to be able to explain a legally defensible position in a public context, even if the government chooses not to act on this legal advice—a tradition symbolized by Sir Gerald Fitzmaurice's advice to the British Foreign and Commonwealth Office against the Suez invasion in 1956.[35] That is, a public responsibility to uphold international law arises, for these national civil servants, from the public nature of the law. Outside the special context of government service, the idea of a quality of publicness as an aspiration in international law seems increasingly, although not universally, accepted by practitioners and professors of the field. But if this aspiration is widely shared, it is tempered by recognition of special functions of public international law in relation to politics. Public international law, perhaps even more so than public law in general, employs gaps and silences as part of the enterprise of establishing, maintaining, and regulating the political sphere.

E. Gaps and Silences in Public Law

The discursive practices of public law also include the use of gaps and silences to accommodate the political. International law, like all public law but often to a greater degree, has such gaps and silences. These gaps and silences are not usually total—they interact with positive principles and legal values in managing different questions in specific contexts. The gaps and silences may circumscribe, but do not necessarily negate, requirements of publicness in law; indeed, such bedrock requirements may help to give meaning to the gaps and silences. The following are illustrative examples of gaps, silences, and abstentions and of their relations to requirements of publicness in international law, in three different structural postures: 1. national public law on national issues; 2.

national public law on foreign policy or trans-border issues; and 3. legal competences of international institutions.

1. Examples of an international legal institution respecting the political dimension of national public law on national issues are readily found in the jurisprudence of the European Court of Human Rights. *Gorzelik v. Poland* illustrates a characteristic line of approach.[36] At the behest of government authorities, the Polish courts had rejected an application to register an organization called the "Union of People of Silesian Nationality" which in its memorandum of association claimed to be "an organization of the Silesian national minority." The EHCR ruled that this did not violate the right to freedom of association. The Court focused on the structure of Polish electoral law, which entitled parties of national minorities to enter Parliament even without reaching the normal 5% threshold, but was operated without any definition in Polish law of a national minority. The electoral procedures seemed to enable any organization registered by the government processes as a national minority organization to claim the benefit of this exemption without further process. The European Court seemed to accept this structure of Polish public law as being relevant to the international public law of the ECHR. The result was that the human rights claim was not allowed to displace the political process for dealing with what are, in Poland, weighty political issues, namely the issues of minority representation in the legislature.[37] In another decision in a similar pattern, the ECHR accepted Turkey's argument that the forced dissolution of the Refah Party in 1997–1998, preventing this Islamic party from contesting an election it may well have dominated, was justifiable because of what the Grand Chamber accepted was incompatibility between some statements of the party's MPs and core values of the Convention and of Turkey's secular democracy.[38] In earlier decades, the ECHR similarly upheld complex Belgian linguistic and region-based electoral arrangements, despite unfairness to some voters which in other circumstances might have been held to be rights-infringing, on the ground that Belgium had adopted a transitional compromise in a fraught political situation that ought not to be destabilized.[39]

2. Illustrations of international law accommodating a special political quality of national public law on trans-border issues abound on security matters,[40] but a more representative illustration be-

cause not overwhelmed by security concerns is the ECHR decision rejecting a claim by Prince Hans Adam II of Liechtenstein. The property of the prince's father was expropriated by the Czechoslovak government in 1945 under the Benes Decrees, and the prince now objected that Germany was allowing this property to be treated as "German" property instead of helping him to recover it.[41] In particular, when a painting from the expropriated collection was sent from Czechoslovakia to an exhibition in Cologne, German courts refused to allow the prince to claim it, on the grounds that German's 1952–1954 treaties put an end to Germany's rights to make World War II–related claims about German property. The ECHR accepted that the exclusion of his claim by German courts did not violate his human rights, broadly on the ground that the public law of the post–World War II settlement ought not to be unraveled by the ECHR.

3. As between international institutions, a comparable approach to public law is particularly evident in attitudes toward the UN Security Council. International courts are generally reluctant to engage in real judicial review of its actions on core security issues,[42] and the limitations to its areas of competence under Chapter VII of the UN Charter have not been closely controlled by judicial bodies. There is indeed a general tendency in international law to allow institutions established by inter-governmental agreement to determine the bounds of their own competence (the power often called Kompetenz-Kompetenz), constrained mainly by political pressures from individual governments or from inter-governmental political bodies who often control the budget and some appointments.

F. Alternatives to the "Publicness of Law" Approach

Some alternative scholarly approaches imply that the approach I have just sketched, with its focus on building a tempered requirement of publicness in international law, is much too modest. Contending positions hold (by implication, albeit not explicitly) that the publicness of international law is just an incidental feature in the project of building a global constitution. I turn now to consider alternatives to the "publicness of law" approach sketched here, beginning with consideration of current approaches to global constitutionalism.

Perhaps the major alternative to the "publicness of law" approach taken here is that of the multifaceted Habermasian school. One line of thought in this school begins the quest for public law not with the relationship of governors and governed, but with the idea of a public, and in particular with the distinction between a weak public and a strong public. As Hauke Brunkhorst puts it, a weak public has communicative power but does not have legally organized access to administrative power–basic rights are respected so it can deliberate, but it lacks constitutional authority to take legally enforceable decisions.[43] By contrast, a strong public exists where protection of basic rights and constitutional arrangements together make a strong coupling between public deliberation and legally effective decision. A weak public emerges where basic rights are protected (whether in hard law or merely in the practice of soft law), and there exist the mass media, political associations, political culture, etc. necessary for common deliberation. A strong public needs these ingredients plus a constitution which organizes the public power legally to take and enforce decisions. This concept of the public draws on Dewey's problem-solving approach to the formation of a political public, and on Arendt's ideas about joint action. It celebrates the "people power" of revolutionary publics, in the Philippines after Marcos, in South Africa and Central Europe in 1989, etc. On this view, trans-border weak publics, or even a global weak public, already exist, within the scope of the general patterns of rights protection now prevalent. The deliberative powers of these publics are only very loosely coupled to any decisional power, but this coupling might be strengthened by the realization of various kinds of global constitutionalism.[44] These global constitutional proposals often involve the elaboration on a global scale of ideas developed to meet the constitutional challenges of European integration. One line of these proposals is promising in that it avoids the familiar traps of simply wishing into being a global public created by communicative action, or of relying on the charters and institutions of global organizations such as the UN or WTO to get constitutionalism going. This proposal seeks to build, around the increasingly dense structure of European institutions and rules, a thick constitutional patriotism, in which the citizens of an emerging European polity embrace and interpret the common values of European constitutionalism not in a uniform manner but in ways that reflect different national politico-legal histories, different ethical commitments, and different politics.[45] Commitments to particular ideas on the purposes and limits of government, individual rights, rule of law, and even democracy are all thus placed at the core of European allegiance even while given detailed meaning in different ways in different national contexts. Even assuming that such an approach can succeed in Europe—a contested assumption—it is doubtful that international law on a global scale can proceed this way. It is very unlikely that any global constitutional-type instruments could soon command the type of allegiance and shared identification from a wide section of humanity that might get any sort of world polity going, even one accommodating considerable variation in interpretations and appropriations depending on variations in national traditions, ethics, and politics. In sum, I think the Deweyan problem-solving too soft and expert-oriented, the Arendtian joint action too limited and erratic, and the strong coupling of a global public with constitutionalist institutions too improbable, for this cluster of Habermasian approaches to be a likely platform for public law on a global basis in the near future, however helpful these ideas may be in world sociology.

Another important alternative to the approach to public law defended here is one that begins not with government and governmentality, nor with any claim for the autonomy of the political, but instead begins with spontaneous orderings in the private sector. Important work on contemporary juridification—the scholarship associated with Niklas Luhmann, Gunther Teubner, Christian Joerges, and others—can be understood as beginning with private ordering and advancing toward a conception of the public and of public law. This work anticipates that private orderings and official regulation will proceed not independently, but interdependently. Even if the rate of technological and market change is so quick that official regulation cannot keep pace, still a demand for elements of public regulation accompanies the more and more complex administration of matters affecting a wide public, particularly issues about risk. This kind of administration is celebrated the more it moves away from rigidified Weberian bureaucracy, and toward the open and flexible models of European Union comitology, the EU's Open Method of Coordination, or perhaps the evolving governance of cyberspace. But even if the form of administration is not particularly Weberian, the new forms are still subject to We-ber's insight about administration necessitating the deformation of law. This approach to transnational juridification thus casts doubt on the place for public law in any traditional sense. One response has been to revive a sources-based definition of private law, and of public law, then to call for a dialectical relationship between them.[46] I doubt, however, that a traditional sources-based account is adequate. My understanding of public law focuses on practice and principles as well as sources theory. It expects variation de-pending on the nature of the issues addressed as well as functional and value dimensions, and is not reducible to a sources-based defi-nition of public or private law. I conclude that the transnational juridification approach, while illuminating for legal theory and generative of an important research agenda, is unlikely at present to provide a way to frame scope conditions for a re-theorized pub-lic international law.

III. The Inter-Public Quality of International Law

A. Law Between Public Entities

The idea that international law is made by entities that are them-selves public—operating under their own public law, and oriented toward publicness as a requirement of law—has implications for how we think about international law. Instead of international law simply as agreements between juridical units, it points to the pos-sibility of understanding public international law as law meeting publicness requirements that is made between entities whose pub-lic nature qualifies them as having jurisgenerative capacity. This is, in short, the possibility of understanding international law as inter-public law rather than simply as *jus inter gentes*. The most important of these public entities are likely to be states. They are accustomed to the operation of the principles of public law of the kind in the indicative list sketched earlier. They are each equipped with a raft of institutions operating in a public law environment, and which will be involved in the international law process. Associations and citizens' groups within the state bring similar public values to their participation in international law. However, there is no strong rea-son to limit the category of public law entities—and of participants in inter-public law—to states. As trans-border interactions among all such public entities increase, situations where they bump up against each other multiply, generating conflicts of laws arrangements in the public law sphere.

A conceptual shift of this sort, if accepted, would be fundamental, even though its practical consequences might be felt only very slowly. Such a shift would probably be operationalized primarily by specification of the relevant (types of) public entities, rather than by routine international law specification of publics. In relation to any particular entity (and especially states), the meaning of "public" for international law purposes would routinely be described in terms of a renvoi to the relevant entity's legal and political arrangements, much as the ICJ in the Barcelona Traction case (1970) concluded that the identity and core governance rules of a "corporation" depend simply on the national law of the corporation, which international law recognizes and follows but does not tinker with. Thus one state may have a corporatist system, with political groups organized and represented by profession or industry or university, while another state has a mixed system of ethnic and territorial groupings and representation, and an industry governance association may have only regional peak groups as its members, but international law will simply accept the heterogeneity of forms and categories.[47] Efforts will be made to limit this tolerance. But they are unlikely to entail the robust commitment to political equality that has been embraced in most democracies for many decades; any prescription of equality would probably operate only to rule out egregious exclusions and abuses. Political equality would be at best a regulative ideal; and inter-region equity would be something less than that. Participation rules would also be loose. As is at present the case in global governance, some of the public entities might be virtually self-appointed.[48]

Operationalization in terms of entities rather than publics is likely to be juridically much more practicable (much in the way that self-determination in international law has generally been applied to juridical units such as colonially defined territories with arbitrary borders, rather than to ethno-linguistic peoples). In practice, public entities and publics will often go together. But situations in which the public entity is not an adequate representative of the relevant public are common. For example, a public entity with governing power may decide an issue, with full participation of its public under a deliberative model, and careful framing of arguments and reasons so as genuinely to encompass all of those who spoke; yet the decision may be taken by an entity whose public is not the public truly affected.

B. The Inter-Public Conception Illustrated: Global Administrative Law

I will offer here one example of this inter-public law in operation: the emerging field of global administrative law. A legal commonality is introduced to the innumerable permutations of contemporary global governance forms, through the idea that the various mechanisms for accountability, for participation, and for the strengthening or eroding of legitimacy in these different governance structures, are evolving not simply in parallel but in increasingly interconnected ways. This loose unity may be described as an emerging global administrative law, by which is meant the legal mechanisms, principles, and practices, along with supporting social understandings, that promote or otherwise affect the accountability of global administrative bodies, in particular by ensuring these bodies meet adequate standards of transparency, consultation, participation, rationality, and legality, and by providing effective review of the rules and decisions these bodies make.[49] It is practiced at multiple sites, with some hierarchy, some inter-site precedent and borrowing of principles, but considerable contextual variation. Thus the WTO Appellate Body now requires (e.g., in the *Shrimp-Turtle* case, mentioned above) member states to follow certain administrative procedures before excluding imports, the Basel Committee of central bankers now puts out drafts of its proposals on capital adequacy for wide comment before adopting them, the UN Security Council has adopted a limited review mechanism to make it possible for people listed as terrorist financiers to be delisted, the World Bank operates a notice and comment process before adopting policies and has an Inspection Panel to hear complaints that it has breached its policies, and the International Olympic Committee follows an elaborate procedure for athletes suspected of doping and has a review process culminating in arbitration at the International Court of Arbitration for Sport. This body of practice is normative and cross-referential. It is influenced by treaties and fundamental customary international law rules, but it goes much beyond these sources and in places moves away from them. It is a prime example of the inter-public international law of the era of global governance.

C. *Implications of the Inter-Public Approach to International Law*

Three implications of adopting such an inter-public approach to international law may be noted.

First, the inter-public approach may provide a way of encompassing jurisgenerative activity of market actors—activity that was placed largely outside the emerging *jus inter gentes* model as states (public) and markets (private) came to be separated in liberal theory. The inter-public approach may provide a basis, without great disruption of entrenched liberal positions, for addressing market actors as public actors when they exercise governing power (i.e., when they regulate), and for defining the relevant public in terms of those they govern.

A second implication of the approach sketched here is that some things should be non-public. This will entail fundamental normative argument about where lines between public and non-public should be drawn, and what their consequences should be. Some will defend the non-public (not necessarily the same as the private) as a zone of freedom, and of voluntarism; others will criticize it as a zone of oppression and evasion. To give one example of the cashing out of this in practical international law doctrines, it has been argued that the standard for review by a national court of a private international commercial arbitration award should not be the same as the standard of judicial review of public acts of a state.[50]

Third, an attribute of the inter-public approach is that it challenges a relatively untheorized but highly influential functional approach to transnational and international governance. In this functionalist view, there is nothing intrinsically (merely contingently) important about the state, nor even about an articulate conception of the public, as a basic unit in governance. This view favors any way in which governance can best be organized in terms of criteria such as efficiency, effectiveness, aggregate welfare maximization, and political viability. If in practice this means that some strong states do most of the governing, and other states are eclipsed in many spheres by markets or by specialized international institutions or by private governance actors, nothing of great value is lost. If this counsels for particular attention to states at risk of failing, and to supplanting their institutions in order to protect basic human needs or suppress terrorism or drug trafficking, so be it. I believe that one of the costs of this approach is that it misses the intrinsic value for people of the public sphere—the value of performing, and debating, and updating public values—activities that coexist comfortably with markets and private associations but are not reducible to these. States often provide important elements for a public sphere; but some states barely do this, and public spheres are also being built in other forms under conditions of globalization. The inter-public approach expects that states and state institutions will feature prominently, and indeed provides normative and functional reasons for expecting them typically to be the primary jurisgenerative actors, but it emphasizes that public values and public orientation should also be features of other forms of governance.

D. Does Gunther Teubner's Global Legal Pluralism Offer an Alternative?

Gunther Teubner, wrestling with the problem of identifying law in 21st century practices called lex mercatoria or the law of cyberspace, produces a concept of law that is more radically unmoored from the state.[51] However, the test of validity he proposes for this kind of governance is simply one of social coding: legal pluralism is "a multiplicity of diverse communicative processes in a given social field that observe social action under the binary code of legal/illegal." This is a formal view that has the great merit of not reducing law merely to function (I return to this issue below). As he points out, law cannot simply be any arrangement of norms that perform such functions as social control, conflict resolution, coordination of behavior, shaping expectations, accumulation of power, private regulation, or disciplining and punishing bodies and souls. However, rejection of the relevance of such functional criteria limits the bases on which any content criteria for valid law might be generated. This is a major problem in the absence of any system of authoritative sources, an absence that is probably unavoidable given his assumption of pluralism of normative discourse and networks. Teubner recognizes that the ability of diffuse global governance sub-systems to identify legal norms, or authoritative deciders, is weak. His idea is that such norms emerge in relatively autonomous cross-border social sub-systems, and are in effect self-validated through practices in these sub-systems that stretch the law over time, operate internal hierarchies, and externalize from the parties to arbitration bodies, professional and business associations, etc.

Teubner's account of extra-civil law has not overcome the basic problems of system and proof faced by theorists of international law from Grotius onward. Teubner tries to deal with the problem through anti-foundationalist analysis of discourses and social practices. Teubner's strategy is to shift practice out of domains of morality, or ordinary politics, and into sub-specialized communities of interest and expertise that are barely accessible to civil society or even to most of the educated elite. I do not accept this as a normatively defensible strategy for international law under modern democratic conditions. Instead, I believe it is normatively important to emphasize and build the (tempered) requirements of publicness in law, and I argue that the adoption of an inter-public approach to international law provides the conditions for this to be effectively pursued.

IV. What About Democracy?

The idea that publicness is necessary to international law and to law in general is not in itself democratic, but it raises the question whether someone normatively committed to this quality of publicness should necessarily be interested in giving a normative priority in international law to democracy. The idea that international law has, and should have, inter-public features may well seem also to be a waypoint on the path leading to a commitment to democracy in international law. The possibility that these ideas of publicness in law and inter-public international law aggregate into a democratic commitment raises many challenges I cannot explore here. But several basic problems about the relations between these ideas and democracy should be noted.

The incentives for someone whose highest priority is assuring the flourishing of her own national democracy will not necessarily lead her to support building and maintaining other robust and independent national democracies. The usual view is that each democracy is better off if there are more other democracies, because of the reduced risk of aggressive war between democracies, and because of democratic contagion and inter-democratic buttressing. But these gains may be outweighed by the realpolitik gains of having a pliant leadership installed in other countries of importance (for example, a dependent dictator may do a much better job of supplying oil abroad than does a precarious new democracy).[52] To have the government of a foreign state on the payroll of one's own state dramatically changes the structure of relations with it from the normal posture of international relations, particularly between states with sharply diverging security and resource interests.[53] These gains from pliant leadership may also filter into the political structure of the democracy, enabling its politicians to deliver more benefits to the constituencies to whom they are accountable. Thus in powerful democratic states, in particular, it cannot be taken for granted that pro-democratic commitments nationally translate into genuinely pro-democratic commitments with regard to all other countries. If this is correct, it is to be expected that democratic leaders involved in making international law will vary in the degree to which they seek to make international law genuinely pro-democratic. Those leaders who have been elected by democratic processes in fragile democracies are likely to try to use international law and institutions to lock in their current democratic institutions and raise the costs for coup plotters or foreign invaders.[54] Leaders of strong states with well-entrenched democracies will seek an international law that is not incompatible with their own national systems and those of their allies, and are very likely to favor an international law that advocates electoral processes as a means of legitimating fragile governments elsewhere which they have helped to constitute. But they are also likely to want international law to allow some play for pursuit of their political interests while impeding pursuit of the conflicting political interests of others.

If those committed to national democracy in the national society cannot uniformly be relied on to seek to promote genuine democracy in all other countries, or to favor an international law system which gives high priority to this, can they nevertheless be expected to favor democratic-type mechanisms and principles in transnational or inter-governmental governance? (I use the phrase "democratic-type mechanisms" here because I do not think there is any realistic scheme for international democracy on a global scale that is remotely comparable to the idea of democracy as understood nationally. So as a practical matter it is necessary to consider not an international analog of national democracy, but the application in international governance of some of the mechanisms and principles which currently help in the realization and operation of democracy nationally.) The starting point is that those who are committed to their own national democracy are right to see that globalization is potentially a threat to the realization of this commitment in its current form. It is true that globalization is in many respects operating to empower the state, and to increase aggregate wealth and welfare even if heightening intra-state inequalities as well as global inequality. But it remains the case that the people of state X are increasingly affected by, but unable to influence, decisions by policymakers of state Y or of intergovernmental or transnational networks: their votes do not elect these policymakers, their legislature often cannot legislate over them, their courts usually cannot judicially review them, and their power of the purse is seldom effectively exercisable to control them.[55] Given that isolationism is impractical or impossibly costly for most, the obvious response is to build stronger non-national systems of accountability in global governance, and to strengthen participation rules within transnational bodies. Paradoxically, in transnational governance this response is likely to intensify a particular kind of rule by technocratic experts, buttressed by other experts financed by industry or a few sophisticated NGOs with stakes in the issue—experts who are subject to forms of accountability related to professional reputation or to institutional financing, but who are largely beyond the reach of any general democratic politics. In so far as the oversight and checking of expert rule nationally has been a sustaining task of judicial review, and of small local groups organizing politicians and news media to intervene on an issue, the transfer of governance processes beyond their reach, to transnational expert groups, makes it more difficult for such vibrant national systems to thrive.[56] This may be a double loss–less and less governance is within democratic control, and the performative civic experience of enacting democracy may be felt less widely if such institutions wilt from diminished significance.

So while those whose highest normative priority is national democracy may also be unreserved advocates of an international law system that promotes democracy elsewhere, and that builds democratic-type mechanisms and principles in international governance, there are strong reasons why these agendas do not uniformly march together. Therefore, I do not think the inquiry into the value of the quality of "publicness" in international law can have as its normative starting point the commitment to national democracy. The Habermasians go along with all of this, but then assert that it is now wrong to have as one's highest normative priority the maintenance of national democracy, because we now live in the era of the post-national constellation, and democratic normative projects must address this in framing ideas of international law. There is much to sympathize with in this approach. But with regard to the subject of the present paper, my view is that, since I do not think there is any imminent prospect of a true international democracy (in global terms; I leave aside the EU and any similar regional projects), I do not see the inquiry into the quality of publicness in international law as being in itself part of the quest for a democratic jurisprudence, even though the agendas overlap.

If cosmopolitan democracy is not presently viable, what of the traditional attraction of the current states system, namely that it is possible, and indeed normal, for the states all to assemble and deliberate? Assemblies continue to be held regularly among all of the states of the world (in the UN General Assembly, or in the vast range of conferences on great issues such as environment, development, habitat, equality of women, etc.), or all of the states interested in a particular topic (the diplomatic conference to draft and debate the Statute of the International Criminal Court, for instance) or which have agreed on a framework instrument for it (the Conferences of the Parties under many major treaties). The more the states are understood as primordial actors, rather than merely functional institutions among many others, the more it is possible to sustain the image of the assembly as one of primal participation rather than legislative representation. But once the state ceases to be coherently univocal, and once states cease to be monopolists, the image of the Athenian assembly breaks down. This breakdown is by no means complete—but the topics in which it has occurred least, such as military security, are also those in which the assemblies have been least effective. In fields where the assemblies might work well, they cannot simply be redefined as representative legislatures, as they do not include all of the key actors and cannot generally assume the exclusive or preemptive hierarchical competence in the international lawmaking process that national legislatures typically claim.

The considerations just mentioned lead me to bracket the possibilities that a requirement of publicness in international law, or an inter-public approach to international law, or the two in combination, are intrinsically democratic. Democracy is an important aspiration, but I myself am only able to formulate the analytic implications of the two ideas discussed here much more cautiously.

V. Conclusion: Inter-Public International Law as Pluralism-in-Unity

The approach to international law outlined in this paper, if coherent, holds at least three conceptual attractions. First, it provides a structure for theorizing the pursuit and actualization through law of distinctly public values, responsibility for which falls on the society and its public actors rather than on individual law-subjects. Second, it provides one of the elements needed in the important theoretical enterprise of distinguishing law from the morass of approaches to governance into which it threatens to disappear. Finally, and perhaps most important, it provides an organized way to connect law to democratic state politics and to the politics of governance institutions other than states.

The argument of this paper represents an aspiration for international law as a kind of pluralism-in-unity. The argument for a requirement of publicness provides a basis for an international law that accommodates separate publics and their values but within the unity of a solidarism of public values; in so doing it overcomes the voluntarist contractualism that informs an international law based on bilaterality alone. The argument for an inter-public conception of international law, with multiple sites that are separately constituted but normatively linked and with some inter-site accountability, makes space for a practical and institutional pluralism within a shared global project. These arguments come together to build an international law that makes space for working democracy, but is not in itself democratic—rather, it is an international law of engaged pluralism, unified by a shared, if modest, requirement of publicness in international law.

NOTES

1. This approach to international law is sustained by a realist view of international politics that presumes that the (foreign) policy of the state and its enunciation in international assemblies is tightly controlled by a few key leaders and governmental agencies, that these state institutions are very strong vis-à-vis other institutions and social forces in the polity, and that the leadership acts rationally in identifying and pursuing a reasonably coherent view of the national interest. These presumptions are ideals—the realist tradition from Machiavelli has been much concerned with urging government leaders not to depart from these ideals, and statist international lawyers have built innumerable devices to keep idiosyncratic international institutions and legal arrangements intelligible within this framework. For details and references on statism, see Benedict Kingsbury, "The International Legal Order," in *The Oxford Handbook of Legal Studies*, eds. Peter Cane and Mark Tushnet (Oxford: Oxford University Press, 2003), 271, at 282-287; and Benedict Kingsbury, "Review of Stephen Krasner, Sovereignty: Organized Hypocrisy," *American Journal of International Law* 94 (2000): 591-595.

2. For example, the Forest Stewardship Council, a private entity, has developed detailed sets of criteria for sustainable forest use, and for certification of products from such forests, which are to some extent enforced by NGO monitoring and market pressure. The work of the International Standards Organization (ISO), which consists of one national standard-setting body (public, private, or hybrid) from each of country, is a further illustration. At present, this body goes almost unmentioned in general international law works. Yet it has set over 13,000 standards, including many with important economic, social, and environmental implications, and its insufficiently studied procedures include some 180 technical committees, 550 sub-committees, and 2,000 working groups, which altogether involve over 40,000 people. It has direct ties into *jus inter gentes*: while each country is in theory free to apply or not apply a particular ISO standard, the effect of WTO law is to insulate from challenge those national standards that are based on ISO standards, and to place considerable burdens of justi-

fication on countries that choose to set their own standards instead. It is also important in shaping markets. See Steven Bernstein and Ben Cashore, "Non-State Global Governance: Is Forest Certification a Legitimate Alternative to a Global Forest Convention," in *Hard Choices, Soft Law: Voluntary Standards in Global Trade, Environment, and Social Governance*, eds. John Kirton and Michael Trebilcock (Aldershot: Ashgate, 2004), 33-63; and Walter Mattli and Tim Büthe, "Setting International Standards: Technological Rationality or Primacy of Power?" *World Politics* 56 (2003): 1.

3. This argument is explored in Benedict Kingsbury, "Legal Positivism as Normative Politics: International Society, Balance of Power, and Lassa Oppenheim's Positive International Law," *European Journal of International Law* 13 (2002): 401-436.

4. H. L. A. Hart, *The Concept of Law*, 2nd ed. (Oxford: Clarendon Press, 1994), 227.

5. Gunther Teubner's account of law, in terms of the mutual checking between formal and informal elements in a series of self-validating social-economic sub-systems largely autonomous from politics, is one which seems to eschew any claim that a unified system of law is needed. See, for example, his contributions to Gunther Teubner, ed., *Global Law Without a State* (Aldershot: Dartmouth, 1996).

6. This is one of the lines of accretion illuminated by Joseph Weiler in his ongoing work on a "geologic" approach, see, for example, J. H. H. Weiler, "The Geology of International Law: Governance, Democracy, and Legitimacy," *Zeitschrift für ausländisches öffentliches Recht und Völkerrecht* 64 (2004): 547-562.

7. In this paragraph and the preceding one I have drawn heavily on an elegant and economical summary of my argument by Melissa Williams, who in summarizing it also contributed much clarity to it.

8. Jeremy Waldron, "Can There Be a Democratic Jurisprudence?" (March 2004 revised draft of Wesson Lectures presented at Stanford University, Stanford, CA, January 21-22, 2004). I refer to this presently unpublished draft because its brief discussion of this issue is important and has been a stimulus to my project. But I do not here enter into debate about particular formulations.

9. This claim seems to sit uneasily with the role of many national democratic legislatures in adjusting entirely particular and private matters by legislation—the vast number of private bills in the U.S. Congress and state legislatures, for instance. But we might defend Waldron by saying that these private bills are classified as private, in the U.S. Congressional Record for example, precisely to distinguish them from public laws, which do indeed present themselves as oriented in the direction of the public good.

10. Lon Fuller, *The Morality of Law*, revised ed. (New Haven, CT: Yale University Press, 1969). See also Neil MacCormick, *Questioning Sovereignty: Law, State, and Nation in the European Commonwealth* (Oxford: Oxford University Press, 1999). The Lon Fuller-type claim that the orientation of law is toward the general, not simply to particular commands, is treated by Waldron as separate from the claim about publicness, but seems to me to fold into it.

11. Joseph Raz, "The Rule of Law and its Virtue," in *The Authority of Law* (Oxford: Clarendon Press, 1979), 210.

12. See for instance Samuel Pufendorf, *Of the Law of Nature and Nations: Eight Books*, 4th ed., trans. Basil Kennett (London, 1729; reprint, Clark, NJ: The Lawbook Exchange, 2005), I.vi.5: "Now, altho' there are many other Things which have an Influence on the Will, in bending towards one side rather than the contrary, yet *Obligation* hath this peculiar Force beyond them all, that whereas they only press the Will with a kind of natural Weight or Load, on the Removal of which it returns of its own Accord to its former Indifference; *Obligation* affects the Will in a moral Way, and inspires it inwardly with such a particular Sense, as compels it to pass Censure itself on its own Actions, and to judge itself worthy of suffering Evil, if it proceed not according to the Rule prescrib'd."

13. Hart, *The Concept of Law*.

14. Part of Waldron's argument for a greater interest in democratic jurisprudence is that topics such as the quality of publicness in law have been insufficiently attended to in recent analytic legal theory.

15. Jeremy Waldron suggests, en passant, that in a democracy it is the business of society to be concerned with the whole of the law that stands in its name, even law focused only on private actors, so that a requirement of publicness prima facie applies to private and public law without fundamental distinction. But his argument is made against those who would in some way insulate private law, or private property and markets, from ordinary public-political engagement. This does not necessarily reach the question whether special requirements might apply to public law.

16. Cicero, *De Legibus*, III.6; Hobbes, *De Cive*, XIII.2; Pufendorf, *De Officio Hominis*, II.xi.3.

17. Duncan Kennedy, "The Structure of Blackstone's Commentaries," *Buffalo Law Review* 28 (1979): 205; and his "Form and Substance in Private Law Adjudication," *Harvard Law Review* 89 (1976): 1685.

18. See generally David Dyzenhaus, ed., *The Unity of Public Law* (Oxford: Hart, 2004), esp. Michael Taggart, "The Tub of Public Law," 455-480.

19. An illustration is Richard Fallon, "The Rule of Law as a Concept in Constitutional Discourse," *Columbia Law Review* 97 (1997): 1.

20. Ronald Dworkin, "Political Judges and the Rule of Law," in *A Matter of Principle* (Oxford: Oxford University Press, 1985), 12.

21. Jeremy Waldron, "The Rule of Law as a Theater of Debate," in *Dworkin and His Critics*, ed. Justine Burley (Oxford: Blackwell, 2004), 319, 323.

22. See David Dyzenhaus, "Aspiring to the Rule of Law," in *Protecting Human Rights: Instruments and Institutions*, eds. Tom Campbell, Jeffrey Goldsworthy, and Adrienne Stone (Oxford: Oxford University Press, 2003), 195-209.

23. Steve Charnovitz, "The Emergence of Democratic Participation in Global Governance (Paris, 1919)," *Indiana Journal of Global Legal Studies* 10 (2003): 45; Steve Charnovitz, "Two Centuries of Participation: NGOs and International Governance," *Michigan Journal of International Law* 18 (1997): 183–286.

24. Société Française pour le Droit International, Colloque de Genève, *La pratique et le droit international* (Paris: Pedone, 2004).

25. In 2005 the Appellate Body for the first time held such a session in public, with the agreement of the disputing parties. Many other international rule-making and decision-making bodies try to find a way of both being jurisgenerative and not too constrained by the public, by finding ways to avoid publicity for their documents and proceedings while also not keeping them formally secret—they want to be part of international law, but they fear that their good work as technocratic experts will be slowed down by NGO agitators or self-serving industrialists.

26. Kai Alderson and Andrew Hurrell, eds., *Hedley Bull on International Society* (Basingstoke: MacMillan, 2000).

27. John Meyer et al., "World Society and the Nation State," *American Journal of Sociology* 103, no. 1 (1997): 144.

28. Georges Abi-Saab, "International Law and the International Community: The Long Road to Universality," in *Essays in Honour of Wang Tieya*, ed. R. MacDonald (The Hague: Nijhoff, 1994), 31.

29. Robert Keohane and Joseph Nye, "The Club Model of Multilateral Cooperation and the World Trade Organization: Problems of Democratic Legitimacy," in *Efficiency, Equity, and Legitimacy: The Multilateral Trading System at the Millennium*, eds. R. Porter et al. (Washington DC: Brookings Institution Press, 2001), 264-294.

30. I say that international law requires this, because this is what most experts globally believe. But the U.S. Supreme Court in *Republic of Austria v. Altmann*, 541 U.S. 677 (2004) said that this is a matter of comity, not international legal obligation.

31. Not surprisingly, the subordination of foreign public autonomy to competing interests in pursuing claims against foreign states came initially with regard to financial markets. The U.S. Supreme Court holding in *Republic of Argentina v. Weltover*, 504 U.S. 607 (1992), that Argentina had no immunity in U.S. courts when sued on bonds it had issued as part of a

restructuring to prevent financial collapse of the Argentine private sector, was based on the commercial nature of a bond default, without giving any weight to circumstance of the bonds being issued by the government acting for public purposes.

32. See dicta in *Al-Adsani v. the United Kingdom* (35763/97) [2001] ECHR (21 November 2001), Grand Chamber, although the Court held that the United Kingdom did not breach the Convention by applying foreign state immunity to prevent a Kuwaiti bringing a torture claim against Kuwait in UK courts. See also dicta in *Waite and Kennedy v. Germany* [GC], no. 26083/94, ECHR 1999-I, in which the Court implied that in upholding immunity of an international organization from labor rights claims in a national court, it was relevant that other remedies achieving an equivalent level of rights protection were available against the international organization.

33. WTO Appellate Body, 12 October 1998, (1999) 38 ILM 121.

34. See, for example, the reflections of the then French Foreign Ministry Legal Adviser: Guy Ladreit de Lacharrière, *La Politique juridique extérieure* (Paris: IFRI, 1983).

35. Geoffrey Marston, "Armed Intervention in the 1956 Suez Canal Crisis: The Legal Advice Tendered to the British Government," *ICLQ* 37 (1988): 773-817. Press reports of the resignation of Elizabeth Wilmshurst from the FCO legal department after the invasion of Iraq in 2003 indicated that she did not regard the invasion as lawful under international law.

36. *Gorzelik v. Poland* (44158/98) [2004] ECHR 72 (17 February 2004), Grand Chamber.

37. The Court emphasized the roles of political parties and of all kinds of associations in the realization of democracy and pluralism, and noted that "freedom of association is of particular importance for persons belonging to minorities" (para. 93). But the Court was not prepared to condemn the structure of the Polish legal arrangements, even though they entailed non-recognition of a plausible group. In essence, the Court accepted that the state's actions (taken through the Polish courts) were to prevent disorder and "to protect the existing democratic institutions and procedures in Poland."

38. *Refah Partisi (The Welfare Party) v. Turkey* (41340/98) [2003] ECHR 87 (13 February 2003), Grand Chamber. The language and reasoning of parts of this judgment have very problematic aspects, discussed at the conference "The Turkish Welfare Party Case: Implications for Human Rights in Europe," Central European University, Budapest, June 12-15, 2003, proceedings forthcoming.

39. *Mathieu-Mohin and Clerfayt v. Belgium* (9267/81) [1987] ECHR 1 (2 March 1987).

40. For example, the resistance of the European Court of Human Rights to judging the legal merits of the military actions by various NATO states against Yugoslavia taken in 1999, *Bankovic v. Belgium* (2001) 11 BHRC 435; or the ECHR holding that a cross-border abduction of an accused person by one state with the connivance of the state from which the abduction occurs is not itself a breach of the human rights of the abductee, *Öcalan v. Turkey* (2003) 37 EHRR 238.

41. *Prince Hans-Adam II of Liechtenstein v. Germany* (42527/98) [2001] ECHR 463 (12 July 2001).

42. Bernd Martenczuk, "The Security Council, the International Court, and Judicial Review: What Lessons from Lockerbie?" *European Journal of International Law* 10 (1999): 517-548.

43. Hauke Brunkhorst, "Globalising Democracy Without a State: Weak Public, Strong Public, Global Constitutionalism," *Millennium* 31 (2002): 675-690.

44. For a social solidarity approach see Hauke Brunkhorst, *Solidarity: From Civic Friendship to a Global Legal Community*, trans. Jeffrey Flynn (Cambridge, MA: MIT Press, 2005); and for a systems-theoretic approach, Andreas Fischer-Lescano, "Die Emergenz der Globalverfassung," *ZaöRV* 63 (2003): 717.

45. Jürgen Habermas, *Der gespaltene Westen* (Frankfurt: Suhrkamp Verlag, 2004); Mattias Kumm, "The Idea of Thick Constitutional Patriotism and its Implications for the Role and Structure of European Legal History," *German Law Journal* 6 (2005).

46. See, for example, Christoph Moellers, "Transnational Governance Without a Public Law?" in *Transnational Governance and Constitutionalism*, eds. Christian Joerges, Inger-Johanne Sand, and Gunther Teubner (Oxford: Hart Press, 2004), 329, 337: "The discussion on transnational constitutionalism can be reconstructed by a distinction between two forms of laws. A private law framework defines law as the result of spontaneous co-ordination efforts. A public law framework defines law as the result of a political process, which is not autonomous, but is intentionally steered. . . . But an adequate theory of law needs a dialectical synthesis of both approaches."

47. Consider the slowness of international law, and indeed of many national public law systems, to deal in a sophisticated way with political parties.

48. Thanks to Jeremy Waldron for discussion of these issues.

49. The Global Administrative Law Project of NYU Law School's Institute for International Law and Justice (www.iilj.org) focuses on the extent to which there are, or should be, principles and rules common to this diverse regulatory practice. See, for example, Benedict Kingsbury, Nico Krisch, and Richard B. Stewart, "The Emergence of Global Administrative Law," *Law and Contemporary Problems* 68 (2005).

50. Gus van Harten makes this normative argument in forthcoming work on national court review of NAFTA investor-state arbitral awards.

51. Gunther Teubner, "Global Private Regimes: Neo-spontaneous Law and Dual Constitution of Autonomous Sectors?" in *Public Governance in the Age of Globalization,* ed. Karl-Heinz Ladeur (Aldergate: Ashgate, 2004), 71-87; Gunther Teubner, ed., *Global Law Without a State* (Aldershot: Brookfield, 1997).

52. Bruce Bueno de Mesquita et al., *The Logic of Political Survival* (Cambridge, MA: MIT Press, 2003).

53. Stephen Krasner, *Sovereignty: Organized Hypocrisy* (Princeton, NJ: Princeton University Press, 1999).

54. Andrew Moravcsik, "The Origins of Human Rights Regimes: Democratic Delegation in Postwar Europe," *International Organization* 54 (2000): 217-252.

55. Martin Loughlin, "The Impact of Globalization on the Grammar of Public Law" (paper presented at NYU-Oxford Workshop on Global Administrative Law, Oxford, United Kingdom, October 29-30, 2004).

56. This point has been incisively made in the work of Martin Shapiro. See, for example, Martin Shapiro, " 'Deliberative,' 'Independent' Technocracy v. Democratic Politics: Will the Globe Echo the E.U.?" *Law and Contemporary Problems* 68 (2005): 341-356. See also Janet McLean, "Divergent Legal Conceptions of the State: Implications for Global Administrative Law," *Law and Contemporary Problems* 68 (2005): 167-187.

9

"THE CENTER CANNOT HOLD"

A RESPONSE TO BENEDICT KINGSBURY

WILLIAM E. SCHEUERMAN

Benedict Kingsbury tackles one of the most significant issues facing normatively minded international lawyers today. In the face of a proliferation of legal developments (e.g., new forms of security governance, the growing popularity of international business arbitration and many forms of "soft" economic regulation, and novel forms of international economic decision making insulated from public scrutiny) in which the specifically *public* character of much international law becomes at best opaque and at worst unintelligible, Kingsbury offers a bold reformulation of the idea of international public law. In the ongoing debate about globalization and the law, Kingsbury follows a middle path between two political extremes. In contrast to neoliberal theorists who celebrate the privatization of international law and the apparent demise of some crucial traditional state functions, Kingsbury provides a robust defense of the public character of important facets of international law. In order to do so, however, he creatively draws on a rich variety of intellectual sources to move beyond conventional ideas of public international law: Kingsbury doubts that a mere nostalgic restatement of traditional legal dogmas suffices as an intellectual response to the challenges posed by globalization. In this way, he simultaneously distinguishes his approach from many on the left who continue to believe that the best way to respond to globalization lies chiefly in strengthening the nation-state's traditional legal and regulatory instruments. The result, as the reader is sure to agree, is a series of rich and multifaceted suggestions about the appropriate normative underpinnings of public international law in the new century.

Kingsbury's approach draws heavily on the English School of international relations theory, as developed over the course of the last half century by writers such as Martin Wight, Herbert Butterfield, and Hedley Bull.[1] Although readers unfamiliar with recent international political theory may miss this debt, it is indispensable for understanding Kingsbury's project. In the simplest terms, the English School has sought to conceive of the possibility of a third theoretical alternative to realist and cosmopolitan approaches to international politics. On the one hand, realists (e.g., E. H. Carr or Hans Morgenthau) are accused of succumbing to a crude Hobbesianism that inaccurately envisions interstate relations as taking the form of an amoral and fundamentally brutal state of nature. Realists oftentimes accurately capture the rough-and-tumble of power politics, the English School concedes, but they nonetheless obscure the extent to which a common moral and normative framework is necessarily shared by states and without which the modern international system could not function. If interstate relations were rigorously Hobbesian in character, how could so many of the familiar practices of international political life ever function with some measure of success, as they often do? According to the English School, realists simply fail properly to understand the significance of international society, defined as operating "when a group of states, conscious of certain common interests and common values, form a society in the sense that they conceive themselves to be bound by a common set of rules in their relations with one another, and share in the working of common institutions."[2]

Only because of the existence of such an international society can states "cooperate in the workings of institutions such as the forms of procedures of international law, the machinery of diplomacy and general international organization, and the customs and conventions of war" in the first place.[3] International society, in short, mitigates the ominous prospect of an international system guided by nothing more than a vicious struggle for survival. It spares us the horrors of a global Hobbesian state of nature by allowing for the possibility of a minimum of shared values among and between otherwise sovereign political entities.

The idea of international society might at first glance seem conducive to cosmopolitanism. In light of the political and moral fact of international society, why not establish a corresponding international political order, perhaps even a world state? Yet the English School has typically resisted the allure of cosmopolitanism, generally underscoring the normatively unattractive as well as politically utopian character of ambitious proposals to extend the scope of transnational legislation and adjudication. One fundamental reason for this is that the morality of international society is typically described as being a decidedly thin morality. Existing states remain legitimate vessels for moral, political, and cultural difference, and the morality of international society should not be conceived as "a mid-point along the path to a universal community of mankind."[4] On the contrary, it represents a reasonable and in many respects even desirable answer to the difficult question of how to accommodate pluralism and provide for a basic measure of order amidst the potential anarchy of the international system. The crucial mistake of cosmopolitanism is to overstate the depth of shared norms and values at the international level and consequently miss ways in which the modern state system serves as a sensible, though by no means ideal, institutional complement to cultural and political pluralism. Not surprisingly, a certain argumentative overlap between realism and the English School can generally be discerned. Both intellectual movements not only typically offer powerful defenses of the existing state system, but also delight in launching jeremiads against those supposedly too naïve to acknowledge both the political unreality and excessive moral risks of cosmopolitanism.

If we translate the English School position into the conceptual terms of the present volume, it might look something like the following. Realists offer a one-sidedly *pluralist* account of the international order to the extent that they (rightly) see existing states as useful containers for moral, political, and cultural difference while obscuring the significance of international society. Cosmopolitans offer a no less one-sided *universalistic* approach since they devalue the fact of pluralism and exaggerate the extent to which shared agreement on deeply controversial issues is possible at the international level. Only the English School supposedly captures the right mix of pluralism and universalism: correctly appreciative of the normative grounds for the present system of states as a way of giving expression to pluralism, its vision of international society simultaneously does justice to crucial universalistic normative elements of international political life.

Kingsbury follows the broad outlines of this argumentative pattern, aptly describing his own vision of public "international law as a kind of pluralism-in-unity," an attractive yet typically underrated theoretical "middle position" between the Scylla of realism and the Charybdis of cosmopolitanism. Directly building on the English School, he locates the intellectual origins of this middle position in the political and legal theory of Hugo Grotius, who—or so Kingsbury and the English School argue—provides a powerful alternative to realist Hobbesian and cosmopolitan Kantian models of international order. It was Grotius who provided a path breaking account of international society, we are told, and it is to him we must turn in order to make sense of the modern international order: Grotius is best interpreted "as embracing a minimum content of universally applicable rules of the *jus gentium* . . . with a pluralist overlay of additional norms based on custom or consent or the values of the peoples concerned."[5] According to Kingsbury, the Grotian framework corresponds well to the present international situation, where we see "pragmatic tolerance of diversity within an overall structure of values embodied in international society."[6] In short, it not only offers an excellent normative starting point, but has already gained substantial empirical footing in the everyday realities of contemporary international law.

Again very much in the shadows of the English School, Kingsbury's Grotius-inspired model recognizes the pivotal role that the existing state system will continue to play in the international order, despite the deep transformations undergone by it in recent decades. The interpublic approach notes that the "most important of these public entities are likely to be states," while remaining distinct from realist theories which fail to do justice to the fact that in contemporary international law the relevant normative practices take place at multiple sites, including some of a non-traditional character. In a separate essay, Kingsbury offers a robust defense of the increasingly unfashionable concept of state sovereignty, arguing that the modern sovereign state continues to perform valuable normative functions unlikely to be accomplished by any feasible institutional alternative.[7] Despite his views about state sovereignty, Kingsbury concedes that "there is no strong reason to limit the category of public law entities—and of participants in inter-public law—to states." For Kingsbury it is precisely the fact that international public law emerges at a multiplicity of decision making sites "so that there is neither a simple unified global hierarchy," as purportedly sought by cosmopolitans, "nor a complete disjunction between different sites of law," in the spirit of realist theory, that vindicates his third approach. In his view, what we today have is an international legal order resting on separately constituted but normatively linked multiple sites or, alternately, an order that "cosmopolitan and univeralist in its normative community, and local and pluralist in specific decisions, but is neither strongly universalist nor radically pluralist in the authoritative derivation of norms or in their application" (p. 173, this volume).

Much of Kingsbury's essay is devoted to the difficult matter of describing the normative cement that makes this shared global project possible amid the practical and institutional pluralism of present-day international law. But at least one facet of his answer to the question directly reproduces the traditional approach of the English School. The public character of international law apparently derives in part from the fact that "international law should speak to the whole of society," that it gives expression to a normative commonality that transcends state boundaries—in short, that it serves "an expressive function for the realities of international society" (p. 180). In somewhat simpler terms: the normative commonality or shared moral character of inter-public law rests on the existence of an international society which itself embodies common moral commitments that "have become almost immanent in the way international law is understood" (p. 181). Again, reminiscent of the English School, however, Kingsbury points out that this definition of public international law entails no commitment to international or global democracy, along the lines now advocated by cosmopolitan thinkers such as David Held or Jürgen Habermas. His general outlook here again mirrors the deep skepticism of the English School about possible readings of the idea of international society as a conceptual launching pad for global or transnational democracy. In the arena of international administrative law, he accordingly notes, "there are doubts that international society today sufficiently agrees on democratic standards to use them as a foundation for a common, global administration."[8]

What then can we gain by situating Kingsbury's approach in the broader theoretical framework of the English School? The existing critical literature notes that practitioners of this approach typically oscillate between "pluralist" and "solidarist" readings of international society. In some interpretations, writers describe the existence of nothing but the barest of shared moralities among and between states, whereas their competitors offer a thicker reading of the fundamental morality of international society. The pluralist wing of the movement tends to emphasize the fact of deep and probably irrevocable moral, political, and cultural diversity on the international scene, and it remains hostile to the view that much has changed to alter the fundamentally pluralistic character of modern international politics. In contrast, the solidarist version sees "the society of states as having the potential to enforce universalist ethics such as respect for human rights," going so far as to argue that "the collectivity of states has the moral resources within it to enforce new standards of international legitimacy built upon world-order values."[9] Striving to absorb the rational kernel of contemporary cosmopolitan theory, the solidarist wing is more open to the suggestion that recent trends—including globalization—have helped make possible a far thicker conception of international society than anticipated by the original theorists of the English School. What makes the story even more complicated and potentially confusing, as Tim Dunne observes in his insightful history of the movement, is that even individual authors within the English School—most notably, its leading theoretical light, the late Hedley Bull—probably embraced both views of international society over the course of their careers, depending on the historical constellation and particular policy issues at hand. During the heydays of the Cold War, for example, Bull worried that international society was becoming too fragile to support a more-or-less functioning system of international relations. At later historical junctures, in contrast, English School thinkers, including Bull, were more willing to embrace solidarist interpretations of international society and at least consider the possibility of ambitious forms of international institutions and modes of law.

This conceptual oscillation might be taken as evidence that the attempt to stake out a middle ground between realism and cosmopolitanism is more difficult than Kingsbury and his English School predecessors concedes. The conceptual tension looks something like the following. To the extent that English School authors embrace a pluralistic reading of international society, their views risk becoming indistinguishable from those of realism; to the degree that solidarist tendencies become dominant, their approach becomes ever more akin to cosmopolitanism.[10] For example, even the arch-realist Hans J. Morgenthau, despite his soft spot for polemics and occasional eulogies for Thomas Hobbes, acknowledged that international law and even international morality perform invaluable functions in preserving international order. It would be a terrible caricature of Morgenthau's ideas to miss the many ways in which he recognized elements of what the English School describes as international society.[11] Indeed, at closer look, there is probably more in common between the two approaches than initially meets the eye. Just to mention one example: a careful perusal of the English School writings suggests that much of its animosity against cosmopolitanism is in fact directed against proposals for a world-state which, of course, arguably represent one possible but by no means necessary institutional expression of a cosmopolitan normative perspective. In fact, most cosmopolitan thinkers today are hesitant to embrace the idea of a world state.[12] Unfortunately, Morgenthau shares this rather flat reading of cosmopolitanism, also misleadingly reducing its complex normative insights to the indisputably unattractive institutional demand for a centralized world-state outfitted with total sovereignty.[13] Although the story is a complicated one requiring further investigation, it arguably is hard to see how a rigidly pluralistic reading of international society necessarily might correct the alleged excesses of realism. On many practical matters, their positions are likely to prove quite close. By no means coincidentally, many international relations theorists continue to describe the English School as nothing more than a specific variant of realist theory.[14] The direct source of this misunderstanding is the fact that a pluralistic interpretation of international society functions to blur identifiable differences between the two approaches.

Alternately, as thin international society arguably evolves into a thick global society based on far-reaching shared normative commitments, the middle ground of Grotian international society potentially gives way in the other (cosmopolitan) direction. At least according to some influential accounts of globalization, this development is precisely what we have witnessed over the last course of the last fifty years or so: many writers now plausibly argue that the human community has taken significant steps toward realizing a far-reaching global consensus concerning many previously controversial normative and political ideals. Cosmopolitanism, in short, is more than a mere Kantian "ought"; it has gained a firm footing in many facets of contemporary political and legal experience.[15] If in fact we now find ourselves located in an increasingly global society, characterized by a far-reaching set of shared transnational and not simply inter-state norms, what sound normative grounds do we really possess for criticizing potentially ambitious models of global governance? After all, a truly cosmopolitan—that is, shared or "universal" global society—might quite sensibly culminate in demands for fundamental modifications to the existing state system, including a far-reaching abrogation of the principle of state sovereignty. If democracy and the rule of law, for example, are now indeed universally embraced, why not then try to extend their scope dramatically to the international level?[16] As their critics have long noted, the English School tradition probably makes things too easy for itself on this point. As Stanley Hoffmann has pointed out in an otherwise appreciative discussion, the English School occasionally caricatures cosmopolitan models of global decision making, even incorrectly attributing the unattractive idea of a world state or government to Kant.[17] By doing so, its representatives avoid confronting one of the tougher questions at hand: to the extent that international society is becoming both more intensive and extensive and thereby (at least in certain senses of the term) universal in character, does it not cry out for novel forms of no less universal lawmaking and adjudication?

This is why I believe Kenneth Baynes is absolutely right to worry that Kingsbury remains overly dismissive of cosmopolitan attempts to synthesize democracy and the rule of law at the international level. Like too many of his predecessors in the English School, Kingsbury's critical comments about cosmopolitanism remain at best underdeveloped and at worst misleading. In light of the many nuanced cosmopolitan institutional proposals on the table, does it really suffice to discard them as nothing more than the latest examples of old-fashioned utopian demands for a "simple unified global hierarchy"? This sounds all too reminiscent of one of the English School's favorite straw men, the centralized world state. But few cosmopolitans today endorse anything approaching the world state. In any event, one would like to learn much more about why writers like Habermas—or, for that matter, the German critical theorist Hauke Brunkhorst, who has offered one of the most subtle defenses of global democratization available thus far[18]—are necessarily utopian in character. As Baynes correctly points out, such proposals are both normatively and institutionally more sophisticated than Kingsbury's comments reveal.[19]

The fundamental conceptual problem here probably stems from the fact that in the intra-paradigmatic English Society debate, Kingsbury ultimately comes down on the "solidarist" side. Yet, like many of his English School predecessors, he wants to avoid endorsing the cosmopolitan implications of this interpretation of international society. As Kingsbury observes in a recent contribution to the Oxford Handbook of Legal Studies, "No longer is international society simply a minimum structure of basic order—it is more and more a purposive association based on solidarity. . . . This purposive quality is most evident in the emerging structures of economic governance, but also in the assertion and transmission of values, in occasional collective mobilization of force or sanctions, and in pressing demands for global structures of equal concern and respect and for global distributive justice (largely unmet)."[20]

In fact, in another recently published essay Kingsbury worries that even the solidarist reading of international society fails to go far enough in acknowledging the extent to which existing legal practice has become deeply transnational—and not simply international—in character. In his view, even the most creative English School thinkers have failed to cut "across the inside/outside distinction that has structured traditional public law analysis," and thereby inadvertently obfuscated the far-reaching ways in which globalization processes are altering international law.[21] In accordance with this seeming admission that thin international society is now well on its way to becoming a thick global society, Kingsbury's contribution to the present volume quite sensibly tries to sketch out a corresponding normative model of public international law.

But the resulting model may be more ambitious both normatively and institutionally than Kingsbury concedes. In his view, public international law needs to rest on normative principles of legality, rationality, proportionality, the rule of law, and human rights, and he devotes a section of his essay to outlining what these normative principles entail. Yet, this arguably represents a no less demanding model for an emerging "global rule of law" than we encounter in prominent cosmopolitan theories.[22] What precisely separates Kingsbury's model from more openly cosmopolitan approaches? If his main answer is that his approach, in contrast to that of Habermas and other cosmopolitans, avoids endorsing legal centralism or a "simple unified global hierarchy," he is making things too easy for himself. If I understand Kingsbury's redefinition of international public law correctly, it would require—or perhaps presuppose—significant agreement on many complicated and indisputably controversial matters concerning the legitimacy of law, not the least of which are much contested ideas of the rule of law and human rights. In his essay, Kingsbury's discussion of these issues borrows heavily from the legal theorist David L. Dyzenhaus' ideas about the legitimacy of law. A student of Dworkin who follows his teacher in underscoring the moral core of the rule of law, Dyzenhaus has formulated his ideas as an alternative to legal positivism and its attempt to separate legality clearly from morality: Dyzenhaus understands that his model rests on a number of normative assumptions that are by no means uncontroversial in character.[23] Even if Kingsbury eschews "principles of substantive justice in the Dworkinian sense," one might still legitimately doubt whether anything approaching agreement on such controversial moral matters on the global stage is likely, especially in light of the fact that they remain controversial even at the existing national level. If we consider such consensus non-existent or improbable, why claim that Kingsbury's views are somehow less utopian than those of cosmopolitanism? Alternately, if we agree with him that such consensus now exists, why is this model any less ambitious than many more openly cosmopolitan views?

Perhaps it is unfair to suggest that Kingsbury's approach cannot be clearly distinguished as neatly as he hopes from cosmopolitanism. Perhaps the center *can* hold, and Kingsbury is right to envision his model as a sensible alternative to the ills of both hard-headed realism and fuzzy-brained utopian cosmopolitanism. Unfortunately, the recent history of the English School suggests another flaw in Kingsbury's approach.

In his final years, Bull revealingly tended to move away from a rigidly pluralist interpretation of international society in order to emphasize new possibilities for what Tim Dunne aptly describes as "cosmopolitan solidarism" in international affairs. In part as a theoretical response to the seemingly worldwide embrace of human rights, Bull arguably anticipated the emergence of a thick transnational or global society resting on far-reaching shared political, moral, and cultural ideals. At the very least, he was increasingly willing to consider the possibility that reforms to the international order might be able to bring about greater justice on the world scale. International society need not be a limited to a thin morality that chiefly functioned to achieve a modicum of order and peace. There was now also the possibility of a thick morality, Bull implied, that might provide a starting point for achieving a just global order. Bull even occasionally suggested that the achievement of this thick morality might constitute nothing less than an epochal change in the history of international relations.[24]

By taking the idea of a transnational or global society seriously, while simultaneously trying to outfit it with an appropriate normative framework, Kingsbury can be fairly interpreted as trying to extend this line of reflection from Bull's late writings. Yet one striking difference separates the two positions. Bull argued that a necessary presupposition for the achievement of a thicker solidarist international society was that the wealthy countries of the North would need to accommodate the South's demands for far-reaching economic redistribution. Without a greater measure of economic and material commonality on the world scene, he grasped, ambitious solidarist versions of international society remained at best precarious. Indeed, only by accepting the necessity of economic redistribution was it realistic to expect the South to begin to see the North's emphasis on the virtues of the rule of law and human rights as more than normative fig leafs for great power political manipulation. In this argument, the aspiration for a thicker version of international and perhaps even global society required that the rule of law and far-reaching social and reform go hand-in-hand.

To put the point even more bluntly: a global society committed to humanitarian ideals of the rule of law and universal rights can only thrive on the basis of dramatically increased social and economic equality. Western ideals of the rule of law and human rights are unlikely to gain a firm footing if they continue to be plausibly associated with economic and social policies which exacerbate the economic misery of hundreds of millions of our fellow human beings. When they face starvation, otherwise curable diseases, and unnecessarily exhausting forms of hard and even humiliating labor, global society is unlikely to take an attractive normative form or even gain much of a basis in global political or legal life. This simple but oftentimes neglected intuition provides yet another reason why we should probably worry about Kingsbury's rather unsympathetic reading of contemporary cosmopolitan theory. In many regions of the developed world, the strongest political and institutional check on economic inequality over the last century or so has arguably been the deepening of democratic political institutions: it was political democratization that made possible the welfare state and social democracy. Liberal democratic society and culture flourished at the domestic level only because universal suffrage and mass-based political parties worked to mitigate the harshest features of the modern capitalist economy. Although it would be problematic to assume dogmatically that transnational political development necessarily needs to parallel the history of the democratic nation-state, it nonetheless remains difficult to imagine how we might combat material inequality at the global level without new experiments in cosmopolitan democracy there as well.

This salient point receives short shrift in Kingsbury's essay. The stunning economic asymmetries of contemporary economic globalization constitute a decisive feature of the emerging international society described by Kingsbury. If I am not mistaken, Kingsbury's predecessors in the English School were right to argue that we will need to tackle those asymmetries if our emerging global society, as well as Kingsbury's revised model of public international law, are to flourish.

NOTES

1. The two crucial texts are probably: Hedley Bull, *The Anarchical Society: A Study in World Politics* (New York: Columbia University Press, 1977) and Martin Wight, *International Theory: The Three Traditions* (London: Royal Institute of International Affairs, 1991). The latter is based on Wight's LSE lectures from 1950s, which Bull attended.

2. Bull, *Anarchical Society*, 13.

3. Ibid.

4. Tim Dunne, *Inventing International Society: A History of the English School* (New York: St. Martin's Press, 1998), 11. I have relied on Dunne's useful history in many different ways.

5. Benedict Kingsbury and Adam Roberts, "Introduction: Grotian Thought in International Relations," in *Hugo Grotius and International Relations*, eds. Hedley Bull, Benedict Kingsbury, and Adam Roberts (Oxford: Clarendon Press, 1990), 48.

6. Kingsbury and Roberts, "Introduction: Grotian Thought in International Relations," 14. Kingsbury's work is clearly part of a broader Grotian renaissance in international political and legal theory. For reasons I cannot go into in this response, I think there are good reasons to be skeptical of this trend.

7. Benedict Kingsbury, "Sovereignty and Inequality," *European Journal of International Law* 9 (1998): 599-625.

8. Benedict Kingsbury, Nico Krisch, and Richard Stewart, *The Emergence of Global Administrative Law* (New York: NYU Institute for International Law and Justice Working Papers, 2004), 35.

9. Dunne, *Inventing International Society*, 11.

10. Stanley Hoffmann sees a similar tension in the work of Hedley Bull ("International Society," in *Order and Violence: Hedley Bull and International Relations*, eds. J. D. B. Miller and R. J. Vincent [Oxford: Clarendon Press, 1990], 24).

11. Hans J. Morgenthau, *Politics Among Nations: The Struggle for Power and Peace*, 2nd ed. (New York: Alfred Knopf, 1954), esp. Parts V and VI.

12. See, for example, the essays collected in Jim Bohman and Matthias Lutz-Bachmann, eds., *Perpetual Peace: Essays on Kant's Cosmopolitan Ideal* (Cambridge: MIT Press, 1997).

13. Morgenthau, *Politics Among Nations*, 287-310, 469-485. On Morgenthau's ideas about the world state, see also William E. Scheuerman, "Carl Schmitt and Hans J. Morgenthau: Realism and Beyond," in *Realism Reconsidered: The Legacy of Hans J. Morgenthau in International Relations*, ed. Michael Williams (Oxford: Oxford University Press, 2008).

14. This reading appears, for example, in a recent work by a leading

German IR theorist, Michael Zuern, who classifies Bull as a "neo-realist." See Zuern and Bernhard Zangl, *Frieden und Krieg* (Frankfurt: Suhrkamp, 2003), 141.

15. For example, see David Held, *Democracy and the Global Order* (Stanford: Stanford University Press, 1995).

16. This is a central theme in Held's model of cosmopolitan democracy, for example.

17. Hoffmann, "International Society," 23-24.

18. Hauke Brunkhorst, *Solidarity: From Civic Friendship to a Global Legal Community*, trans. Jeffrey Flynn (Cambridge: MIT Press, 2005).

19. For the latest rendition of Habermas' ideas on these issues, see his *Der gespaltene Westen* (Frankfurt: Suhrkamp, 2004).

20. Benedict Kingsbury, "International Legal Order," in *Oxford Handbook of Legal Studies*, eds. Peter Cane and Mark Tushnet (Oxford: Oxford University Press, 2003), 295.

21. Benedict Kingsbury, "People and Boundaries: An 'Internationalized Public Law' Approach," in *States, Nations, and Borders: The Ethics of Making Boundaries*, eds. Allen Buchanan and Margaret Moore (Cambridge: Cambridge University Press, 2003), 303. This essay both underscores Kingsbury's debts to the English School, as well as eagerness to augment it.

22. For a discussion of recent cosmopolitan views of the rule of law, see William E. Scheuerman, "Cosmopolitan Democracy and the Rule of Law," *Ratio Juris* 15 (2002): 239-257.

23. See, for example, David L. Dyzenhaus, *Legality and Legitimacy: Carl Schmitt, Hans Kelsen, and Hermann Heller in Weimar* (Oxford: Clarendon Press, 1997).

24. Dunne, *Inventing International Society*, 149-151.

10

COSMOPOLITANISM AND INTERNATIONAL LAW[1]

KENNETH BAYNES

In the past decade or so there have been various calls for "global" or "cosmopolitan" democracy—most notably, perhaps, by David Held.[2] Sometimes these calls are based on empirical and quasi-functional claims about the supposed trends of globalization, the increasing obsolescence of the nation-state and Westphalian order, and the need for democratic politics to "catch-up."[3] One influential theorist, Alexander Wendt, has even spoken in this context of the "inevitability of a world-state."[4] More often, however, the calls for global democracy invoke various normative arguments—about justice, fairness, autonomy, or the further expansion of democratic rights. Some of these normative approaches look more promising than others. However, here I want to set these normative considerations aside in order to consider a different argument for cosmopolitan democracy—one that explores its relation to the idea of an emergent international (or global) rule of law.

In fact, the idea of cosmopolitan democracy covers a wide variety of institutional proposals and, contrary to some of its critics, rarely calls for replicating at a global level the institutional design of democratic governance in the nation-state or for establishing a world-state.[5] Held has been the most specific in his proposals. He distinguishes between short-term and long-term reforms.[6] For the short-term, his proposals concerning political governance include reform of the UN Security Council, the creation of a second chamber within the UN that would not be limited to representation of nation-states, enhanced regional representation and use of transnational referenda, and the establishment of a new international Human Rights Court that would include a broad set of basic rights and compulsory jurisdiction for their implementation.[7] Longer-term reforms include the entrenchment of cosmopolitan democratic law within national and supranational constitutions, a global parliament with limited revenue-raising capacities, and the creation of an interconnected global legal system.[8] As William Scheuerman has pointed out, Held's proposals depend heavily not only on global networks of IGOs and NGOs of various sorts, but, perhaps even more important, on transnational courts and judicial bodies to which these other agencies would in some sense be accountable and "so that groups and individuals would have an effective means of suing political authorities for the enactment and enforcement of key rights."[9] Moreover, according to Scheuerman, since global governance on Held's model would require relatively flexible forms of regulation, such reforms thus mark a significant departure from the classical conception of the rule of law. In his own work, he suggests that Held's proposals must be supplemented by closer attention to the role of reflexive law within a framework of more traditional rule of law virtues (e.g., the demand that procedural and organizational norms are relatively clear and cogent).[10] In short, while cosmopolitan democracy may demand more flexible forms of legal regulation as Held suggests, the new paradigm of reflexive or procedural law to which it appeals must itself be situated within a constitutional framework of relatively transparent and stable democratic procedures. This, I suspect, is the major challenge confronting advocates of institutional (as opposed to moral) cosmopolitanism.

The responses to calls for cosmopolitan democracy have been equally varied. Some have been highly critical of proposals to move beyond the Westphalian order suggesting that they are either premature, since there is no corresponding demos at the global level, and/or inherently dangerous, since they seem to open the way for a centrist and bureaucratic legal order that may prove to be rather despotic.[11]

Still others have argued that, however attractive in theory, global democracy is practically speaking both implausible and unnecessary.[12] Benedict Kingsbury, for example, argues that, short of a world government still conceived more or less along the lines of the democratic nation-state, there are other developments at the global level, particularly developments within international law, that may be able to address some of the concerns about globalization noted by cosmopolitans. Kingsbury mentions several important conceptual innovations that have shaped the character of international law and may play a role here: for example, the emergence of a concept of sustainable development among the OECD nations that has influenced the formation of both environmental law and economic regulation, the concept of international criminal responsibility (and final ratification of the International Criminal Court in 2003), and the concept of "transnational civil responsibility," expressed, for example, in the increasing ability of foreign plaintiffs to pursue damage awards for human rights abuses in domestic courts—primarily in the United States. It also is in this context that Kingsbury points to the increasingly public character of international law. These and other developments suggest to Kingsbury an expanding if precarious international legal system that is gradually establishing the rule of law at the international level. However, rather than buttressing calls for cosmopolitan democracy along the lines proposed by Held, Kingsbury suggests that the emerging international society is more likely to be pluralist or Grotian in character.[13]

I believe that Kingsbury points to some interesting and important developments and that he is right to draw attention to the emerging forms of global governance that stop short of some of the proposals associated with more robust forms of cosmopolitan democracy. However, if he is right about the various ways in which aspects of the rule of law are being realized at the international level, then I think there is also a basis for expecting the emergence of cosmopolitan democratic institutions as well, perhaps even along the lines indicated by Held. This is primarily because, as I shall suggest in a moment, just as there is a relation of mutual presupposition between the ideas of democracy and the rule of law at the level of the nation-state, I see no particular reason for not assuming that this should be true as well at the global level at least in some measure.

Let me begin with a brief summary of Kingsbury's argument. According to Kingsbury, recent reflection on the character of international law has been insufficiently attentive to its distinctively public character or what he calls its "publicness." This failure, in turn, has impeded an interpretation of international law that is distinct from both skeptical or realist models, on the one hand, and excessively normative ones or, in his phrase, "fanciful cosmopolitanism," on the other. The realist model, I gather, strictly speaking reserves the label "public" for laws created by the sovereign of the respective nation-state and so denies that international law could have a truly "public character"—much as it also denies there could even be any genuine international law. The normative or cosmopolitan model, on the other hand, might similarly argue that the public character of international law would require a global democratic sovereign and, accordingly, real steps toward supra-national democratic institutions. The originality of Kingsbury's proposal lies in a refashioned notion of the "public" that is detached from a claim about its source in a sovereign legislator (whether a nation-state or world-state)—it concerns most broadly and most generally "the relationship of governors and governed" (p. 186, this volume). For Kingsbury, "Public law is here understood as the law that empowers the state and that regulates state power. National public law usually has its locus within the state, but it is internationalized insofar as it is shaped by, and shapes, traditional international legal rules, international public policy, and transnational ethical norms."[14] He then further links this notion of (international) public law with the idea of a dispersed sovereignty or exercise of law from multiple and overlapping sites. As he describes it, "the relevant normative practices are conducted at multiple sites, each site subject to local considerations as to legal principles, institutional meshing, and sources of authority, so that there is neither a simple unified global hierarchy on the internationalist model, nor a complete disjunction between different sites of law" (p. 175). The result is accordingly a return to the Grotian *jus gentium,* but at the same time it is a modest proposal that stops short of a call for a more robust cosmopolitan democracy.

I would first like to unpack Kingsbury's idea of the publicness of international law and suggest that, in contrast to Hobbes and Kant, respectively, it parallels at least in some respects Rawls's strategy in

The Law of Peoples. This is most evident in Kingsbury's emphasis on the "political" character of public law and the contrast he draws, for example, between his own and Dworkin's justice-based approach.[15] I will then suggest that it also shares some of the same weaknesses of Rawls's approach. Finally I will suggest that his embrace of a (restricted) pluralism is not unique to his particular approach but also finds support among at least some cosmopolitans if only as one element in a more explicitly democratic or "republican" approach.

Let me indicate what I consider to be distinctive about Kingsbury's notion of the public character of law. There are, of course, a number of senses of public law. Traditionally, public law deals with the powers and limits of the state or political rule or with what concerns the "commonweal."[16] In Hobbes, it refers more directly to the law (or will) of the political sovereign, such that all law is public that, with only a few constraints, issues from the established sovereign power.[17] This traditional account of public law can also be found in Kant. However, Kant also introduced his own novel conception of publicity and public reason that goes beyond this traditional account. In "What is Enlightenment?" Kant proposed an idiosyncratic account of the public and private uses of reason. A public use of reason refers, not to the reasoning of citizens in their role as civil servants or state bureaucrats, but to the reasoning of citizens directed at the enlightened ("reading") public. Thus, in something of a reversal of familiar terminology, a private use of reason is "that which a person may make of it in a particular civil post or office," where the audience is restricted, while a public use of reason occurs when the same person "as a scholar addressing the real public (i.e., the world at large) . . . speaks in his own person."[18] As Onora O'Neill points out, what distinguishes the public use of reason is its appeal to an unrestricted audience in which, to borrow a phrase, nothing but the force of the better argument prevails. For Kant, this notion of public reason could in turn serve as a check on the exercise of legislative power and, in that context, Kant introduces a variant of the categorical imperative that he calls "the transcendental principle of public right": "All actions affecting the rights of other human beings are wrong if their maxim is not compatible with their being made public."[19] Public reason (and hence the further "publicness" of public law sanctioned by it) can thus claim its public character on three grounds. Its publicness arises from the specific actors exercising it, its particular content, and the practices associated with it:[20] namely, private citizens deliberating collectively about the common good via both formally and informally instituted practices. Indeed, Kingsbury appears to endorse a similar view when he states that "[p]ublicness is a way of describing that quality of law which entails law claiming both to stand in the name of the whole society, and to speak to that whole society" (p. 180). For Kant, the principle of public right or publicity, together with the widening scope of the public use of reason, is arguably also one basis for his call for cosmopolitan law and a confederation of free republics oriented to perpetual peace.[21]

Kingsbury's conception of the public character of law, however, is ultimately neither Hobbesian nor Kantian. He proposes a third model that has it roots in the political thought of Grotius and, more recently (if I have read him correctly), in Hedley Bull's notion of an international society. The public character of law does not have its source exclusively in the political sovereign (who acts in a unitary and rational manner), nor is it the same as that associated with Kant's notion of the public use of reason by private citizens seeking the common good. Kingsbury proposes a more pragmatic and "political" approach that fashions a notion of public from the practice of international law and from customary norms and values that have taken shape in international society. The public character of international law arises from an "inter-public process" that includes multiple actors in addition to states and draws on principles and norms not limited to universal moral norms: "The key point is that the normative content of law arises not in its derivation from or consonance with universal moral principles, nor in the self-governing power of each and every politically organized community, but in the public nature of law itself" (p. 173). Among the various elements that compose this alternative notion of publicness, Kingsbury mentions its "political character" (p. 182), its claim "to speak to the whole society" (p. 180), its inclusion of fundamental human rights (p. 182), its integrative role in a conception of "world political order," and its relation to a notion of social solidarity or a "solidarism of public values" (p. 197). However, these elements are not all given equal weight or attention. Kingsbury, for example, says little about the connection between the public character of law and the basic rights and liberties of citizens. He emphasizes more than once the claim that public law speaks to (and in behalf of) society as a whole (p. 174 and 181). However the principal feature seems to be that it is law that defines and enables the complex relationship between the governors and the governed. He also stresses at several points that it builds on a solidarism of public values rather than a narrower conception of instrumental rationality. I want to suggest, very briefly, some similarities this approach has to Rawls's "political" approach in *The Law of Peoples*.[22]

As is often noted by critics, Rawls's *The Law of Peoples* departs significantly from the liberal and egalitarian framework of *A Theory of Justice*.[23] The parties to the social contract at the international level are, importantly, not representatives of individuals but representatives of "peoples." Further, the representatives include not only liberal regimes but also what Rawls calls "decent" political societies. Finally, their motivation is not to secure the same set of primary social goods, but rather their political independence together with a more limited set of rights and liberties. This refashioning of the character and terms of the international contract has been highly criticized by egalitarian and cosmopolitan theorists. However, fewer critics have noted the deeper continuity between *The Law of Peoples* and *Political Liberalism* and, in particular, the similar role played by the idea of a free-standing political conception, together with a principle of toleration. In fact, in contrast to Kantian model of public reason, in Rawls, as the potential audience of public reason widens—now to include decent societies as well as liberal regimes—the constraints imposed by public reason are reduced. The motivation for this seems to be Rawls's conviction that a principle of reciprocity is violated and liberal regimes fail to show toleration if they expect agreement on the same set of liberal rights and liberties that it is reasonable for them to acknowledge at the level of the domestic contract. Or, to put it differently, his "political" approach looks for an agreement on a more limited set of public values it is reasonable for decent but not liberal societies to accept.

Though I can't develop the claim in any detail here, I would argue that Kingsbury's approach has many similarities with Rawls's position in *The Law of Peoples*, especially Rawls's "political" approach which looks for an agreement on a limited set of public values it is reasonable for decent but not liberal societies to accept. There are no doubt differences between Rawls's position and Kingsbury's neo-Grotian model as well. For example, at least according to Hedley Bull, Grotius importantly held that it is individual citizens (not only states or peoples) who are members of the international society.[24] On the other hand, it does seem to parallel the pragmatic approach advocated by Rawls. Kingsbury's call for an "autonomous" or free-standing political conception of international law—though presented within a more explicitly Schmittian framework—also parallels Rawls's political conception. Further, Kingsbury's contrast between his conception and a Hobbesian or "rational agent" model of public entities is similar to Rawls's claim that peoples are moral and not solely rational actors. Most important, however, is the shared focus on an "overlapping consensus" or "solidarism" of core political values.

Rawls also describes his "law of peoples" as a "realistic utopia." It seeks what is feasible given the fact of international pluralism. Kingsbury's contribution is less explicit on this score. He describes his position as "a broader view of the entities responsible for making international law, and a more demanding view of what is needed to make international law" (p. 167). At the same time, the general tone of the paper is certainly favorable toward the shifts he sees in international law while his reservations about a greater emphasis on democracy seem, at least in part, to be a judgment about what is both feasible and desirable at the international level. It thus does not seem inappropriate to describe his contribution as an exercise in "realistic utopianism" as well.

However, these similarities with Rawls also point to some potential weaknesses in Kingsbury's position. In particular, it is difficult to assess the role played by the corresponding empirical and normative claims, and the call for a "realistic utopia"—or dismissal of "fanciful cosmopolitanism"—can operate in ways that undermine normative commitments. For example, Kingsbury writes, "Interpublic law consists, in part, of the internationalization of public law, and in part of an international law dimension of public law" (p. 175). To repeat, Kingsbury surely considers the increase in the public character of law a positive trend. However, it is less clear what more specific public values are to be included and what the normative limits of publicity are—why, for example, does it not include a demand for greater democratization? Kingsbury's own position—like Rawls's—seems to be more political or pragmatic at this point (p. 175). However, again like Rawls, it is at just this point that a clearer distinction between empirical interpretation and normative commitments would be helpful.[25]

Kingsbury suggests that the public (and "interpublic") character of law advances pluralism but not necessarily democracy (pp. 193–194). By pluralism, I assume he means more or less the trend to dispersed and multi-level sovereignty. However, this trend has been recognized and embraced by many cosmopolitans as well. As David Held points out, modern republican theory, including recent democratic theory, generally works with an unquestioned conception of political sovereignty in which the state is conceived as "a circumscribed structure of power with supreme jurisdiction over territory accountable to determined citizen body."[26] Democratic theory in particular traditionally assumes a remarkably unitary conception of sovereignty in its commitment to what Held calls a "symmetrical" and "congruent" relationship between political decision makers and the recipients of political decision or "stakeholders": "In fact, symmetry and congruence are assumed at two crucial points: the first between citizen-voters and the decision-makers whom they are, in principle, able to hold to account; and secondly, between the output (decisions, policies, etc.) of decisionmakers and their constituents—ultimately, 'the people' in a delimited territory."[27]

Yet, as Held notes, this conception of sovereignty is barely recognizable in the contemporary world. Trends toward global interconnectedness have both modified and constrained the exercise of sovereignty and called into question its assumptions about symmetry and congruence. Processes of globalization have produced structures of decision making that are less tied to the legal jurisdiction of the nation-state and hence also less accountable; at the same time those decisions still made within the legal framework of the nation-state frequently have consequences that go well beyond national territorial borders.

Following a suggestion of Hedley Bull, Held describes the results of these trends as a kind of neo-medieval international order—"a modern and secular counterpart to the kind of political organization that existed in Christian Europe in the Middle Ages, the essential characteristic of which was a system of overlapping authority and multiple loyalties."[28] In apparent contrast to Bull, however, Held suggests that the model of overlapping authorities and criss-crossing loyalties continues to offer some normatively attractive features.

Similarly, Thomas Pogge has also proposed a model of differentiated or dispersed sovereignty in connection with the cosmopolitan ideal: "What I am proposing instead is not the idea of a world State, which is really as variant of the preeminent state idea. Rather, the proposal is that governmental authority—or sovereignty—be widely dispersed in the vertical dimension. What we need is both centralization and decentralization—a kind of second-order decentralization away from the now dominant level of the state."[29]

As Pogge goes on to point out, differentiated or dispersed sovereignty is not simply the product of actual social, political, and economic trends; considerations of peace and security, global economic justice, and environmental preservation provide reasons for preferring such dispersed sovereignty from a normative point of view as well. Equally important for Pogge is the consideration of democracy itself: "Persons have a right to an institutional order under which those significantly and legitimately affected by a political decision have a roughly equal opportunity to influence the making of this decision—either directly or through elected delegates or representatives."[30] For Pogge, as for Held, increasing global interdependence requires that new forms of decision making be developed that are able to secure simultaneously mechanisms for local autonomy and effective input and accountability on global issues that impact individual lives—in other words, both centralization and decentralization in a dispersal of state sovereignty.

I mention the views of Held and Pogge to suggest that cosmopolitans too have looked favorably on this idea of pluralism yet, apparently in contrast to Kingsbury, don't see it as conflicting with democracy. Rather, many of them see it as the basis for a new and emerging form of cosmopolitan democracy and alternative form of global governance.[31] Archibugi for example locates cosmopolitan democracy "midway" between a confederation of states and a global federal system, and Habermas too, in his reflections on the "postnational constellation," describes not a centralized world-state, but rather multi-level forms of governance within an "international negotiating system."[32] This leads me to propose a different interpretation of the various phenomena that Kingsbury has identified. To repeat my earlier conjecture, if there is indeed an emergent rule of law at the international level, then this equally both encourages and demands the development of democratic institutions at the global level.

The central claim I wish to advance then, in response to Kingsbury, is that there is an important normative connection between democracy and the rule of law.[33] At the level of the democratic *Rechtsstaat*, Habermas has described this connection as "gleichursprunglich" (co-original) or one of mutual supposition. It is not immediately obvious what the force or basis of this claim is: clearly, not all democracies consistently adhere to the rule of law; and the rule of law—at least in one of its narrower senses—can be found in non-democratic regimes. It is also not obvious that there is a strong analytic or conceptual connection between these two ideals—and at least some theorists have resisted that proposal.[34] My own suggestion is that the best way to understand this claim about the reciprocal dependence or mutual supposition of democracy and the rule of law is in terms of a kind of immanent developmental tendency contained in each of these ideas—somewhat along the lines of Hegel's views about the inner logic of a "Begriff." More specifically, in an increasingly "rationalized" world (in Weber's sense), the virtues traditionally associated with the rule of law can only be secured procedurally through processes of democratic will-formation. Let me, by way of conclusion, offer a few remarks in support of this hypothesis and briefly note its relevance for cosmopolitan democracy.

It is sometimes supposed that the rule of law is in conflict with the idea of democratic rule or "popular sovereignty." Similarly, it is also argued that the related idea of legal adjudication is undemocratic, at least if judges are not subject to direct means of democratic accountability.[35] However, I believe this is a misunderstanding that arises from an overly concrete interpretation of what these ideals demand, especially concerning the institutional conditions required for realizing the idea of the rule of law. Of course, if the rule of law is contrasted with the "rule of men" then no reconciliation will be possible. However, recent analyses of the rule of law suggest that this ideal incorporates a variety of political values and that it cannot be adequately described by reference to only one of these values (such as legal formality).[36] Thus, in a comprehensive review, Richard Fallon suggests that there are at least four "types" of rule of law (historicist, formalist, process, and substantive) and that no one of these types alone captures its role in contemporary legal practice.[37] Rather, elements of each type are important and if, as he suggests, one looks to the various "interests" served by the rule of law (clarity, predictability, accountability, public justification, etc.), then a case can be made, not only that the rule of law is compatible with democracy, but that democracy (itself conceived as set of institutions for public debate and decision making) itself both requires the rule of law and anticipates some institutional structures well-suited for its realization. As Jean Hampton has argued in the context of a friendly amendment to Hart's conception of law as a system of primary and secondary rules, democracy offers a set of rules for how legal rules are to be changed.[38] Of course, at some level, these rules must themselves be included in what Hart called the "rule of recognition"; but it is a distinctive feature of a democracy that the rules for changing the rules of the game themselves be legally specified, at least in a broad sense (e.g., through inclusion in a democratic constitution). At the same time, one function of the rule of law (and the role of law, generally) is to provide a relatively stable, predictable, and publicly justifiable set of norms in accordance with which citizens can regulate their interactions with one another. An institutional account of the relation between deliberative democracy and the rule of law, as well as the separation of political powers more generally, certainly needs to be explored empirically and allows for a variety of institutional forms. But, such a conception, I believe, allows one to see how the rule of law can play an important constitutive role in realizing a deliberative democracy, and, more specifically, how processes of legal adjudication as the task of a (more or less) autonomous legal community can be "rational," without invoking an overly rule-based conception of law.[39] The idea is that both institutions of legal reasoning and legal argument and institutions of political deliberation and will-formation necessarily complement one another in seeking to express a more general conception of public deliberation. More important, it also suggests how the idea of the rule of law expresses a commitment to forms and procedures of practical reasoning—a "theatre of debate," to borrow Dworkin's phrase—

that both complements yet requires other institutions of public reason and deliberation best expressed in the idea of a deliberative democracy. Neil McCormick has also recently emphasized the "public reasoning" aspect of the rule of law as an indispensable complement to the dimension of "legal certainty."[40] Further, to return now to Kingsbury's thesis, I also see no particular reason not to see this same relation between democracy and the rule of law as relevant at the international level as well.

In fact, there is substantial empirical basis for claiming that a "democratic entitlement" is emerging at the international level not only as a "moral prescription" but also as a "legal obligation." In his comprehensive study, Thomas Franck has identified three "generations" in the development of this entitlement.[41] The first generation, dating from at least 1918, is a right to self-determination that applies primarily to "peoples." The second generation centered on the human right to free expression and civil association. The third generation of normative entitlement is that of a participatory electoral process. This generation is potentially the most radical since it raises the question of international monitoring of democratic processes in ways that greatly challenge traditional conceptions of internal sovereignty. Franck's claim is not that these entitlements have been fully realized and even less that they constitute a claim for cosmopolitan democracy as outlined above. Rather, his claim is that a democratic entitlement has already received wide recognition as a basic human right at the international level and that the three generations together constitute a coherent normative entitlement that has a firm basis in established international law. Franck writes:

> A bright line links the three generations of democratic entitlement. The rules and the processes for implementing self-determination, freedom of discursive expression, and electoral rights, have much in common. They evidently aim to achieve a coherent purpose: allowing all persons to assume shared responsibility for shaping the civil society in which they live and work. There is a large normative canon for promoting that objective: the UN Charter, the Universal Declaration of Human Rights, the International Covenant on Civil and Political Rights, the International Convention on the Elimination of all Forms of Racial Discrimination, the International Convention of the Suppression and Punishment of the Crime of Apartheid, the

Declaration on the Elimination of All Forms of Intolerance and of Discrimination Based on Religion or Belief, and the Convention on the Elimination of All Forms of Discrimination Against Women.[42]

Again, Franck's claim is not that this "democratic entitlement" provides the basis for an individual human right to global or cosmopolitan democracy—as perhaps a fourth generation of democratic entitlement. Rather, it is meant to suggest that with the increasing thickening or juridification of international relations— itself still quite uneven both in terms of its content and its application—there is some basis for recognizing a corresponding democratic entitlement. As such, it may present some counter-evidence to Kingsbury's thesis that there is an important alternative between what he calls Kantian cosmopolitanism and a Grotian *jus gentium* that supports pluralism rather than global democracy.

In fact, it seems to me that there is some reason to anticipate a growing convergence between the processes of juridification described by Kingsbury and processes of global governance that might claim some degree of democratic legitimation. In her recent book A New World Order, Anne-Marie Slaughter offers a comprehensive overview of developments in global governance, especially in connection with transgovernmental networks.[43] In contrast to transnational networks, transgovernmental organizations occur primarily in the context of a "disaggregated" state in which sub-national governmental bodies develop global networks with like-minded bodies in other states. She describes these in the three areas of regulatory bodies, judicial bodies, and (to a lesser extent) legislative bodies. Examples include regulatory agencies in which private corporations work with IGOs, NGOs, and other organizations to develop more socially responsible policy, judicial bodies that take on a more global awareness, even to the point of incorporating international judicial viewpoints within their own judicial decisions.[44] Slaughter goes on to describe a process of both horizontal and vertical networking in which, within an increasingly "disaggregated sovereignty," a global governance is taking shape that offers some prospect for achieving democratic accountability: "The defining feature of government networks is that they are composed of government officials and institutions— either national to national, in horizontal networks, or national to supranational, in vertical networks. Yet they coexist and increasingly interact with one another informally, as least in the eyes of the law and traditional diplomacy of the international system. Yet their networks exist alongside and within formal international organizations."[45] The process of "disaggregation" of state sovereignty she describes does not necessarily support Hauke Brunkhorst's more pessimistic claim that "every weakening of the strong public sphere of national democracies is, first of all, to the advantage of the thicker and thicker interweaving of economy and law, and thereby shifts the balance of the 'separation of powers' set up between 'solidarity' and 'money' (Habermas) in favor of the medium of money."[46] On the contrary, her claim is that the process of horizontal networking may allow for more democratic policy-formation than is possible within the traditional model. Of course, thus far the horizontal networking (among regulatory, judicial, and legislative bodies) is much more extensive than the vertical networking; and whether such networking will secure genuine democratic accountability is an open question. Indeed, Slaughter herself describes the need for a "network of networks"—what I described in my opening remarks as a "constitutional framework of democratic procedures"—including the creation of more vertical government networks that "pierce the shell of state sovereignty by making individual government institutions—courts, regulatory agencies, or even legislators—responsible for the implementation of rules created by a supranational institution."[47]

In addition to Slaughter's own observations, one could also point to some of the recent literature on a global public domain which note the quantum increase in NGOs assuming various governmental responsibilities—John Ruggie notes some 30,000—in the past two decades, and their increasing ability to shape global policy (Ruggie notes in particular the defeat by CSOs of the OECD-sponsored Multilateral Agreement on Investment [MAI]).[48] Ruggie does not underestimate the real antagonisms between a (diverse) public domain and private governance, but nonetheless finds some basis for optimism that a newly emergent public domain might exercise some control over private corporations. (Ruggie has himself been associated with the UN's Global Compact, which seeks in various ways to promote social responsibility among private corporations.) Taken together with Slaughter's observations on the formation of vertical and horizontal networks, there may thus be some basis for regarding the thickening juridification as also securing some degree of democratic accountability, at least to the extent that the horizontal networks are open to a wide range of voices and viewpoints.

Curiously, like Brunkhorst, Kingsbury also expresses some caution about the prospects of the "spontaneous" legal orders that emerge independently of states as proposed by Teubner and others (p. 187).[49] Thus, the reflexive law of relatively distinct, autonomous systems (evidenced primarily in lex mercatoria), though certainly relevant for the thickening or juridification of international relations, does not seem to capture the phenomena of "publicness" that Kingsbury has in view. Similarly, he distances himself from more radical pluralists, including the recent proposal by Hardt and Negri for a "democracy of the multitude."[50] However, if cosmopolitanism is no longer identified solely with the idea of a world state or world republic, it is no longer obvious what Kingsbury's specific disagreements with it might be. After summarizing Hauke Brunkhorst's recent suggestion that the already existent "weak public sphere" of a global civil society might be strengthened via a "constitutionalization of international law" (Habermas), Kingsbury rather hastily (and somewhat unfairly) remarks, "In sum, I think the Deweyan problem-solving too soft and expert-oriented, the Arendtian joint action too limited and erratic, and the strong coupling of a global public with constitutionalist institutions too improbable, for this cluster of Habermasian approaches to be a likely basis for public law on a global basis in the near future, however helpful these ideas may be in world sociology" (p. 187). On the contrary, it would seem that Kingsbury's observations regarding an emergent global law might well describe at least one aspect of just the kind of intermeshing and exchange between weak and strong publics that Brunkhorst envisions.

Of course, many difficult questions about the prospects—indeed, even the very idea—for a global democracy remain. In particular, the question of how to detach democratic accountability from its historical links with the territorial nation-state is especially relevant for the idea of "disaggregated sovereignty" within a vast system of vertical and horizontal networks or (if it amounts to the same thing) what Habermas calls "the organizational forms of an international negotiation system."[51] Habermas's suggestion that democratic legitimacy might be linked more to an "expectation of rationally acceptable results" of diverse and overlapping deliberative fora than the decisions of a territorially delimited political body is certainly worthy of further consideration (despite the fears of a "technocratic" or "expert-oriented" elitism).[52] Similarly, questions about the appropriate role of the principle of symmetry— the claim that those affected by a political decision should have an equal voice in that decision—within a conception of democracy become even more troublesome at the global level.[53] However, difficult as these questions are, they do not alone offer support for the view that we can have global law without global democracy, and they do not seem to threaten the basic thesis I have sought to defend here: namely, the claim that if the mutual supposition of the rule of law and democracy is valid at the level of the nation-state, there would seem to be at least prima facie grounds for expecting the same relation of mutual supposition at the global level as well.

NOTES

1. These comments are based on Benedict Kingsbury's chapter, "International Law as Inter-Public Law," presented at the Society for Legal and Political Philosophy meeting in December 2004. His contribution to this volume, though shorter, presents essentially the same position. I was provoked by Kingsbury's essay, along with an earlier essay by William Scheuerman, to think further about the connection between international law and various proposals for cosmopolitan democracy.

2. See David Held, *Democracy and the Global Order: From the Modern State to Cosmopolitan Governance* (Stanford: Stanford University Press, 1995), and, most recently, David Held, *Global Covenant: The Social Democratic Alternative to the Washington Consensus* (Cambridge, UK: Polity Press, 2004).

3. See Jürgen Habermas, "The Postnational Constellation and the Future of Democracy," in *The Postnational Constellation: Political Essays*, trans. Max Pensky (Cambridge: MIT Press, 2001), 58-112.

4. Alexander Wendt, "Why a World State is Inevitable," *European Journal of International Relations* 9 (2003): 491-542.

5. For an overview, see Daniele Archigugi, "Cosmopolitan Democracy and its Critics," *European Journal of International Relations* 10 (2004): 437-473.

6. Held, *Democracy and the Global Order*, chap. 12.

7. Ibid., 279.

8. Ibid.

9. William Scheuerman, "Cosmopolitan Democracy and the Rule of Law," *Ratio Juris* 15 (2002): 446; for some of Held's fairly limited remarks on "cosmopolitan democratic law," see "The Transformation of the Political Community: Rethinking Democracy in the Context of Globalization," in *Democracy's Edges*, eds. Ian Shapiro and Casiano Hacker-Cordon (New York: Cambridge University Press, 1999), especially 105-108.

10. William Scheuerman, "Reflexive Law and the Challenges of Globalization," *Journal of Political Philosophy* 9 (2001): see especially page 99, where Scheuerman draws on the work of Ingeborg Maus.

11. See, for example, Danilo Zolo, "The Lords of Peace" and Michael Saward, "A Critique of Held," both in *Global Democracy: Key Debates*, ed. Barry Holden (New York: Routledge, 2000); see also M. Koskenniemi, *From Apology to Utopia: The Structure of International Legal Argument* (Helsinki: Coronet Books, 1989), 35.

12. See, for example, Michael Saward, "A Critique of Held," in *Global Democracy*, 32-46.

13. Benedict Kingsbury, "The International Legal Order," in *Oxford Handbook of Legal Studies*, eds. Peter Cane and Mark Tushnet (Oxford: Oxford University Press, 2003), 290.

14. Benedict Kingsbury, "People and Boundaries: An 'Internationalized' Public Law Approach," in *States, Nations, and Borders: The Ethics of Making Boundaries*, eds. Allen Buchanan and Margaret Moore (Cambridge: Cambridge University Press, 2003), 303.

15. For another moral- or justice-based approach, see Allen Buchanan, *Justice, Legitimacy, and Self-Determination: Moral Foundations for International Law* (Oxford: Oxford University Press, 2004).

16. For a survey, see Martin Loughlin, *Public Law and Political Theory* (New York: Oxford University Press, 1992), and Martin Loughlin, *The Idea of Public Law* (New York: Oxford University Press, 2003).

17. See David Gauthier, "Hobbesian Public Reason," in *Contemporary Political and Social Philosophy*, eds. Ellen Paul, Fred D. Miller, and Jeffrey Paul (New York: Cambridge University Press, 1995), 19-42.

18. Hans Reiss, ed., *Kant's Political Writings* (New York: Cambridge University Press, 1970), 55-57; see Onora O'Neill, "The Public Use of Reason," in *Constructions of Reason: Explorations of Kant's Practical Philosophy* (New York: Cambridge University Press, 1989), and Gerald Postema, "Public Practical Reason: An Archaeology," *Social Philosophy and Policy* 12 (1995): 43-86.

19. Reiss, *Kant's Political Writings*, 126.

20. See John Ruggie, "Reconstituting the Global Public Domain: Issue, Actors, and Practices," *European Journal of International Relations* 10 (2004): 499-531.

21. Kant, "Perpetual Peace," in Reiss, *Kant's Political Writings*, 108; see also Habermas, "Kant's Idea of Perpetual Peace, with the Benefit of Two Hundred Years' Hindsight," in *Perpetual Peace: Essays on Kant's Cosmopolitan Ideal*, eds. James Bohman and Matthias Lutz-Bachmann (Cambridge: MIT Press, 1997), 124, and, recently, Seyla Benhabib, *The Rights of Others* (New York: Cambridge University Press, 2004).

22. John Rawls, *The Law of Peoples* (Cambridge: Harvard University Press, 1999).

23. See especially Thomas Pogge, "An Egalitarian Law of Peoples," *Philosophy and Public Affairs* 23 (1994): 195-224, Leif Wenar, "The Legitimacy of Peoples," in *Global Justice and Transnational Politics: Essays on the Moral and Political Challenges of Globalization*, eds. Pablo De Greiff and Ciaran Cronin (Cambridge: MIT Press, 2002), 53-76, and Andrew Kuper, "Rawlsian Global Justice," *Political Theory* 28 (2000): 640-674.

24. "The members of international society in the view of Grotius are not merely states or the rulers of states but include groups other than states and, indeed, individual human beings. International society for Grotius is not just the society of states, it is the great society of all mankind," in Hedley Bull, "The Importance of Grotius in the Study of International Relations," in *Hugo Grotius and International Relations*, eds. Hedley Bull, Benedict Kingsbury, and Adam Roberts (New York: Oxford University Press, 1990), 83.

25. See Thomas McCarthy, "On Reconciling Cosmopolitan Unity and National Diversity," in *Global Justice and Transnational Politics*, eds. Pablo De Greiff and Ciaran Cronin (Cambridge: MIT Press, 2002), 235-274.

26. David Held, "Democracy and the Global System," in *Political Theory Today*, ed. David Held (Stanford: Stanford University Press, 1991), 223.

27. Ibid., 198.

28. Ibid., 223.

29. Thomas Pogge, "Cosmopolitanism and Sovereignty," in *Political Restructuring in Europe*, ed. Chris Brown (New York: Routledge, 1994), 89-122.

30. Ibid., 105.

31. For other political cosmopolitans, see David Held and Anthony McGrew, eds., *Governing Globalization: Power, Authority, and Global Governance* (Cambridge, UK: Polity Press, 2002).

32. Daniele Archibugi, "Principles of Cosmopolitan Democracy," in *Re-imagining the Political Community: Studies in Cosmopolitan Democracy*, eds. Daniele Archibugi, David Held, and Martin Köhler. (Cambridge, UK: Polity Press, 1998), 215, and Habermas, *The Postnational Constellation*, 110; see

also Jürgen Habermas, "Does the Constitutionalization of International Law Still Have a Chance?" in *The Divided West*, trans. Ciaran Cronin (Cambridge, UK: Polity Press, 2006), 115-194, esp. 141.

33. See Jürgen Habermas, "On the Relation Between the Nation, the Rule of Law, and Democracy," in *The Inclusion of the Other: Studies in Political Theory*, eds. Ciaran Cronin and Pablo De Greiff (Cambridge: MIT Press, 1998), 129-153, and Jürgen Habermas, *Between Facts and Norms*, trans. William Rehg (Cambridge: MIT Press, 1996), chap. 4; this is, of course, a corollary of the "co-originality" of public and private autonomy, introduced in chapter 3.

34. Joseph Raz, "The Rule of Law and Its Virtue," in *Authority of Law: Essays on Law and Morality* (Oxford: Clarendon Press, 1979), 210-232; but see also Joseph Raz, "The Politics of the Rule of Law," in *Ethics in the Public Domain: Essays in the Morality of Law and Politics* (New York: Oxford University Press, 1994), 354-362.

35. For a criticism of this popular view, see Stephen B. Burbank, "The Architecture of Judicial Independence," *Southern California Law Review* 72 (1999): 315-351.

36. See, for example, Brian Tamanaha, *On the Rule of Law: History, Politics, Theory* (New York: Cambridge University Press, 2004), who speaks of different "themes" in the rule of law; Richard Fallon, who speaks of different "types" of the rule of law, and their "fusion" in "'The Rule of Law' as a Concept in Constitutional Discourse," *Columbia Law Review* 97 (1997): 1-56; and Cass Sunstein, *Legal Reasoning and Political Conflict* (New York: Oxford University Press, 1996).

37. Fallon, "The Rule of Law."

38. Jean Hampton, "Democracy and the Rule of Law," in *NOMOS XXXVI: The Rule of Law*, ed. Ian Shapiro (New York: NYU Press, 1994), 34f.

39. See Jeremy Waldron, "The Rule of Law as a Theatre of Debate," in *Dworkin and His Critics*, ed. Justine Burley (Malden, MA: Blackwell, 2004), 319-336; see also my own "Disagreement and the Legitimacy of Legal Adjudication," in *Multiculturalism and Law: A Critical Debate*, ed. Omid Payrow Shabani (Cardiff: University of Wales Press, 2007), 224-243.

40. Neil MacCormick, "Rhetoric and the Rule of Law," in *Recrafting the Rule of Law*, ed. David Dyzenhaus (Oxford: Hart Publishing, 1999), 163-177.

41. Thomas Franck, *Fairness in International Law and Institutions* (New York: Cambridge University Press, 1995).

42. Ibid., 123.

43. Anne-Marie Slaughter, *A New World Order* (Princeton: Princeton University Press, 2004).

44. Justice Kennedy, for example, cited the European Court of Human Rights in the Texas sodomy case, *Lawrence v. Texas*, 539 U.S. 558, at 570

(2003) (overturning *Bowers v. Hardwick*, 478 U.S. 186 [1986]), and even legislative bodies that seek to become more globally informed. (Newt Gingrich, to take an even more surprising example, is a member of the Twenty-first Century International Legislators Network!)

45. Slaughter, 131-132.

46. Hauke Brunkhorst, *Solidarity: From Civic Friendship to a Global Legal Community*, trans. Jeffrey Flynn (Cambridge: MIT Press, 2005), 150.

47. Slaughter, 132.

48. John Ruggie, "American Exceptionalism, Exemptionalism, and Global Governance," in *American Exceptionalism and Human Rights*, ed. Michael Ignatieff (Princeton: Princeton University Press, 2005), 304-338.

49. See, for example, Gunther Teubner, ed., *Global Law Without a State* (Aldershot: Dartmouth, 1997).

50. Michael Hardt and Antonio Negri, *Multitude: War and Democracy in the Age of Empire* (New York: Penguin, 2004).

51. Habermas, *The Postnational Constellation*, 109.

52. "The democratic procedure no longer draws its legitimizing force only, indeed not even predominantly, from political participation and the expression of political will, but rather from the general accessibility of a deliberative process whose structure grounds an expectation of rationally acceptable results." Ibid., 110; see also Erik Eriksen, "Deliberative Supranationalism in the EU," in *Democracy in the European Union: Integration through Deliberation?*, eds. Erik Eriksen and John Erik Fossum (New York: Routledge, 2000), 42-64.

53. Held offers a few remarks on this question in *Global Covenant*, 99.

11

DEMOCRACY AND INTERNATIONAL LAW

A PERIL FROM THE "PUBLIC"?

GOPAL SREENIVASAN

In his stimulating and instructive paper, Benedict Kingsbury aims to develop a theory of international law that can stand as an alternative to the orthodox model of *jus inter gentes*. Of the various distinguishing features of Kingsbury's "inter-public" model of international law, perhaps the chief is that his model broadens the category of entities whose practice is recognized as making international law to include more than simply "states." International law is understood as "law meeting publicness requirements that is made between entities whose public nature qualifies them as having jurisgenerative capacity" (this volume, p. 180); and *public* entities, so understood, are not limited to states. Toward the end of his discussion, Kingsbury also briefly takes up the relationship between international law and democracy—or, more specifically, between a commitment to the public quality of international law and a commitment to democracy. His conclusions here are largely cautionary, in the skeptical sense.

My comment will focus on this secondary theme in Kingsbury's paper. In the first instance, I shall try to add a significant new polarity to the range of connections between international law and democracy that Kingsbury himself considers. As we shall see, the principal upshot of my addition is cautionary in a different sense: I shall suggest that, under certain conditions, international law can actually be a *positive threat* to national democracy. Since this at least raises a question about the legitimacy of (certain aspects of) international law, and since any general theory of law needs to account for its legitimacy, the outcome I describe has some bearing on Kingsbury's project. Now the conditions that trigger the threat I have in mind are realized, at present, by certain agreements among states. While this may appear to give an advantage to the *jus inter gentes* model, I shall argue next that this appearance is illusory. I shall close by considering how far reliance on the "public" character of international law helps to defuse the indicated threat to national democracy.

§1. Kingsbury is skeptical about any close connection between the public quality of international law and democracy. His view is that, on the inter-public model, international law "makes space for working democracy, but is not in itself democratic" (p. 193). Let me begin with a summary catalog of the various paths between international law and democracy that Kingsbury considers—paths, that is, by which the two might be connected. All of them are paths by which international law might *contribute* to the development of democracy, either international democracy or domestic. As I see it, four such paths can be distinguished in Kingsbury's discussion (pp. 193–197): International law might facilitate

    (i)   the export of national democracy, from one country to another;

   (ii) the export of democracy, from national governance to international governance;

  (iii) control/influence in country X over X-affecting decisions either in country Y or in international decision processes; or

  (iv) attempts by "leaders who have been elected by democratic processes in fragile democracies . . . to lock in their current democratic institutions and raise the costs for coup plotters or foreign invaders" (p. 194).

For the most part, Kingsbury emphasizes various impediments to the operation of these paths; he also seems to regard some of them (e.g., [iv]) as comparatively unimportant in determining the overall dynamic between international law and democracy. Hence his skepticism.

Kingsbury's position is developed in counter-point to the greater optimism of the Habermasian school (pp 186–187). But, even taking this context into account, his own view seems to be that the relationship between international law and democracy is—at worst, as it were—one of neutral indifference (p. 193, quoted above). By contrast, I wish to suggest that international law can sometimes *shrink* the space for national democracy. The conditions under which this shrinkage occurs are generated—in today's world, anyhow—by certain features of agreements between states. I shall first describe the relevant conditions in general terms and then add some illustrative detail afterward.

By the "space for national democracy" here, I mean the power of a domestic population to decide various legal questions concerning its own state, i.e., to decide the law of its land. Alternatively, we might consider it as the range of such questions—call them *domestic legal questions*—whose answer depends on the exercise of domestic legislative power. This range is restricted, and the space for national democracy correspondingly shrunken, whenever the answer to some domestic legal question *cannot* be decided by domestic legislation. Let us refer to this situation as one in which (the majority of) a given domestic population suffers from a *disability* to decide some domestic legal question—either a *strict* disability (when the majority literally lacks the valid power to legislate on the question) or an *effective* disability (when, strictly speaking, the majority has a valid power, but is prevented by practical realities from exercising it).

In very general terms, an international legal agreement effectively disables the majority in a signatory state from deciding a given domestic legal question when three conditions are satisfied: First, compliance with the obligations entailed by the agreement dictates a specific answer to the relevant domestic legal question. Second, the signatory state(s) have no realistic option of quitting (or simply abrogating) the agreement. Third, the prospective cost of having the agreement's obligations enforced makes compliance with them the only worthwhile option for the signatory state(s).

To put it more intuitively, domestic majorities in state X are effectively disabled from deciding what the law of X will be on a given point whenever state X is signatory to an international agreement that already settles what X's law on that point should be *and* state X has no viable option of evading that agreement's prescription. Now, in this sense, international agreements have (i.e., international law has) always had the *potential* to disable domestic populations from deciding the law of their land. However, since viable options to evade the force of international legal prescriptions have typically been either plentiful or unnecessary (because enforcement was not feasible), the threat to national democracy implicit in these potential disabilities has traditionally been rather theoretical at best.

What is different in the contemporary situation, if anything is, is the extent to which the prescriptions of international law can be effectively enforced. Of course, one should not exaggerate. By and large, evading these prescriptions remains a fairly viable option for domestic majorities (or other national decision-makers). Still, in some quarters, the enforcement of international law has become much more effective, and the prospective cost of non-compliance notably higher. In particular, the advent of the World Trade Organization (WTO) and the development of its (economic) sanctions regime has arguably made the international *trade* agreements it administers effectively enforceable, especially for smaller states. As a result, WTO agreements can plausibly be seen as effectively disabling domestic majorities in signatory states from deciding the law of their land on a range of domestic legal questions that fall with the scope of WTO prescriptions.

Let me offer an example from the General Agreement on Trade in Services (GATS).[1] Among other things, the GATS prohibits the introduction of new service monopolies (or the expansion of old ones) in sectors that have been explicitly placed within its purview. To take a specific instance, this provision applies to the health insurance sector in Canada, which is presently organized as a public monopoly for (insurance for) many medical services, but not for outpatient pharmaceuticals. While recent proposals to reform the Canadian health system have included recommendations to expand the public health insurance monopoly to outpatient pharmaceuticals, implementing this reform would run afoul of the GATS prohibition against expanding service monopolies. Hence, if Canada cannot afford either to quit the GATS altogether or to suffer its enforcement by the WTO, domestic majorities in Canada are effectively disabled from deciding how health insurance should be organized in Canada.

As I have suggested, the connection between international law and democracy illustrated by this example differs fundamentally in its polarity from any of the connections Kingsbury considers: here international law facilitates an *anti*-democratic upshot, whereas along all of Kingsbury's paths (i)-(iv) it facilitates a *pro*-democratic upshot. Notice, however, that in another respect the GATS example has something in common with path (iv), which thereby differs significantly from paths (i)-(iii). To wit, in both my example and (iv), international law serves to transmit an influence on democracy—either positive or negative—between a particular state *and itself.* By contrast, along paths (i)-(iii), the (pro-democratic) influence is always transmitted from one state to something *else,* be it another state or some international process.

To put it another way, both the GATS example and Kingsbury's fragile democracy example (i.e., path [iv]) feature effective disabilities to decide some domestic legal question that have been *self-imposed* by a domestic majority in a given state, albeit with the assistance of international law. Yet, in one case, I have characterized the disability as anti-democratic and, in the other, as pro-democratic. What explains the difference? A reasonable initial answer might be that the opposing characterizations are explained by the fundamentally different *contents* entrenched by the respective disabilities. In the fragile democracy example, what the effective disability entrenches is precisely (a set of) *democratic* institutions, while in the GATS example what it entrenches is merely a particular social or economic policy.

§2. While this initial answer may be reasonable, one might nevertheless object to it. One might deny, for example, the "fact" it aims to explain—deny, that is, that the effective disability in the GATS example *is* anti-democratic, and thereby deny any difference in the polarity of the two examples. *Any self-imposed* disability to decide a domestic legal question, according to this objection, is necessarily consistent with democracy, at least when it is self-imposed by a democratic majority. It does not matter, then, which domestic legal questions a domestic majority disables itself from deciding:

all contents entrenched by such means are equally consistent with democracy.

If this objection is correct, the *jus inter gentes* model of international law may appear to have a certain advantage over Kingsbury's inter-public model, so far as the preservation of democracy is concerned. For on the *jus inter gentes* model, international law always arises, in effect, from an *agreement* between states. Nothing counts as international law unless its genesis involved some such agreement; furthermore, no international law applies to a given state unless that state is party to the relevant agreement. It follows that any disability to decide a domestic legal question "imposed" on a nation's decision-maker(s) by international law is, in a sense, actually always *self*-imposed. As a result, it may seem that, at least in the case of democratic states, any disability imposed by international law is necessarily consistent with democracy.

On the *jus inter gentes* model, in other words, international law may therefore seem, at least in certain cases, to be *incapable* of threatening democracy. By contrast, on Kingsbury's model, some international laws can validly apply to a state that has never been party to any agreement generating the laws in question. Since enforcement of *that* sort of international law may also effectively disable a domestic majority from deciding various domestic legal questions, and since the consequent disabilities will be in no sense self-imposed, potential threats to democracy exist on Kingsbury's model where none seems possible on the orthodox model.

However, despite these appearances, the *jus inter gentes* model has no genuine advantage over the inter-public model with respect to the preservation of democracy. In any given case, the threat to democracy entailed by the enforcement of a particular international law arises, so far as it does, equally well on either model. The basic reason has nothing to do with international law *per se*, but is rather due to the very limited reach of the principle on which the objection relies, namely, that any disability to decide a domestic legal question self-imposed by a democratic majority is necessarily consistent with democracy. This principle is perfectly valid whenever the democratic majority that *suffers* the disability to decide a particular domestic legal question and the democratic majority that *imposed* that disability are majorities of one and the same generation of co-citizens. But as soon as a generation gap enters to distinguish the two majorities, the principle ceases to apply without ambiguity.

Consider, for example, a democratic majority of Canadians in generation B who find themselves effectively disabled by the GATS from deciding whether public health insurance in Canada should be extended to cover outpatient pharmaceuticals. Whether or not their effective disability is consistent with democracy, the issue cannot be settled by appealing to the fact that, a generation earlier, (representatives of) a democratic majority of Canadians in generation A ratified the GATS and thereby imposed it on themselves. Since generation B did not even exist when generation A ratified the GATS, A's ratification hardly counts as a "self-imposition" by B—not, at least, without an equivocation on "self." Hence, the self-imposition principle says nothing about the consistency of B's effective disability with democracy.

Of course, the validity of the GATS as international law survives the (generation of the) various national decision-makers who signed and ratified it, including generation A of Canadians. Unlike the scope of the self-imposition principle, the validity of international law is trans-generational. That is precisely what both limits the applicability of the self-imposition principle to the issue at hand and sets the stage for a threat to national democracy. Any international agreement that effectively disables a domestic majority in a signatory state from deciding certain domestic legal questions will inevitably continue so to disable later majorities in the same state,[2] once the signatory generation passes into history, as it eventually must. For the later generations, this inherited restriction in their power to decide the law of their own land will not be self-imposed in any ordinary sense, but rather imposed by the dead hand of the past (albeit, *their* past). Since this threat to national democracy arises even with a paradigm instance of *jus inter gentes*, and even when our attention is confined to democratic states, we may conclude that the *jus inter gentes* model has no advantage in the preservation of democracy after all.

§3. Although threats to national democracy from the enforcement of international law can *arise* equally well on either the inter-public model or the *jus inter gentes* model, it remains to be seen whether one model is better than the other at defusing such threats. Here, I assume that the value of democracy does not always "trump" everything else in the moral assessment of legal arrangements (including international legal arrangements).[3] Hence, while democracy is of great value, some (international) legal arrangements that are inconsistent with democracy may still prove to be justified, all things considered. As I am using the expression, a model of international law *defuses* threats to national democracy when it counts laws that are inconsistent with (national) democracy as "international law" *only if* they are also justified, all things considered. To emphasize the obvious, this involves a somewhat exacting standard of what counts as international law. But might this exacting standard nevertheless be satisfied by Kingsbury's inter-public model of international law?

A central aspect of Kingsbury's model holds some promise in this context. I have in mind his idea that "'publicness' is a necessary element in the concept of law under modern democratic conditions," whereby "publicness is meant the claim made for the law that it has been wrought by the whole society, by the public, and the connected claim that law addresses matters of concern to the society as such" (p. 175). Now it is not entirely clear what it means to "address matters of concern to the society as such." But let us suppose, not implausibly, that it means to satisfy the fundamental common interests of a population.

In that case, one might argue that disabilities suffered by a domestic majority are justified, all things considered, *when* the laws the majority is disabled from revising are laws that protect the fundamental common interests of the population in the relevant society. Disabilities of this sort are justified—so the argument might go—because, in the stipulated cases, the population's interest in deciding domestic legal questions for itself is *outweighed* by its interest in simply having a certain legal arrangement in place. For example, one might think that a population's interest in deciding for itself whether or not free speech should be legally protected is outweighed by its fundamental common interest in (having legally protected) freedom of speech.

To achieve plausibility, this argument may have to lean heavily on its stipulation that the interests it privileges are both *fundamental* (i.e., weighty enough to defeat a population's significant interest in having the majority decide a given domestic legal question) and *common* (i.e., shared by all the individuals in the population). But if the quality of "publicness" in law already entails that the interests a *public* law protects are both fundamental and common, and if the inter-public model makes "publicness" a necessary quality of international law, then Kingsbury's model may well help to defuse the threats to national democracy posed by the enforcement of international law.

I do not know whether Kingsbury intends his model to require every international law to be a public law as I have construed it. One reason for doubt is that, in the international context, only strictly universal interests qualify as "common," i.e., shared by everyone on earth. Hence, no law that protects only less-than-universal interests will count as "international law," since no such law will be a public law. So construed, the publicness requirement would restrict the scope of international law considerably.[4]

In fact, that is not the end of the problem. For the publicness requirement, as it stands, is not even sufficient to defuse the most serious threats to national democracy. As we saw in discussing the *jus inter gentes* model, the most serious threats have an *inter-generational* dimension—they arise, that is, from effective disabilities to decide a domestic legal question that are simply *inherited* by (domestic majorities in) later generations in the affected states. In order for *these* disabilities to be justified, all things considered, the affected later generation(s) will also have to *inherit the interest* in the particular legal arrangement entrenched by the disability in question. Otherwise, the later generation's interest in deciding the corresponding domestic legal question for itself will not begin to be outweighed. To illustrate with our previous example: a later generation effectively disabled from revising the legal protection it inherits for freedom of speech would also have to inherit the interest in having legally protected free speech.

Let me recast the point in slightly different terms. The argument under consideration appeals to the fundamental character of a population's interest in a specific legal outcome (e.g., having legally protected free speech) in order to outweigh that same population's interest in deciding the corresponding legal question for itself. If this justification is to be extended to a disability inherited by later generations of the same society, the fundamental character of the privileged interest has not only to be shared across individuals in the original generation (i.e., to be "common"), but also shared *across the generations* (i.e., to be "inter-generationally stable" or, perhaps better, "permanent"). Accordingly, to defuse the most serious threats to national democracy, the publicness requirement actually has to be strengthened—so that what a *public** law, as we might call it, protects are the *permanent* fundamental common interests of the population in the relevant society.

I assume that Kingsbury does not want his inter-public model to incorporate this strengthened publicness requirement. While it may be plausible that laws protecting freedom of speech (and other very basic rights and liberties) qualify as protecting permanent fundamental common interests, and so qualify as public* laws, many other apparently valid international laws will not qualify as public*. Elsewhere, for example, I argue that certain provisions of the GATS (including the one featured in our initial illustration) do not protect the permanent interests of any population.

In that case, however, there seems to be a tension between the descriptive ambitions of an adequate model of international law and its normative ambitions. For it seems that certain international laws (e.g., certain provisions of the GATS)—indeed, perhaps most international laws—would, if effectively enforced, restrict national democracy in ways that are not justified, all things considered. Yet, normatively, it is at least puzzling if a theory of law makes the legitimacy of a law depend on its not being effectively enforced. How to resolve this puzzle is a question I leave open to theorists of international law.

NOTES

1. I have described this example in greater detail in my "Does Today's International Trade Agreement Bind Tomorrow's Citizen?," *Chicago-Kent Law Review* 81, no. 1 (2006): 119-145. I also elaborate there on various of the points sketched here and below in the text.

2. Assuming, that is, no change in the external conditions that give rise to an effective disability. The disability can lapse if the state in question later acquires a realistic option to quit (or abrogate) the agreement or later finds it worthwhile to have the agreement enforced against it.

3. This largely reflects a preference for a normatively modest defini-

tion of "democracy." One *can* always define democracy in such a way that it entails the legal arrangements that are justified, all things considered.

4. One might reduce the problem somewhat by distinguishing, within international law, between bilateral or multilateral laws and omnilateral laws. The strict universality of the publicness requirement would only apply to *omni*lateral international law. But the remaining restriction is far from trivial.

INDEX

251